THE NEW

GEOGRAPHY

OF GLOBAL

INCOME

INEQUALITY

GLENN
FIREBAUGH

THE NEW GEOGRAPHY OF GLOBAL INCOME INEQUALITY

HARVARD UNIVERSITY PRESS

CAMBRIDGE, MASSACHUSETTS

LONDON, ENGLAND

First Harvard University Press paperback edition, 2006

Library of Congress Cataloging-in-Publication Data

Firebaugh, Glenn.
The new geography of global income inequality / Glenn Firebaugh.
    p.   cm.
Includes bibliographical references and index.
ISBN 0-674-01067-1 (cloth)
ISBN 0-674-01987-3 (pbk.)
1. Income distribution.   I. Title.

HC79.I5 F565   2003
339.2′1—dc21   2002038724

Designed by Gwen Nefsky Frankfeldt

To Heather, Joel, and Rosie—
you will shape the future

Contents

Preface

This book is about global income inequality—the uneven distribution of economic activity and welfare worldwide. The first and principal objective of the book is to set the facts straight about trends in global income inequality, an area in which there is much controversy and misunderstanding. For example, the World Bank's *World Development Report 2000/2001* (p. 51) claims that "income inequality between countries has increased sharply over the past 40 years," and as recently as April 2001, an article in *The Economist* proclaimed that "new evidence suggests that global inequality is worsening rapidly" (Wade 2001, p. 72). Such claims are commonplace. An examination of the data, however, suggests that income inequality across nations peaked in the last third of the twentieth century and is now declining. At the same time, inequality *within* nations—which had been declining over the first half of the twentieth century—has begun to rise. Because of industrialization's spread to poor nations and the prospect of a demographic windfall for many of them, I expect these trends to continue. The result is a new geography of global inequality, where—contrary to trends that dominated the nineteenth and early twentieth centuries—income inequality declines across nations and rises within nations. This book documents this new geography, shows that the new geography has led to declining global income inequality, and explains why other analyses have wrongly concluded that global income inequality continues to grow.

These claims are likely to be met with skepticism in some quarters, so the bulk of the book documents and describes the new geography—the first objective. The second objective of the book is to determine what is behind the change in the contours of global inequality. The most important cause is the spread of industrialization to the world's poor regions. Determining this and other causes puts us in a better position to determine whether the new patterns are likely to continue—the book's third objective. The final chapter predicts that the patterns will continue in the twenty-first century. If that forecast proves to be correct, then we are in the middle of an inequality transition that will slowly reduce the link between nationality and income, so that in the future your income might be determined more by what you know than by where you live.

There is a great deal of interest these days in the topic of globalization and income inequality, and I seek to clear up misconceptions and to advance our knowledge in this important area. The book is written for scholars and students alike, and it is appropriate for a variety of undergraduate- and graduate-level courses, such as political science courses on international affairs or globalization, sociology courses on social stratification or social problems, and economics courses on economic development or income distribution and inequality.

Writing a book is a solo task embedded in a social context, and in the course of my work I have benefited greatly from the counsel of others. I begin by thanking David Grusky for his advice and encouragement throughout this project, and Jacob Felson, Christopher Jencks, Telle Kjetil, Dan Lichter, Jeff Manza, and Evan Schofer for their written comments on one or more of the chapters. At Penn State I have benefited from discussions with (and in some cases written comments from) David Baker, Cristina Bradatan, Jeffrey Cohen, Gordon DeJong, Richard Felson, Roger Finke, Brian Goesling, Mark Hayward, Barry Lee, John McCarthy, Sal Oropesa, Sean Reardon, Assata Richards, Robert Schoen, Pam Short, David Shapiro, and Alan Sica. I have also benefited from the good offices of the Population Research Institute (PRI) at Penn State, and I thank in particular Tonya Allen and Tara Murray for bibliographic assistance and Erica Gardner for programming assistance. The figures and maps in this book were prepared by Jim Detwiler (assisted by Jason Smith) in the Geographic Information System group in PRI.

I also thank Susan Welch, Dean of the College of the Liberal Arts, who saw enough potential in this project to grant a timely research leave. A cabin in Maine in the fall is an ideal place for putting together one's thoughts. The Sociology Program of the National Science Foundation also provided material support for the research underlying this book (grants SBR-9515153 and SBR-9870870), as did the National Institute of Child Health and Human Development through its Center Grant to PRI. Tables

6.1 and 7.3 and Figure 7.1 are adapted from my article "Empirics of World Income Inequality," *American Journal of Sociology* 104 (© 1999 by The University of Chicago; all rights reserved).

Over the past four years I have presented preliminary findings from this research in talks at the universities of Michigan and Wisconsin and at Cornell, Indiana, and Oxford universities, as well as at various academic conferences. Some in the audiences provided probing questions or criticisms, some provided timely encouragement, and some provided both. The list of those who provided at least one of the above includes Art Alderson, David Brady, Tom DiPrete, Steven Durlauf, Robert Hauser, Albert Hermalin, Michael Hout, David James, Leslie Kish, David Lam, Noah Lewin-Epstein, Michael Macy, Karl Ulrich Mayer, Patricia McManus, Victor Nee, David Sahn, Karl Schuessler, Donald Treiman, Wout Ultee, Pam Walters, Franklin Wilson, and Yu Xie. I have also benefited from email correspondence with Ian Castles, Ryan Hobert, Branko Milanovic, and Tim Smeeding on various issues related to global inequality.

I thank Michael Aronson at Harvard University Press, a superb editor, and Elizabeth Gilbert, a superb manuscript editor.

Finally, I thank my wife, Judy Rae, and my valued friends Barb, Carole, Dan, Don, Emory, Joan, Judy, Larry, and Lynda for their support—you know who you are.

September 2002

THE NEW
GEOGRAPHY
HYPOTHESIS

Massive Global Income Inequality: When Did It Arise and Why Does It Matter?

At THE TIME of the first Industrial Revolution, Thomas Malthus (1960 [1798]) and other classical economists feared that humans might be doomed to near-subsistence levels of living. A century earlier Thomas Hobbes had warned that a powerful sovereign was needed lest life be "solitary, poor, nasty, brutish, and short" (Hobbes 1962 [1651], p. 100). Malthus was even more pessimistic, warning that poverty is the likely human lot with or without a powerful ruler. Malthus's fear was based on a population-trap model positing that economic growth is unlikely to outpace population growth over the long run. In this model, economic gains are short-lived, because the geometric growth of population inevitably catches up with linear economic gains. Unless there are other checks on population growth, income per person will inevitably return to a low equilibrium level. A new round of economic expansion will upset that equilibrium in the short run, but in the long run income per capita will track back down to its preexpansion level. In other words, economic growth will serve to increase the size of the human population, but it will not boost living standards over the long run.

The Growing World Income Pie

The pace of population growth and economic growth over the last two centuries has proved Malthus right about the expansion of the human population but wrong about the population trap. In line with Malthus, the productivity gains of the Industrial Revolution were accompanied by an era of unprecedented population growth. In 1820 the world's population was about 1.1 billion (Maddison 1995, table 1.1a). Today the world's population has surpassed 6 billion. But contrary to Malthus's warning that rapid population growth will undermine economic growth, the quintupling of the world's population has not resulted in stagnant incomes and living standards. The economic historian Richard Easterlin recently wrote that "a revolution in the human condition is sweeping the world. Most people today are better fed, clothed, and housed than their predecessors two centuries ago. . . . Although the picture is not one of universal progress, it is the greatest advance in the condition of the world's population ever achieved in such a brief span of time" (Easterlin 2000, p. 7). In the face of unprecedented growth in world population, world income has grown even faster. In fact economic growth over the past two centuries has so greatly outpaced population growth that, according to the standard source for such historical comparisons, income per capita for the world as a whole has, in constant dollars, increased roughly eightfold since 1820 (Maddison 1995, table 1.1a).

So over the past two centuries a world population explosion has been outdone by a world income explosion. The world income pie has expanded not only in an absolute sense, but also in a per capita sense, as most people today enjoy a much higher standard of living than their ancestors had in the preindustrial world. Although scholars have tended to pay more attention to the population explosion than to the income explosion, the growth in per capita income is the defining feature of our historical epoch. Moreover, the remarkable growth in world per capita income has shown no signs of leveling off in recent decades. As Robert Lucas (2000, p. 159) notes, "The real income of an average person has more than doubled since World War II and the end of the European colonial age." Before that time, during the first half of the twentieth century and during the nineteenth century, there is strong evidence (despite the fact that income estimates before 1950 tend to be less reliable than those after 1950) that world income growth was not doubling as rapidly (see Maddison 1995, table G-3).

The best estimates of world and regional incomes over the last two centuries are from the economic historian Angus Maddison. Maddison's (1995) monumental income series begins with 1820, and Figure 1.1 depicts Maddison's estimates of per capita income for the whole world for 1820, 1950, and 1990. The figures are in 1990 U.S. dollars, so the observed growth is not due to inflation. Although the estimates for the nineteenth century in particular are based on gross approximations for many nations, the general pattern of sustained growth is unmistakable. As these figures indicate, recent growth has been especially remarkable. In terms of

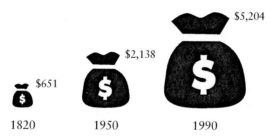

FIGURE 1.1 World average income in 1990 U.S. dollars: 1820, 1950, and 1990. Based on Maddison 1995.

absolute change, average income in the world increased twice as much over the 40-year period 1950–1990 as it did over the previous 130 years combined (an increase of $3,066 from 1950 to 1990 versus an increase of $1,487 from 1820 to 1950). The 1950–1990 interval also exhibits a faster growth rate, as average income increased by a factor of 2.4 over the 40 years from 1950 to 1990 after increasing by a factor of 3.3 over the much longer period of 1820 to 1950.

Other Welfare Changes

In addition to rising incomes over the past two centuries, there are two other significant changes that bear on the issue of changing human welfare. The first is that we tend to live longer now than before. Life expectancy today is estimated to be sixty-six years at birth for the world as a whole (World Almanac 2001), which is likely almost double what it was at the beginning of the twentieth century.[1] This dramatic increase in life expectancy is one of the singular features of the past hundred years. Not only do people live better than before, they also live much longer—a fact not captured by statistics on income growth per se. No doubt most people agree with C. P. Snow's (1963, p. 78) statement that "it seems to me better that people should live rather than die . . . [and] that they shouldn't have to watch their children die." Although it is difficult to place a dollar value on longer life, most would agree that length of life is part of human welfare. Because the analysis in this book focuses on change in per capita income without also factoring in rising life expectancy, one could argue that I in fact understate the rise in human welfare since the early nineteenth century. Moreover, the change in average income fails to capture the increased welfare that results from the new choices that we have in the twenty-first century that were not available earlier. Our ancestors in the early nineteenth century knew nothing of automobiles, computers, telephones, air travel, and other inventions of the past two centuries. So if human welfare is largely about options and freedom—as Amartya Sen (1999) has argued—then on that basis the estimated rates of income growth given above most likely understate the rise in material welfare over the last century, since they fail to factor in the new choices available to many today.

The Rise in Income Disparities over the Nineteenth and Twentieth Centuries

There are two big stories about world income trends over the past two centuries. The first story is the remarkable growth in the world's average income, just described. The second story is that the growth has disproportionately benefited different regions of the world, with richer regions generally benefiting much more than poorer regions. As a result global income inequality has worsened dramatically since the early nineteenth century. (In this book the terms "global income inequality" and "world income inequality" are used as synonyms to refer to the total level of income inequality across all the world's people.) A central message of this book is that the enormous growth in global inequality occurred during the period of Western industrialization, that is, during the nineteenth century and the first half of the twentieth century. Today, during the period of Asian industrialization, global inequality is no longer growing. (A note on terminology: "Period of Western industrialization" is shorthand for the era when industrialization was led by Western nations. Not all industrialization occurred in the West during this era, of course, but Western nations took the lead in industrializing during this period. Similarly, Asian nations have been industrializing the most aggressively in recent decades, so I use the term "period of Asian industrialization," even though recent industrialization obviously has not been restricted to Asia. Historians sometimes distinguish a "first Industrial Revolution"—about 1760 to 1830, centered in England—from a "second Industrial Revolution"—about 1860 to 1900, occurring simultaneously in the United States and Europe—but in the case of global inequality, the distinction between the first and second Industrial Revolutions is much less significant than the distinction between the Western and Asian periods of industrialization, as we shall see.)

This book focuses on the second story, the unevenness of the income growth. The remarkable rise in average income over the past two centuries has produced massive global income inequality, as income growth in the world's richer regions and nations has outpaced growth in poorer regions and nations. The practical implication for individuals is that in today's world, one's income is determined largely by one's residence. Figure 1.2 shows the magnitude of the regional disparity in incomes by disaggregating the world averages for 1820 and 1990 and mapping the regional averages with China and India separated out from the rest of Asia. These maps, based on the data in Table 1.1 below, reveal at a glance not only the striking growth in world per capita income over the past two centuries but also the striking unevenness of that growth across space. Incomes have surged ahead in Europe and lagged behind in Africa and (until recently) in Asia. So the eightfold increase in average world income since 1820 is easy to misinterpret, because it masks huge differences in income growth across the world's major regions.

An important part of the global inequality story is that the world has divided into three income camps. As Table 1.1 shows, although the three camps were discernible in 1820, the divisions are much sharper today. It is important to note, however, that the divisions are no longer becoming more and more distinct, because the era of global "trifurcation" in income occurred during the period of Western industrialization and now appears to be behind us. Compare the two columns under Income Growth in Table 1.1. If we rank regions on the basis of their estimated income levels in 1820, we find that over the course of the nineteenth century and first half of the twentieth century the initially richer regions got richer much faster than the poorer regions did (first column under Income Growth). From 1820 to 1950—the period of Western industrialization—per capita income increased by a multiple of 4.0–7.7 for the initially higher-income regions, by a multiple of 2.5–3.7 for the middle-income regions, and by a multiple of 1.8 or less for the lower-income regions. Since 1950—the period of Asian industrialization—income growth rates no longer line up with initial incomes. Some regions in the low-income group have been growing faster than some regions in the high-income group. These results point to the possibility that the era of big-time growth in global income inequality may be ending.

In the meantime the legacy of the big-time growth in inequality remains. To appreciate the unevenness of the income growth across regions during the period of Western industrialization, compare income growth in the Western offshoots (Australia, Canada, New Zealand, and the United States) to income growth in Africa from 1820 to 1950. Average income is estimated to have been about $1,200 in the Western offshoots in 1820 compared with about $450 in Africa in 1820—a ratio of less than 3 to 1 at the early stages of Western industrialization.[2] By 1950 the ratio had ballooned to about 11 to 1 ($9,255 versus $830). Unless income estimates are wildly off the mark (I address data reliability in Chapter 3), regional differences in average incomes are profound.

In sum, the world income pie has expanded greatly over the past two centuries, but not everyone's piece has expanded at the same rate. Be-

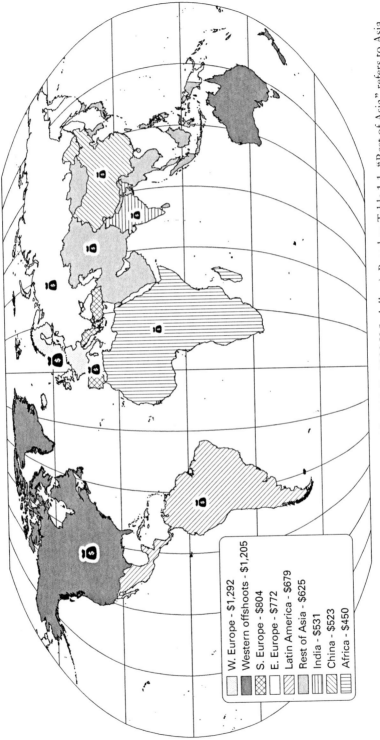

FIGURE 1.2a Average incomes in major regions of the world, 1820 (in 1990 U.S. dollars). Based on Table 1.1. "Rest of Asia" refers to Asia outside China and India; "E. Europe" includes Russia.

W. Europe - $1,292
Western offshoots - $1,205
S. Europe - $804
E. Europe - $772
Latin America - $679
Rest of Asia - $625
India - $531
China - $523
Africa - $450

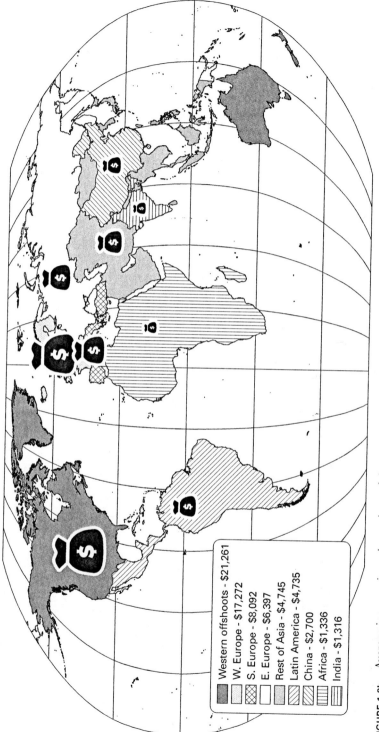

FIGURE 1.2b Average incomes in major regions of the world, 1990 (in 1990 U.S. dollars). Based on Table 1.1. "Rest of Asia" refers to Asia outside China and India; "E. Europe" includes the Soviet Union.

Legend:

- Western offshoots - $21,261
- W. Europe - $17,272
- S. Europe - $8,092
- E. Europe - $6,397
- Rest of Asia - $4,745
- Latin America - $4,735
- China - $2,700
- Africa - $1,336
- India - $1,316

TABLE 1.1 World "trifurcation" since 1820: Average income in major regions of the world in 1820, 1950, and 1990

Region	Income per capita			Income growth	
	1820	1950	1990	1950/1820	1990/1950
High-income group					
Western Europe (23 nations)	$1,292	$5,126	$17,272	4.0	3.4
Western offshoots (4 nations)	1,205	9,255	21,261	7.7	2.3
Middle-income group					
Southern Europe (7 nations)	804	2,021	8,092	2.5	4.0
Eastern Europe (9 nations)	772	2,631	6,397	3.4	2.4
Latin America (44 nations)	679	2,487	4,735	3.7	1.9
Low-income group					
Asia (56 nations)					
China	523	614	2,700	1.2	4.4
India	531	597	1,316	1.1	2.2
Rest of Asia	625	1,081	4,745	1.7	4.4
Africa (56 nations)	450	830	1,336	1.8	1.6
World totals	651	2,138	5,204	3.3	2.4

Source: Calculated from Maddison (1995), tables G-1 and G-3 for regional data; tables A-3e and D-1e for data for China and India.

Note: Regional incomes are population-weighted averages, in 1990 U.S. dollars. The ratios 1950/1820 and 1990/1950 are calculated from the income data. "Western offshoots" refers to Australia, Canada, New Zealand, and the United States. "Asia" includes Oceania.

cause incomes tended to grow more rapidly in the richer regions in the nineteenth and early twentieth centuries, income inequality has increased across the world's major regions. This book examines the income inequality issue in the context of the expanding world economy. Three chapters of the book (Chapters 6–8) are devoted to between-nation income inequality, that is, to trends in the distribution of income across nations. I emphasize between-nation income inequality, first, because most of the world's total income inequality lies between nations and, second, because there has been a historic turnaround in between-nation income inequality that has gone virtually unnoticed.

Why Nations?

There are two answers to the question of why nations are strategic in the study of global income inequality. The simple answer is that one uses nations because the income data come that way, packaged in national chunks. Nations have national accounting offices charged with collecting data on the nation's annual productivity, and these data are combined with price data, aggregated, and combined with demographic data to estimate national per capita income. The United Nations, the World Bank, and other international agencies assemble these data and make them readily available.

Yet there is much more than convenience involved in the choice of nations as the unit of analysis for a study of world income inequality. To appreciate why the nation is a strategic unit for studying world income inequality, consider the following thought experiment: Suppose we had income data for every individual in the world (unfortunately, we do not have such data)—over six billion cases in all. Then with a powerful enough computer we could summarize the level of income inequality for the whole world by calculating some standard summary inequality measure such as the Gini index or the Theil index (described in Chapter 4). Now suppose that we were required to aggregate the data to reduce the cases by a factor of 50 million, that is, from 6 billion cases down to 120 cases. One strategy would be to aggregate by assigning individuals the mean income for the nation where they live. This strategy would pare the 6 billion cases to 120 cases since there are about 120 nations with significant populations.[3] In effect we would be replacing six billion cases with 120, and we would calculate the inequality in income across nations instead of across individuals.

How much information about world income inequality would be lost by collapsing 6 billion cases down to 120 nations? Not as much as one would expect for such a drastic reduction in cases. By assigning each individual the national mean on income, we ignore all the variance in income within nations—so within each nation the rich and the poor are assigned the same income. In short, our method of aggregation discards all the within-nation income inequality. But within-nation income inequality accounts for only about one-fourth to one-third of the world's total income inequality (Schultz 1998; Goesling 2001; Milanovic 2002), so if we magically eliminated all income inequality within nations, the world's total income inequality would shrink by only one-third at most (skeptical readers can look ahead to Table 5.1 if they like).

The central point here is that nations are key in the production and distribution of the world's income. By knowing only one piece of information about individuals—where they live (nation)—we can explain about 70 percent of the variance in individuals' incomes worldwide.[4] The link between national residence and income is strong not because within-nation income inequality is so small, but because the disparity in income across nations is so large. To understand global income inequality, then, we begin with income inequality across nations.

Why Not Focus on Poverty Rather than on Inequality?

As we have just seen, between-nation income inequality matters because it constitutes the major portion of global income inequality. But why should we care about income inequality in the first place—isn't it poverty that we should really be concerned about, not inequality? Why should we care if some are rich, so long as no one is poor? Aside from ethical arguments about equality and justice,[5] there are two compelling reasons for studying world inequality. The first reason is to understand world poverty. As this book will make clear, if we were to study world poverty without also studying world inequality then we would miss an essential element of the story about world poverty: that the poverty problem changed from a production problem to a distribution problem over the course of the Industrial Revolution of the nineteenth and twentieth centuries. Hence the study of global inequality is critical to the study of global poverty. By examining the big picture on global inequality we understand the changing roots of global poverty.

Second, the study of global inequality is critical to major theoretical traditions in sociology and economics (to cite a familiar example, the assumption of income bifurcation is a key component of Marx's theory of history). Here we examine inequality and poverty. Subsequently (in Chapter 10) we examine how the trend in global inequality bears on major theories of development.

INEQUALITY AND POVERTY

Income inequality matters because poverty in the world today is largely a problem of distribution, not production. As shown in Figure 1.1, the growth in total world production has outpaced the growth in world population over the past two centuries. So the average person today is much richer than the average person in the past.

With respect to the trend in the world's *average* income, then, the news has been encouraging over the past two centuries. Although the rise in world incomes does not appear to be accompanied by rising human happiness or contentment (see the Epilogue), at the least it can be said that at this juncture in history there is greater potential than there was in earlier eras for meeting the essential human needs for food, shelter, clothing, and medical attention. The central economic issue in Malthus's era was whether or not there was enough to go around, so the problem of poverty was primarily a problem of insufficient production. According to the estimates of François Bourguignon and Christian Morrisson (1999, p. 8), in the early nineteenth century about three-fourths of the world's people were poor when poverty is defined as a consumption level of less than $1 per day (in constant 1985 U.S. dollars), and 90 percent were poor if a threshold of $2 per day is used. Adjusting for inflation between 1985 and 1990 and for investment's share of gross domestic product (GDP), $1 per day in 1985 equals an annual income of roughly $625 in 1990 dollars and $2 per day equals an annual income of roughly $1,250 (Bourguignon and Morrisson 1999). Note that $625 is just below the estimated 1820 world *average* income of $651 in Figure 1.1. Because both income figures are in the same unit (1990 U.S. dollars), they imply that the average person in 1820 was close to the poverty line using the severe standard of $1 consumption per day (in 1985 dollars) and well below the poverty line using the standard of $2 per day (both standards based on the World Bank 1990). In short, as recently as two centuries ago the vast majority of our ancestors were poor, and the cause of that poverty was not income concentration, since according to the $2 per day standard *all* would have been poor if incomes had been distributed equally. For our ancestors the poverty problem was primarily a production problem, not a distribution problem.

Today the situation is quite different. According to the Bourguignon-Morrisson (1999, p. 8) estimates, about 40 percent of the world's people are poor today if we use the $2 per day threshold and about 16 percent are poor if we use the $1 per day threshold. These declines—from 75 percent down to 16 percent poor according to the $1 per day criterion, and from 90 percent down to 40 percent poor according to the $2 per day criterion[6]—certainly provide historical support for the argument of David Dollar and Aart Kraay (2000) that income growth *is* good for the poor. Also note, however, that in 1990 the world's average income in 1990 dollars was about $5,200 (Figure 1.1), more than four times the poverty threshold of $1,250 (in 1990 dollars) if the higher poverty threshold is used. So if incomes were distributed equally across the world today, all would have incomes well above the World Bank's poverty thresholds. In today's world, then, absolute poverty is primarily a problem of distribution, not production. Today there is more to go around than ever before and, with regard to poverty, the issue is not whether we are producing enough, but how evenly the total product is being distributed.

World poverty evolved from a production problem into a distribution problem during the period of Western industrialization. As we have seen,

Western industrialization brought growing global income inequality along with growing global income, as the world divided into three income camps, with Western Europe and its offshoots at the high end and Asia and Africa at the low end. So if you live in Germany or Switzerland or the United States, you are probably enjoying a standard of material comfort that your ancestors could scarcely imagine. If you live in Nepal or Ethiopia or Chad, your standard of living might differ little from that of your ancestors. In short, some populations benefited much more than others from the increased bounty of the Industrial Revolution, and the demarcation between winners and losers over the past two hundred years has largely coincided with regional and national boundaries. The distribution of income at the beginning of the twenty-first century is highly spatially based. Can we expect to see a reduction in the spatial basis of income over the next decades? Although no one expects a sudden change in the world income distribution, there is much talk in the globalization literature of a new global economy where nations diminish in importance. If so, then as national forces yield to global forces in the production of income, we might expect the association of income and nation to diminish over time. One of the key issues addressed in this book is whether nations are in fact declining in significance as sites for income production.

WHY STUDY GLOBAL INEQUALITY IF WE ALREADY KNOW THE ANSWERS?

Finally, some may see no point in studying global inequality because they believe the essential facts are already well established—namely, income disparities continue to widen between nations, and global inequality is worsening. What this book demonstrates, however, is that much of the conventional wisdom on global income inequality is wrong. This demonstration commences with Chapter 2, which describes five myths of what I call the Trade Protest Model of global inequality. The description of the myths sets the stage for introducing the New Geography Hypothesis.

The Reversal of Historical Inequality Trends

THIS CHAPTER presents the book's central hypothesis, which posits a new geography of global income inequality. The new geography of inequality—not to be confused with the "new economic geography" that arose in economics in the 1990s (Fujita, Krugman, and Venables 1999)—refers to the new pattern of global income inequality caused by the recent phenomenon of declining inequality across nations accompanied by (in many places) rising inequality within nations. This phenomenon, which began in the last third of the twentieth century and continues today, results in a "new geography" because it represents the reversal of trends that trace back to the early stages of Western industrialization. Put in the perspective of an individual, the new geography of global income inequality means that national location—while still paramount—is declining in significance in the determination of one's income.

Despite a recent surge of interest in global inequality, researchers have largely overlooked its changing contour. Studies of global income inequality over the last decades of the twentieth century have been preoccupied with the problem of global divergence, that is, the presumed problem of worsening income inequality for the world as a whole (for example, Wade 2001; Milanovic 2002). This preoccupation with global divergence is misguided, first, because global income inequality almost certainly declined over this period (Chapter 11) and, second, because the focus on the level of global income inequality has diverted attention from the changing nature of global income inequality in recent decades. Global income inequality is no worse today than it was in the 1960s and 1970s, but global income inequality is nevertheless changing—it is gradually shifting from inequality across nations to inequality within nations. The rising importance of within-nation inequality and declining importance of between-nation inequality represents a historic change, since it involves the reversal of a trend that began with the uneven industrialization of the world that started more than two centuries ago.

This chapter contrasts the New Geography Hypothesis with the popular view that globalization—by which I mean the increased interconnectedness of localities, particularly the deepening of economic links between countries—has led to growing global income inequality:

Globalization → global inequality.

For short, I call this popular view the Trade Protest Model, because the protests against the World Trade Organization in Seattle and elsewhere were driven at least in part by the assumption that global trade is exacerbating global inequality. To place the New Geography Hypothesis in context, it is useful first to examine five myths that underlie the globalization → global inequality model.

Myths of the Trade Protest Model

Under the heading "Siege in Seattle," the December 13, 1999, issue of the U.S. magazine *Newsweek* gave this account of the protests surrounding the meeting of the World Trade Organization in Seattle, Washington:

> Until last week, not so many Americans had even heard of the WTO. Fewer still could have identified it as the small, Geneva-based bureaucracy that the United States and 134 other nations set up five years ago to referee global commerce. To Bill Clinton, it is a mechanism that can allow America to do well and good at the same time. But to many of the 40,000 activists and union members who streamed into Seattle—a clean, scenic city that has grown rich on foreign trade—the WTO is something else again: a secretive tool of ruthless multinational corporations. They charge it with helping sneaker companies to exploit Asian workers, timber companies to clear-cut rain forests, shrimpers to kill sea turtles and a world of other offenses.

Media accounts grappled with the sheer diversity of the protesters, from leaders of U.S. labor to members of environmental groups to a leading Chinese dissident.[1] The common thread seemed to be, as the *New York Times* (1999) put it, the view that the WTO is a "handmaiden of corporate interests whose rulings undermine health, labor and environmental protections around the world." According to *The Economist* (1999), "The WTO has become a magnet for resistance to globalisation by both old-fashioned protectionists and newer critics of free trade."

Some of the protest groups emphasized rising inequality as among the most noxious consequences of increasing trade globalization. For example, Ralph Nader's Public Citizen group portrays the WTO as a tool of big business "which is harming the environment and increasing inequality" (*The Economist* 1999), and representatives of 1,448 nongovernmental organizations protesting the WTO signed a statement claiming that "globalisation has three serious consequences: the concentration of wealth in the hands of the multinationals and the rich; poverty for the majority of the world's population; and unsustainable patterns of production and consumption that destroy the environment" (*New Scientist* 1999). Note that two of the three consequences—concentration of wealth and impoverishment of the majority—tie globalization directly to growth in inequality.

Global income inequality is the result of the interplay of multiple causes, of course, so serious analyses are unlikely to give an unqualified endorsement to the notion that globalization has automatically resulted in an explosion in global income inequality. Global inequality existed before the recent growth in world trade, and it would persist if nations suddenly stopped trading. Nonetheless, popular literature on globalization has tended to fuel the belief in a globalization-led explosion in global income inequality by making claims that purport to be grounded in the findings of serious scholarly analyses. Upon closer inspection, however, many of the claims fly in the face of available empirical evidence. This section examines the key myths that underlie the globalization → global inequality model.

Myth 1. The myth of exploding global income inequality. A steady drumbeat of reports and articles claims that the world's income is becoming more and more unequally distributed. Here is a sample:

- "Globalization has dramatically increased inequality between and within nations" (Jay Mazur, 2000, in *Foreign Affairs*).

- "The very nature of globalization has an inherent bias toward inequality. . . . One would have to be blind not to see that globalization also exacerbates the disparity between a small class of winners and the rest of us" (Paul Martin, Canada's prime minister, June 1998, quoted in Eggertson 1998).

- "Along with ecological risk, to which it is related, expanding inequality is the most serious problem facing world society" (Anthony Giddens, 1999).

- "Thus, overall, the ascent of informational, global capitalism is indeed characterized by simultaneous economic development and underdevelopment, social inclusion and social exclusion. . . . There is polarization in the distribution of wealth at the global level, differential evolution of intra-country income inequality, and substantial growth of poverty and misery in the world at large" (Manuel Castells, 1998, p. 82, emphasis omitted).

What we will find subsequently is that global income inequality has not exploded but in fact leveled off and then declined in the last part of the twentieth century. Although income inequality rose somewhat in the average nation, income inequality declined across nations. Since between-nation inequality is the larger component of global income inequality, the decline in between-nation income inequality more than offset the rise in within-nation income inequality. As a result, global income inequality declined in the last years of the twentieth century. Sherlock Holmes was right: it *is* a capital mistake to theorize in advance of the facts (Doyle 1955, p. 507). With respect to global income inequality, much mischief has been done by theorizing about global income inequality on the basis of the views expressed above. Theorizing based on the widespread view of exploding global income inequality is theorizing based on facts that aren't.

Myth 2. The myth of growing income inequality across nations, as rich nations surge ahead and poor nations fall further behind. The first myth—exploding global inequality—is based on a second myth, the myth that inequality is growing across nations. The second myth is as widespread as the first, and it has been fueled by widely circulated reports of international agencies:

- "Figures indicate that income inequality between countries has increased sharply over the past 40 years" (World Bank 2000b, *World Development Report 2000/2001*, p. 51).

- "The average income in the richest 20 countries is 37 times the average in the poorest 20—a gap that has doubled in the past 40 years" (International Monetary Fund 2000, p. 50).

- "Gaps in income between the poorest and richest people and countries have continued to widen. In 1960 the 20% of the world's people in the richest countries had 30 times the income of the poorest 20%—in 1997, 74 times as much . . . Gaps are widening both between and within countries" (United Nations Development Program 1999, *Human Development Report 1999,* p. 36).

- "It is an empirical fact that the income gap between poor and rich countries has increased in recent decades" (Ben-David, Nordström, and Winters 1999, World Trade Organization special study, p. 3).

- "In 1960, the Northern countries were 20 times richer than the Southern, in 1980 46 times. . . . [I]n this kind of race, the rich countries will always move faster than the rest" (Sachs 1992, *The Development Dictionary,* p. 3).

The myth of growing income inequality across nations is based in large part on a misinterpretation of the widely cited finding (for example, World Bank 2000b, p. 50) that income growth has tended to be slower in poor nations than in rich nations. As we shall see, this positive cross-country association between income level and income growth rate conceals the critical fact that the poor nations that are falling badly behind contain no more than 10 percent of the world's population, whereas the poor nations that are catching up (largely in Asia) contain over 40 percent of the world's population. When nations are weighted by population size—as they must be if we want to use between-nation inequality to draw conclusions about global income inequality—we find that income inequality across nations peaked sometime around 1970 and has been declining since. This peaking of between-nation income inequality circa 1970 is particularly interesting in light of Manuel Castells's (1998, p. 336) well-known claim that a "new world" originated in the late 1960s to mid-1970s. Ironically, though, Castells characterizes the world born in this period as a world of sharply increasing global inequality, and many other globalization writers make the same error. (We return to the work of globalization writers such as Castells in the final chapters of the book.)

This book will debunk myth number 2 first by replicating the United Nations/World Bank results and then by demonstrating how they have been misinterpreted. In addition to the weighting problem just mentioned, the claims of growing inequality often ignore nations in the middle of the income distribution, focusing instead on selected nations at the tails. When the entire income distribution is used, and when individuals are given equal weight, we find that—far from growing—income inequality across nations declined in the late twentieth century.

Myth 3. The myth that globalization historically has caused rising inequality across nations. Contrary to this myth, the trend in between-nation inequality historically has not followed changes in the trend in world economic integration. First, although it is true that between-nation income inequality increased dramatically over the nineteenth and early twentieth centuries, Peter Lindert and Jeffrey Williamson (2000) argue that the period of rising inequality across nations began *before* the period of true globalization started, so globalization apparently did not cause the upturn. Second, the sharp decline in globalization between World War I and World War II did not result in declining inequality across nations (to the contrary, between-nation income inequality shot up rapidly over the period). Finally, as this book emphasizes, income inequality across nations has declined in recent decades, during a period when globalization has presumably reached new heights. (I say "presumably" because globalization is itself a contentious issue: see Guillén 2001. Nonetheless virtually all agree that the world has become more economically integrated over recent decades, even if the degree of globalization is often overstated, as Chase-Dunn, Kawano, and Brewer 2000, among others, have noted.) In short, the rise in global inequality predates the rise in globalization, global inequality has risen while globalization was declining, and currently global inequality is declining while globalization is rising. It is hard then to make the case historically that globalization is the cause of rising income inequality across nations (O'Rourke 2001).

Myth 4. The myth of a postindustrial world economy. In reading the globalization literature it is easy to lose sight of the fact that, until recently, most of the world's people were engaged in agriculture. So the world's workforce is barely postagricultural, much less postindustrial. This book makes the point that the primary engine still driving the growth in world production is more manufacturing. A new information age might be on the way, but it is not here yet—at least it is not here for most of the world's people. It is important to look ahead, of course, and it is hard to argue against the view that the world will eventually be postindustrial. The death of industrialization is nonetheless much exaggerated, as is the view that we are rapidly approaching an information-based global economy (Quah 1997). Estimates of the composition of global output, albeit rough approximations, rule out the claims of some globalization writers that we live in a new economic era quite unlike the era of the last generation. Industrialization was important in the nineteenth century, it was important in the twentieth century, and it remains important in most regions of the world in the twenty-first century. A preoccupation with postindustrialization in the face of the continuing diffusion of industrialization results in an incomplete and distorted story of global income inequality that deemphasizes the critical role of the continuing spread of industrialization to all regions of the world. Computers are important, but they are not all-important. In accounting for recent trends in global income inequality, this book argues that the bigger story is industrial growth in Asia, not technological growth in the West.

Myth 5. The myth of international exchange as inherently exploitative. Globalization involves increased exchange over national boundaries. One might posit that increased exchange worsens global inequality under some historical conditions and reduces it under other conditions. Until those historical conditions are identified and understood, the effect of globalization on global income inequality at any point in time is an open question to be settled empirically.

But if international exchange is inherently exploitative, as some theories of world stratification insist (Chapter 10), then rising exchange implies rising exploitation, and the Trade Protest Model is true virtually by definition. The Trade Protest Model then becomes:

Globalization → more exploitation of poor nations by rich nations → greater global inequality

Note that this elaboration of the Trade Protest Model reveals how high the theoretical stakes are with regard to empirical tests of the globalization → global income inequality model, since the failure of globalization to lead to rising global income inequality would undermine exploitation theories (for example, dependency theories) as well as undermining the Trade Protest Model.

This book presents evidence that increasing international exchange over recent decades has been accompanied by declining—not rising—income inequality across nations. Other studies also document declining between-nation income inequality over recent decades, as we shall see. The decline in between-nation inequality has significant theoretical implications. The assumption of inherent exploitation favoring rich nations in international exchange is the linchpin of some theoretical schools. But if international exchange were inherently exploitative, we would not expect to observe declining inequality across nations during a period of rising international trade. Yet the assumption persists, suggesting that in some theories the notion of inherent exploitation is so essential that it enjoys creedal status as a doctrine to be believed rather than as a hypothesis to be tested.

Causes of the Reversal: An Overview

I argue that the world's spreading industrialization and growing economic integration in the late twentieth century and the early twenty-first have reversed the historical pattern of uneven economic growth favoring richer nations. The conventional view, just elaborated, is that globalization has exacerbated global income inequality. The evidence presented here challenges that view. In reality globalization has offsetting effects—by spurring industrialization in poor nations, globalization raises inequality within many nations and compresses inequality across nations. The net effect has been a reduction in global income inequality in recent decades, since the reduction in between-nation income inequality has more than offset the growth in within-nation income inequality.

The new pattern of rising within-nation and falling between-nation income inequality has multiple causes. The most important cause is spreading industrialization—the diffusion of industrialization to the world's large poor nations. The diffusion of industrialization to poor regions compresses inequality across nations and boosts inequality within them. The effect of spreading industrialization on between-nation inequality is reinforced by the effect of the growing integration of national economies. Growing economic integration tends to dissolve institutional differences between nations. The convergence of institutional economic goals and policies compresses inequality across nations by (in some instances at least) removing impediments to growth in poor nations.

There are at least four other significant causes of the new geography of global inequality. The first is technological change that reduces the tyranny of space in general and more particularly reduces the effect of labor immobility across national boundaries. This technological change works to reduce inequality across nations. The second is a demographic windfall that has benefited some poor Asian nations in recent decades and promises to benefit other poor nations in the near future. This effect also operates to compress global income inequality, by reducing between-nation inequality. The third is the rise of the service sector, especially in richer nations. Growth in this sector has boosted income inequality within nations, and it is likely to do so in the future as well. The fourth is the collapse of communism, which also boosted within-nation inequality. This is a nonrecurring event, however, so its effect on within-nation inequality is limited to a specific point in history, the 1990s.

In short, the decline in between-nation income inequality that began in the late twentieth century was caused by deepening industrialization of poor nations, by growing economic integration that dissolves institutional differences between nations, by technological change that reduces the effects of labor immobility across national boundaries, and by a demographic windfall that has benefited some poor nations and promises to benefit others in the future. The growth in within-nation income inequality was caused by the deepening industrialization of poor nations, by the growth of the service sector, and by the collapse of communism. Each of these causes will be elaborated and argued in the last two chapters of the book. To set the context for that discussion—as well as to anticipate the empirical findings that constitute the bulk of the book—it is useful to summarize evidence indicating that we are in fact in the midst of an inequality transition.

The Inequality Transition

The industrialization of richer nations in the nineteenth century and first half of the twentieth caused income inequality across nations to explode. As a result, global income inequality shifted from inequality within nations to inequality across nations. Now, however, poorer nations are industrializing faster than richer ones are, and between-nation inequality is declining while within-nation inequality appears to be rising. If this turnaround continues, future historians will refer to an inequality transition that accompanied world industrialization. That transition is from within-nation inequality to between-nation inequality back to within-nation inequality, with the late twentieth century as the period when the shift back to within-nation income inequality began.

PHASE 1 OF THE TRANSITION: FROM WITHIN- TO BETWEEN-NATION INEQUALITY

Phase 1 of the inequality transition coincides with the period of Western industrialization that began in the late eighteenth century and ended in the second half of the twentieth century. The first phase of the inequality transition was characterized by unprecedented growth in income inequality across nations. As Lant Pritchett (1996, p. 40) puts it, "the overwhelming feature of modern economic history is a massive divergence in per capita incomes between rich and poor countries." The evidence is incontrovertible. First, it is clear that current levels of between-nation income inequality would not have been possible earlier in human history. Again quoting Pritchett (1997, pp. 9–10): "If there had been no divergence, then we could extrapolate backward from present income of the poorer countries to past income assuming they grew at least as fast as the United States. However, this would imply that many poor countries must have had incomes below $100 in 1870 [in 1985 U.S. dollars]. Since this cannot be true, there must have been divergence."

Second, Pritchett's conclusion that "there must have been divergence" is supported by estimates of between-nation income inequality in the nineteenth century. Consider the recent estimates of Bourguignon and Morrisson (1999). Bourguignon and Morrisson use the Maddison (1995) data to estimate changes in the level of between-nation income inequality from 1820 to 1992. Because their objective is to estimate total world income inequality—not just between-nation income inequality—Bourguignon and Morrisson begin by disaggregating national income data into vintiles (5 percent groups, that is, twenty income groups per nation). National boundaries have changed over the past two centuries, of course, and nations have come and gone over the past two centuries. Even in nations where boundaries remained constant, we do not always have income data for the entire period. To overcome these problems, Bourguignon and Morrisson grouped the 199 nations with income data in 1992 into 33 homogeneous groups, each of which represented at least 1 percent of the world population or world GDP in 1950. The 33 groups include single nations (such as China and the United States) as well as large groups of small nations and small groups of medium-sized nations. From these 660 data points (33 nation groups × 20) it is a straightforward matter to apply the population-weighted formulas for the Theil index and the mean logarithmic deviation (MLD)—two measures of inequality (Chapter 4)—to calculate summary measures of the world's total inequality for different years. By collapsing the 199 nations into 33 groups, Bourguignon and Morrisson are able to extend their inequality series back to 1820. Note that, to the extent that their grouping strategy introduces bias, the bias is in the direction of underestimating between-nation inequality and inflating within-nation inequality, since some of the inequality within the nation groups is actually between-nation inequality. But that bias should not affect our basic conclusions about the relative growth in between-nation and within-nation income inequality over the past two centuries.[2]

The results are striking (Figure 2.1). Two facts stand out. First, the B/W ratio—the ratio of between-nation to within-nation income inequality—is much higher now than it was in the early stages of Western industrialization. The increase in the B/W ratio reflects both a rise in between-nation

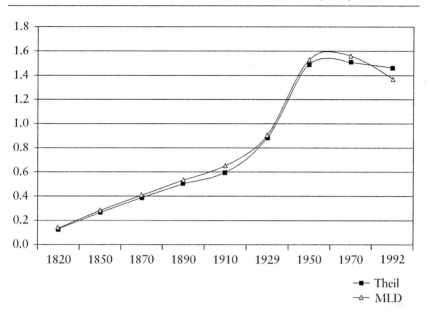

FIGURE 2.1 Ratio of between-nation to within-nation income inequality for 33 nation groups, 1820–1992. Based on Table 2.1. Theil and MLD are measures of inequality.

income inequality and a decline in within-nation income inequality since 1820 (Table 2.1). By far the greater change is in between-nation income inequality, however. The Theil index for between-nation income inequality (actually, inequality between nation *groups*) shot up from 0.061 in 1820 to 0.513 in 1992, and the MLD shot up from 0.053 in 1820 to 0.495 in 1992. As anticipated, then, the Industrial Revolution of the past two centuries has increased income inequality across nations, but the magnitude of the increase is stunning. There has been a metamorphosis from a world where poverty was the norm in all nations to a richer world with much lower poverty rates (Bourguignon and Morrisson 1999, table 1) but also with much greater income inequality across nations. Because the steep rise in between-nation income inequality was not accompanied by an increase in inequality within nations, where you live—your nation—is much more important in determining your income in today's world than it was in the preindustrial world.

The second fact that stands out is that the growth in the *B/W* ratio stalled in the second half of the twentieth century. The *B/W* ratio stopped growing in the second half of the twentieth century because growth in inequality across the nation groups has slowed dramatically since 1950. In

TABLE 2.1 Trends in income inequality between and within 33 homogeneous nation groups, 1820–1992

	Between nation groups		Within nation groups	
Year	Theil	MLD	Theil	MLD
1820	.061	.053	.472	.388
1850	.128	.111	.477	.393
1870	.188	.162	.485	.399
1890	.251	.217	.498	.408
1910	.299	.269	.500	.413
1929	.365	.335	.413	.372
1950	.482	.472	.323	.309
1970	.490	.515	.324	.330
1992	.513	.495	.351	.362

Source: Bourguignon and Morrisson (1999), table 3.

Estimates: Between nation groups: From Bourguignon and Morrisson (1999), based on Maddison (1995) data set. *Within nation groups:* From Bourguignon and Morrisson (1999), based on updating of Berry, Bourguignon, and Morrisson (1983a,b) for the post–World War II period and on various sources (for example, Lindert 1999; Morrisson 1999) for the pre–World War II period. As this book was going to press, Bourguignon and Morrisson (2002) published modestly revised estimates for inequality. By collapsing vintiles to deciles, they report slightly lower estimates of inequality within the nation groups, but the fundamental conclusions are the same.

Note: Income measures are adjusted for purchasing power parity, and inequality measures are based on income vintiles (see Bourguignon and Morrisson 1999 for elaboration).

the four decades after 1950, income inequality across the nation groups increased by 6 percent using the Theil index and by 5 percent using the MLD. Over the four decades prior to 1950, the Theil had grown about 60 percent and the MLD had grown about 75 percent. Apparently the most dramatic effects of Western industrialization on between-nation inequality are over. After more than a century of sharp divergence in national incomes, the trend has been much more stable in recent years. This finding is in line with the findings of others (for example, Schultz 1998; Firebaugh 1999; Melchior, Telle, and Wiig 2000; Goesling 2001) who, drawing on data for individual nations instead of nation groups, find that between-nation income inequality is no longer rising. As we shall see later, between-nation income inequality declined in the late twentieth century when income data for the 1990s are added to data for the 1970s and 1980s.

Finally, it should be emphasized that the results here are so strong that the historical story they tell of increasing inequality across nations and of a rising *B/W* ratio cannot be dismissed as due to error in the data. To be sure, income estimates for the nineteenth century are gross approximations for many nations. But even if we make the extreme assumption that incomes are so drastically overstated for poorer nations in 1820 (or so drastically understated for richer nations in 1820) that the Theil and the MLD estimates understate between-nation income inequality in 1820 by a factor of three, that would still mean that between-nation income inequality tripled from 1820 to 1992 (from 0.18 to 0.51 based on the Theil index and from 0.16 to 0.50 for the MLD), and the B/W ratio still would have more than tripled for both inequality measures.

PHASE 2 OF THE TRANSITION: FROM BETWEEN-NATION BACK TO WITHIN-NATION INEQUALITY

The second phase of the inequality transition began in the second half of the twentieth century, with the stabilization of between-nation income inequality in the 1960–1990 period and the decline in between-nation inequality beginning in earnest in the 1990s. Social scientists hardly have a stellar track record for predictions, especially with regard to sweeping predictions such as the one made here. Nonetheless there is sufficient theory and evidence that we can plausibly forecast that the B/W ratio will continue to decline in the twenty-first century.

The prediction of a declining B/W ratio is based on two separate conjectures. The first conjecture is that between-nation income inequality will decline, and the second conjecture is that within-nation income inequality will rise, or at least will not decline. These conjectures are based on the causes of the current trends, which I expect to continue and in some cases to intensify. (I am assuming that there will be no cataclysmic upheaval in the twenty-first century, such as a global war or a worldwide plague.) Recall the causes listed earlier for the inequality turnaround in the late twentieth century. I expect the major causes to continue, so between-nation income inequality will decline because of the continued industrialization of poor nations, because of the continued convergence of national economic policies and institutions arising from growing economic integration of national economies, because of the declining significance of labor immobility across national borders, and because of a demographic windfall for many poor nations. Within-nation income inequality will rise—or at least not decline—because of the continued industrialization of poor nations and because of continued growth in the service sector. Because between-nation inequality is the larger component, global income inequality will decline (Chapter 11).

The conjecture of declining global income inequality is out of step with much of the globalization literature. A recurring theme in that literature is that we have entered a new information-based economic era where productive activity is becoming less dependent on physical space, as a rising share of the world's economic output is produced in electronic space that knows no national borders (Sassen 2000). This phenomenon is possible because of the emergence of a global economy where income—and hence income inequality—is becoming increasingly rooted in knowledge rather than in capital goods (Reich 1991). What do these developments imply for global income inequality? For many globalization writers, the answer is clear: global inequality is bound to worsen because of the growing "global digital divide" that enlarges the gap between the "haves" and the "have-nots" (Campbell 2001; Ishaq 2001; Norris 2001).

Empirical evidence presented subsequently suggests otherwise, however, and the theoretical argument that a shift to a knowledge-based global economy would worsen global income inequality is shaky as well. It is not hard to think of reasons why the shift from an industrial-based to a knowledge-based global economy would reduce, not increase, inequality across nations. Knowledge is mobile, especially with today's telecommunication technologies that permit virtually instant worldwide codification and distribution of knowledge. In addition, because knowledge can be given away without being lost, the notion of property rights is more problematic in the case of knowledge, so it is harder to concentrate and monopolize knowledge across nations than it is to concentrate and monopolize capital goods across nations. Hence the switch to a knowledge-based global economy should mean that one's income is increasingly determined by how much knowledge one obtains and uses as opposed to where one lives. The tighter link between knowledge and income in turn implies declining income inequality across nations and rising inequality within nations since—absent institutional barriers (an important qualification to be discussed later)—the variance in individuals' ability to obtain and benefit from knowledge is greater within nations than between them.

I return to these issues in Chapter 10, where I examine in more detail the inequality implications of predictions of a fast-approaching information age. It suffices to note here that the issue of how the new information age will affect global inequality in the near term is not as decisive as often imagined, since as already noted, the coming of the information age is often much exaggerated. What is still most important in today's world is industrialization for the many, not digitization for the few. Historically the spread of industrialization has been the primary force driving the growth in between-nation income inequality. The initially richer nations of the West were the first to industrialize, and the poorer nations of Asia and Africa lagged behind. The new geography of inequality is also driven by the spread of industrialization, but the effects are different today: now the spread of industrialization means the diffusion of manufacturing technology to the world's largest poor regions. In recent decades inequality has declined across nations as industrialization has been an engine of growth in the most populous poor regions of the world, especially East Asia. That growth has worked both to compress inequality across nations (Figure 2.2) and to boost inequality within the industrializing nations.

The significance of this continuation of world industrialization has been lost in much of the literature on globalization, because of preoccupation with the idea that we are witnessing the emergence of a new knowledge-based technology regime. To be sure, in the categories used to classify world production, the output of the so-called service sector is estimated to exceed the output of the industrial sector for the world as a whole (World Bank 1997, table 12). Yet much of the service sector—an amorphous sector that includes wholesale and retail trade, the banking industry, government, the transportation industry, the commercial real estate industry, and personal services (including health care and education)—has arisen to grease the wheels of industry. Aside from the growth in personal services and government, much of the growth in the service sector has been for services for producers, not consumers—for example, the rise of an engineering industry to design better machines, and the growth of a banking industry and a commercial real estate industry for commercial transactions. In addition, many of the other so-called service industries—the transportation industry that distributes manufactured goods, for example, and the specialized retailing industry that sells the goods—benefit producers as well as consumers. In short, a significant portion of the growth in service industries over the past century can be seen as ancillary to the industrialization process.

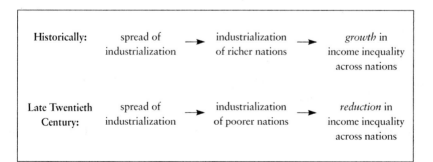

FIGURE 2.2 Industrialization and between-nation income inequality: Historically and in the late twentieth century.

With regard to income inequality within nations, we expect the continuing spread of world industrialization to boost inequality along the lines of the classic argument, from Simon Kuznets (1955), that industrialization boosts inequality (at least initially) as workers move from the lower-wage but larger agricultural sector to the higher-wage industrial sector. Importantly, this argument suggests that income inequality increases in poor nations as they industrialize because of income gains, not income losses. In other words, inequality grows not because some people are becoming poorer but because some people are becoming richer, so the growth in income inequality in poor nations as they industrialize reflects rising rather than declining fortunes. If the industrialization of large poor nations does boost income inequality in those nations, at this juncture in history the continued spread of industrialization implies growth in income inequality in the average nation, because those nations are home to such a large fraction of the world's population. And there are no obvious counterforces on the horizon. Although the jump in income inequality following the collapse of communism in Eastern Europe and the former USSR is not likely to be repeated, there is no good reason to expect income inequality in those nations to fall in the near future. Nor is there any good reason to expect income inequality to decline notably in the West in the near future, either. We lack reliable inequality data for many African nations, but even if inequality were falling rapidly (which is unlikely), the effect of falling within-nation inequality in Africa would not offset the effect of rising within-nation inequality in Asia, given the relative sizes of the two regions. Few expect within-nation income inequality to decline sharply in Latin America in the near future, even though Latin America currently exhibits the highest level of within-nation income inequality of the world's major regions. Indeed, because of the advantage enjoyed by North American farmers with respect to some types of produce, economic integration in the Americas could exacerbate inequality by removing protections for farmers in Latin America. If that reasoning is correct, there is merit in the concern of WTO protesters that globalization may exacerbate income inequality within some poor nations by driving down incomes in the lower-income agricultural sector. But the bigger story is that industrialization (not the collapse of farm prices) will tend to drive up inequality within nations, as least initially. Because many nations are still on the part of the Kuznets (1955) curve where migration from farm to factory boosts inequality, we can anticipate further growth in within-nation income inequality in the early decades of the twenty-first century.

MEASUREMENT

How Is National Income Measured, and Can We Trust the Data?

THIS CHAPTER addresses three questions: What is national income and how is it estimated? Are the estimates of national income plausible? Are the estimates reliable enough to test the notion, advanced in the last chapter, that we are witnessing a turnaround in between-nation income inequality? The claim of this chapter is that, warts and all, the national income data are reliable enough for us to see the big picture regarding between-nation income inequality in the nineteenth and twentieth centuries. More recent data are more reliable than earlier income data, and the data for recent decades indicate that between-nation income inequality was fairly stable or declined slightly from the 1960s through the 1980s, and declined during the 1990s. Income data for the nineteenth and early twentieth centuries are less reliable, but here the signal of growing inequality is so strong that no one can deny the story of rising between-nation income inequality over that period.

In this chapter I describe in nontechnical terms what national income is and how national income is measured, and in the next chapter I describe what inequality is and how inequality is measured. These chapters point out that both the measurement of national income and the measurement of income inequality have a long history in the social sciences, so there is now general consensus about what *national income* and *income inequality* mean and how they should be measured. It turns out, in fact, that virtually all studies of income inequality across nations rely on the same data sets and use the same measures of inequality. This study is no exception, and therefore the claim here of declining income inequality across nations is based on conventional data and measures. Thus readers who are already familiar with the conventions of measuring national income—or readers who do not know much about how national income is measured but are willing to accept on faith that it is done properly—can skip the first section on how national income is measured and go directly to the chapter's second major section, "Are Income Estimates Plausible?" What readers cannot do, however, is dismiss the finding here of declining between-nation income inequality in the late twentieth century as unreliable while accepting as reliable the claims of other studies of growing inequality over the same period, since the contrary findings are based on the same data sets.

How Is National Income Measured?

By convention the term *national income* refers to *national output*, and that is the way the term *income* is used in this book. To compare output across nations, we need production figures (how many bushels of wheat were grown, how many tons of steel were produced, how many pairs of shoes were manufactured) weighted by the prices for the commodities. This is an immense task, and the first part alone—the collection of national production data—has led to a global statistical system of national accounts constituting perhaps the most ambitious data collection effort in history. Using these national accounts, we should be able to determine empirically whether income inequality across nations is growing or shrinking.

National output is measured as gross domestic product (GDP)—the total annual value of all goods and services produced within a nation's borders—or as gross national product (GNP)—the total annual value of all goods and services claimed by a nation's residents. GDP and GNP yield virtually the same results in analyses of between-nation income inequality, since the cross-national correlation of GDP and GNP is close to $r = 1.0$ for the world.[1] As a result, the choice of GDP versus GNP does not matter when estimating the level of between-nation inequality (Chapter 6).

But the question of how to price the output does matter, since nations produce such different bundles of goods and services. Nation A produces lots of steel but little beef and no bananas, Nation B is a leading producer of bananas but produces no steel and very little beef, and Nation C is one of the world's leading producers of beef but produces little steel and no bananas. To compare the output of the three nations we must assign prices to the different commodities—a task complicated by differences in relative prices from country to country as well as by changes in relative prices over time within a country. Historically, prices were set using a shortcut method based on foreign exchange rates. It is now generally recognized that the foreign-exchange-rate method, or FX method, has serious problems that disqualify it for use in academic studies comparing national incomes. The United Nations and the World Bank nonetheless continue to update their FX-based income series by adding FX estimates for recent years, with the warning from the United Nations (1993, para. 1.38) that the FX income estimates are not to be used for comparing living standards across nations. Despite the warning, FX estimates are occasionally still used to make the case for growing income inequality across nations. The next section explains why social scientists generally no longer use estimates based on the FX method for comparing national incomes.

THE EXCHANGE-RATE METHOD FOR ESTIMATING NATIONAL INCOME

Early attempts to compare national incomes relied on official exchange rates to calibrate incomes to a standard yardstick, the U.S. dollar. The problems with this method for estimating national income have long been understood. It is well known, for example, that international travelers commonly find that their money will buy more in India than in Switzerland, which points to the systematic undervaluation of the currencies of poor nations on the basis of official exchange rates. What accounts for this undervaluation? The key is to note that real wages tend to be low in nations with low labor productivity (that is, in poor nations), so in those nations labor-intensive goods are cheap relative to capital-intensive goods. But it is the relatively expensive capital-intensive goods that are more likely to be traded on the international market. Because market exchange rates tend to equate prices in the traded sector rather than in the nontraded sector, the exchange rates for poor nations tend to be based on their relatively more expensive products rather than on their relatively cheap labor-intensive products. Hence markets tend to undervalue the currencies of poor nations relative to what one can actually purchase domestically. This undervaluation benefits tourists from rich nations but exaggerates the level of income inequality across nations by understating the income levels in poor nations.

To appreciate the severity of the problem, consider these FX-based estimates of 1998 per capita GNP from the World Bank (2000a, table 1.1, in 1998 U.S. dollars): $100 for Ethiopia, $140 for Burundi and Sierra Leone, $160 for Guinea-Bissau. Contrast these income figures with the FX-based estimates of $39,980 for Switzerland and $34,310 for Norway. The former estimates are implausible. First, a daily production of only 27 cents per day (Ethiopia) or even 38 cents per day (Burundi and Sierra Leone) is probably not sufficient to sustain life, as we see subsequently. Second, the cross-nation disparities are not reasonable. Admittedly labor productivity is much greater in Norway than in Ethiopia and Sierra Leone, but it is far-fetched to claim that the average person in Ethiopia or Sierra Leone must work 250 to 350 days to produce what the average Norwegian produces in a single day. By any reasonable accounting of output, Norwegians do not produce in one day what Ethiopians produce in an entire year, as the FX estimates imply.

In addition to producing implausible estimates for poor nations, the FX method very often exaggerates annual fluctuations in a country's income. In this case the FX estimates are implausible not because they are too low, but because they change overnight because of changes in the official exchange rate. This volatility problem applies to income estimates for rich as well as poor countries. Consider, for example, the Japanese experience in the mid-1980s. Using the FX method we conclude that per capita income in Japan virtually doubled from 1985 to 1988 (Horioka 1994, table 1). This stupendous increase in fact is a "statistical illusion" (ibid., p. 297) caused by the too-rapid appreciation of the yen from 238 yen to the dollar in 1985 to 128 yen to the dollar in 1988. More realistic measurement of Japanese economic growth indicates much slower income growth over those three years (ibid., table 1). The same problem besets income estimates for poor agricultural nations as well, as I have noted elsewhere (Firebaugh 1999). Consider a farmer who owns an ox. The ox has local value—it can be used to pull a plow, for example—so it can be sold locally. The price that it would command is its local price. Although the ox also has a foreign-exchange-rate price—its price if it were sold internationally—the local price is the relevant price to the farmer because, as Robert Summers and Alan Heston (1991, p. 360) put it, "Residents of a country face their own prices, not international prices." For example, an ox does not become half an ox when a nation decides to devalue its currency by half relative to the U.S. dollar, so the price the ox would fetch locally is not halved by the devaluation. Yet the FX method assumes that the ox's price is cut in half when currency is devalued by half. In sum, as Daniel Nuxoll (1994, p. 1424) and many others have warned, "exchange rates cannot be used to compare income levels of different nations."

USING PURCHASING POWER PARITY TO ESTIMATE NATIONAL INCOME

In the 1960s the United Nations launched the International Comparison Project (ICP), designed to produce more satisfactory estimates of national incomes on the basis of the concept of "purchasing power parity" (PPP). The basic idea is simple: collect data on the price of goods and services in a given nation using that nation's currency, repeat for all nations, and use those prices to construct an international price for all goods and services that is an average of the national prices. This approach relies on a detailed comparison of the prices of hundreds of goods across nations to establish an international price, based on local prices, for each good. It is important to note that, unlike the FX method, prices are based on data on what goods actually cost in a nation, not on their projected cost using exchange rates. National income is derived by applying the set of international prices to the quantities that constitute "each country's national absorption of final goods" (Kravis and Lipsey 1990, p. 35) and aggregating.

Purchasing power parities are ratios of the prices (in the national currencies) of the same good or service in different nations. The goal is to calculate PPPs about every five years through the International Comparison Program (annual PPPs are then estimated by extrapolation from the benchmark years). This is an ambitious goal that has not been attained for many nations, as critics are quick to note. Despite these shortcomings, there is widespread agreement that PPP estimates of income are much superior to FX estimates (for example, Berry, Bourguignon, and Morrisson 1983a, 1983b, 1991; Grosh and Nafziger 1986; Kravis and Lipsey 1990; Summers and Heston 1991; Nuxoll 1994; Dowrick and Quiggin 1997; Temple 1999; Melchior, Telle, and Wiig 2000; Australian Treasury 2001; Melchior and Telle 2001) and clearly the PPP estimates should be used if the purpose is to compare nations' welfare or living standards. Quoting Jonathan Temple (1999, p. 114): "Instead of using exchange rates, incomes should be converted using special currency indexes which are calculated so that one unit will purchase the same bundle of goods across countries. The calculation and use of these indexes, called purchasing power parities or PPPs, is essential for accurate cross-country comparisons of real incomes." The United Nations System of National Accounts (1993, para. 1.38) instructs that "when the objective is to compare the volumes of goods and services produced or consumed per head, data in national currencies must be converted into a common currency by means of purchasing power parities and not exchange rates." In line with the UN instructions, virtually all recent studies of between-nation or global income inequality use income data adjusted for purchasing power differences (Schultz 1998; Boltho and Toniolo 1999; Bourguignon and Morrisson 1999; Summers and Heston 1999; Firebaugh 1999, 2000; Goesling 2000, 2001; Melchior, Telle, and Wiig 2000; Milanovic 2002; Sala-i-Martin 2002a,b).

Because relative prices vary from country to country, a specific methodology is needed to construct PPP data from the benchmark studies. All methods have weaknesses (Dowrick and Quiggin 1997) and different organizations use somewhat different methods for constructing the PPP estimates. Of the existing PPP income series, the standard is the Penn World

Table income series (Summers et al. 1994), and that is the primary income series used in this book. The international prices used in the Penn series are in effect world averages, so they tend to more closely resemble the prices prevailing in middle-income countries than in poorer countries. The likely effect is that PPP estimates somewhat overstate the income levels, and somewhat understate the recent income growth, of poor countries (Nuxoll 1994). If it is the case that PPP estimates tend to understate income growth in poor countries, then the results reported in this book most likely somewhat understate the rate of decline in between-nation income inequality. The findings of Nuxoll (1994), however, indicate that any biases are likely to be very small.[2]

There are profound differences between the PPP and the FX estimates of income in poor nations. To illustrate using data from the same organization, the World Bank PPP estimates of per capita income (GNP) are 6.7 times higher than their FX estimates for the Democratic Republic of Congo in 1998, 5.7 times higher than their FX estimates for Ethiopia, 4 times higher than their FX estimates for Burundi, 3.6 times higher than their FX estimates for Guinea-Bissau, and 3.2 times higher than their FX estimates for Sierra Leone (World Bank, 2000a, table 1.1).

It is the FX estimates that are dubious. No one believes, for example, that Mozambique's per capita output is only $80 per year, or $6.70 a month, as the FX estimates suggest (World Bank 1997, table 1). The PPP estimates of income are much more believable and, as we verify subsequently, other evidence pertaining to living standards in poor nations is much more congruent with the PPP estimates than with the FX estimates.

By understating income in poor nations, the FX method exaggerates the level of income inequality across nations. When we use PPP estimates instead of FX estimates, we still find huge income disparities between the richest and poorest nations, but the ratios are on the order of magnitude of 25 or 30 to 1 instead of the FX-based ratios of 200 to 1 or 300 to 1. The regional differences also shrink when we replace FX estimates with PPP estimates. For example, the 1988 ratio between the world's richest continents (Western Europe and North America) and the world's poorest continent (Africa) was 26 to 1 using FX measures of per capita income but 11 to 1 using PPP measures (Milanovic 2002).

Finally, it is important to note that the FX and PPP methods also yield divergent results for change in income inequality across nations, with FX estimates indicating that inequality rose over the 1970s and 1980s and PPP estimates indicating that inequality was steady or fell over those decades (Chapter 7). Again it is the FX results that are dubious. First, there is the volatility problem illustrated earlier by the example of Japan in the mid-1980s. The FX trends are subject to change over time arising from exchange-rate fluctuations independent of real income changes. Second, there is evidence that FX estimates have tended to understate income growth (as well as income levels) in poor nations over recent decades. Consider, for example, the relative income growth rates of the United States and China in recent decades. By all accounts income has been growing faster in China than in the United States, so the U.S. versus China income ratio should shrink. According to PPP data, it has, from a ratio of about 20 to 1 in 1965 to about 8 to 1 in 1997 (Melchior and Telle 2001). According to FX data, however, the ratio increased from 37 to 1 to 40 to 1. But no serious student believes that per capita incomes have been growing more slowly in China since 1965. So the FX results clearly are implausible, and we turn our attention to the PPP estimates. How plausible are they?

Are Income Estimates Plausible?

By income estimates I refer to PPP-based estimates, since those are the income estimates I use in this study. We have already noted that PPP estimates of per capita income in very poor nations tend to be much higher than the FX estimates. Despite that upward adjustment, the PPP method still yields estimates that appear woefully low by Western standards. Table 3.1 lists estimated incomes for the ten poorest nations in the Penn income series in 1989 (the last year of the Penn income series available at the time of this study). According to these estimates, Chad was the world's poorest nation in 1989, with an estimated per capita income of about $640 in 2000 U.S. dollars. Do Chadians actually live at such a low level? No one could live on $640 a year in the United States—or at least we think they must not be able to, given that $640 is only a fraction of the U.S. poverty threshold of roughly $3,800 per person for a family of six (a typical household size in poor nations) in 2000, and many consider the $3,800 figure to be ungenerous. So if people in Chad typically live on about $640 a year, how do they do it? This section addresses those questions. To get a sense of what life is like for the masses in poor nations, we begin with nonincome evidence on the living standards that prevail in low-income nations.

HOW POOR ARE MOST PEOPLE IN POOR NATIONS?

How poor are most people in poor nations? The answer is quite poor, by Western standards. In the poorest nations the majority of people are poor, and the poverty is more abject than most poverty one sees in the West. It is well established that the "perception of poverty has evolved historically and varies tremendously from culture to culture" (World Bank 1990,

TABLE 3.1 Incomes and populations of ten poorest countries in 1989

Country	Per capita income	% of world's population
Central African Republic	$913	0.06
Comoros	$910	<0.01
Mali	$868	0.16
Uganda	$855	0.30
Burundi	$830	0.10
Malawi	$819	0.16
Burkina Faso	$810	0.17
Niger	$788	0.15
Zaire (Democratic Republic of Congo)	$662	0.69
Chad	$643	0.11
Total		1.91%

Source: Penn World Table, version 5.6 (Summers et al. 1994).
Note: Per capita incomes in 1989, expressed in 2000 U.S. dollars. The income estimates are adjusted for PPP.

p. 27). The thresholds used to determine poverty in Western European nations are substantially higher than the thresholds used in poor nations in South Asia and sub-Saharan Africa—as they should be, since poverty is in part a relative phenomenon (if I have only a small fraction of what others have in a community, then I am among the poor in that community). And that is precisely one of the points to stress here: because the thresholds are lower in poorer nations, the poor in poor nations tend to be poorer in an absolute sense than the poor in rich nations.

The World Bank's 1990 *World Development Report* provides a useful point of departure for comparing the poor in poor nations with the poor in the United States. The 1990 *Report* is probably best known for suggesting PPP $1 per person per day (in 1985 U.S. dollars, or roughly $1.50 in 2000 dollars) as a threshold for poverty in the world's poor nations. Subsequent studies have adopted the $1 per day criterion to define poverty in poor nations, and some add supplementary analyses based on a more generous $2 per day criterion.

For our purposes one of the most pertinent sections of the 1990 *Report* is the one that profiles three poor families—in Ghana, in Peru, and in Bangladesh—who are typical of the poor in those regions of the world. These are compelling accounts:

- *Ghana.* "In Ghana's Savannah region a typical family of seven lives in three one-room mud huts made from mud bricks, with earthen floors. They have little furniture and no toilet, electricity, or running water. Water is obtained from a stream a fifteen-minute walk away. The family has few possessions, apart from three acres of unirrigated land and one cow. . . . None of the older family members ever attended school, but the eight-year-old son is now in the first grade. The family hopes that he will be able to stay in school, although there is pressure to keep him at home to help with the farm in the busy periods. He and his two younger sisters have never had any vaccinations and they have never seen a doctor" (World Bank 1990, p. 24).

* *Peru.* "In a shantytown on the outskirts of Lima a shack made of scraps of wood, iron, and cardboard houses a family of six. Inside there is a bed, a table, a radio, and two benches. The kitchen consists of a small kerosene stove and some tins in one corner. There is no toilet or electricity. The shantytown is provided with some public services, but these tend to be intermittent. Garbage is collected twice a week. Water is delivered to those who have a cement tank, but this family has been unable to save enough for the cement. In the meantime, the mother and eldest daughter fill buckets at the public standpipe 500 yards away. . . . The family lives on rice, bread, and vegetable oil (all subsidized by the government), supplemented with vegetables and, occasionally, some fish" (World Bank 1990, pp. 24–25).

* *Bangladesh.* "In a rural community in a drought-prone region of Bangladesh a landless laborer and his family attempt to get through another lean season. Their house consists of a packed mud floor and a straw roof held up by bamboo poles from which dry palm leaves are tied to serve as walls. Inside there is straw to sleep on and burlap bags for warmth. The laborer and his wife, three children, and niece do not own the land on which the shack is built. They are lucky, however, to have a kindly neighbor who has indefinitely lent them the plot. . . . The household spends about 85 percent of its meager income on food—predominantly rice. Family members are used to having only two meals a day. They hope to struggle through to the rice harvest without having to cut down and sell their jackfruit tree or the bamboo poles supporting their roof" (World Bank 1990, p. 25).

TYPICAL LIVING STANDARDS IN POOR NATIONS

Although it is true that the *average* families in Ghana, Peru, and Bangladesh are not as destitute as the families described here, these profiles should not be dismissed as being far off the mark with regard to common living conditions in poor nations. Most people in poor nations are not living on the verge of starvation, but there is tangible evidence that the majority of families in poor nations are quite poor by Western standards. This evidence begins with the observation that food constitutes one-half or more of the total budget for the average family in many poor nations (for example, 50 percent in Malawi, 51 percent in Nigeria, 52 percent in Benin, 52 percent in Zambia, 53 percent in Mali, and 61 percent in Madagascar: World Bank 2000a, table 4.11). In poor nations few families spend less than one-third of their resources on food, yet in the United States the poverty line itself is based on the assumption that a poor family spends one-third of its income on food (Orshansky 1965).

Household expenditure surveys conducted in selected low-income nations in the late 1980s and early 1990s provide tangible evidence of the meager living conditions prevailing in poor nations. Consider results from the World Bank's Living Standards Measurement Study (LSMS) surveys of Ghana (conducted 1987–1989), Jamaica (1989), Pakistan (1991), and Peru (1994). To these surveys we add results from a 1993–94 survey of Tanzania and a 1995 survey of rural Guatemala. Two of the six nations (Ghana and Peru) were represented in the family profiles above. Importantly, the six nations span the major regions and per capita income levels of the world's poor nations.[3] The household surveys collected data on the characteristics of household dwellings as well as on household possession of consumer durables such as refrigerators and cars. Table 3.2 reports results for key indicators of living standards. In terms of per capita incomes, Ghana, Pakistan, and Tanzania constitute a group labeled "very poor" (per capita incomes less than one-third of the world average in 1989) and Guatemala, Jamaica, and Peru constitute a second group labeled "low income" (per capita incomes between one-third and two-thirds of the world average in 1989). If stated per capita incomes are reasonably accurate, then Ghana and Tanzania should exhibit the lowest levels on the indicators, followed by Pakistan, then rural Guatemala, then Peru and Jamaica.

The general pattern of results is consistent with the per capita income data, but there are a few anomalies. Consistent with income rankings, households in Ghana and Tanzania are far less likely (than households in the other nations) to have water on the premises, to have flush toilets (rural Guatemala is an exception here), and to possess televisions or refrigerators (again rural Guatemala is an exception). In addition, caloric consumption is lower in Ghana and Tanzania than in the other four poor nations, even though households in Tanzania are estimated to devote two-thirds of their budgets to food (reliable estimates for Ghana are not available). With re-

TABLE 3.2 Indicators of living standards in selected poor nations, compared with the United States

	Very poor nations $(0 < r_i < .33)$			Low-income nations $(.33 < r_i < .67)$			
Item	Ghana	Pakistan	Tanzania	Rural Guatemala	Jamaica	Peru	United States
Housing characteristics							
Water on premises (%)	12.6	38.5	19.8	65.0	60.5	66.8	>99
Flush toilet (%)	6.0	40.7	8.4	8.3	25.2	51.5	>99
Nondirt floor (%)	77.7	51.6	50.6	39.9	—	60.6	>99
Consumer durables							
Radio (%)	26.0	20.3	43.1	73.4	70.0	86.9	—
Television (%)	7.6	—	3.2	33.4	51.9	72.9	98
Refrigerator (%)	7.0	—	7.7	7.4	45.4	42.2	—
Car (%)	3.0	2.9	—	7.9	8.2	6.8	—
Food							
% spent on food (1980s)	—	54	64	36[a]	39	35	13
% spent on food (1998)	—	45	67	—	24	26	13
Daily calories (1986)	1,759	2,315	2,192	2,307[a]	2,590	2,246	3,645
Income per capita							
PPP estimates (1989)	$1,300	$2,180	$930	$3,340	$3,950	$3,480	$28,220

Data sources: For housing characteristics and consumer durables: Montgomery et al. (2000), table 2, for the six poor nations; U.S. Census Bureau (2000) for U.S. data. Data for the six poor nations are circa 1990 (see text) and data for the United States are for 1990. *For food:* World Bank (1990), table 10, for food expenses as percentage of total household expenditures in 1980s; World Bank (2000a), table 4.11, for food expenses as percentage of total household expenditures in 1998; World Bank (1990), table 28, for daily calorie supply per capita in 1986. *For income per capita:* From the Penn World Table, except Tanzania, which is based on Maddison (1995), table D-1. Incomes are expressed in 2000 U.S. dollars.

Note: "Very poor nations" are those whose income ratios (r_i) in 1989 were less than one-third the world average, or roughly $2,250 per capita income in 2000 U.S. dollars (PPP). "Low-income nations" are those whose income ratios were one-third to two-thirds the world average in 1989 (roughly $2,250–4,500 income per capita).

a. Includes Guatemala's urban population.

gard to anomalies, flush toilets are more prevalent in Pakistan than in Jamaica or rural Guatemala and radios are more prevalent in Tanzania than in Pakistan. In addition, nondirt floors are about as common in the poorest three nations as they are in Peru, and more common than in rural Guatemala—but one wonders if that result might reflect the wide range of meanings that could be given to the term "nondirt floor" (for example, a dirt floor covered by a woven grass mat might be considered "nondirt").

With regard to the ranking of poor nations, then, the per capita income data appear to be reasonably consistent with more direct indicators of living standards in the six poor nations. But it still could be the case that the income figures themselves are implausibly low for very poor nations such as Ghana and Tanzania. To gain leverage on that issue, we compare the stated per capita incomes with the percentages in Table 3.2 and ask whether the stated incomes seem reasonable in light of the living standards implied by the percentages. It is convenient to use the United States as the point of comparison since the per capita income figures refer to purchasing power parity in U.S. dollars.

GHANA VERSUS THE UNITED STATES

Ghana is used as the test case since Ghana was among the poorest nations in the world in 1989 and the requisite data—PPP income estimates in 1989 and indicators of living standards for the same period—are available (Table 3.2). The stated PPP income for Ghana in 1989 was about $1,300 per capita in 2000 U.S. dollars, or about $7,800 for a household of six. The household expenditure surveys describe what this sort of household is likely to have (or not have): as of 1989 about one in four households in Ghana has a radio, about one in eight has water on the premises, about one in thirteen has a television, about one in fourteen has a refrigerator, about one in seventeen has a flush toilet, and about one in thirty-three has a car. The estimated daily calorie supply per capita in Ghana is about 1,760—less than half the daily supply in the United States.[4]

Many of us have trouble converting this level of living into a dollar figure, since these living standards are so foreign to our own experience. Probably the best way to assist our intuition is to compare this level of living to the level of living typical of the poor in the United States. We can translate poverty conditions in the United States into dollar amounts using the poverty line established by the U.S. Census Bureau, which is in dollars. By U.S. Census Bureau standards, about 13 percent of the U.S. population is poor. We will use the poverty standards for a six-member household in the United States, since households in Ghana typically are about that size. (Observe that this strategy controls for differences in average household size, so no further adjustments are necessary—more on the relevance of average household size later.) In round figures the current U.S. poverty threshold for a family of six is $23,000 (in 2000 U.S. dollars), or roughly $3,800 per person. As noted earlier, this threshold is based on the assumption that poor families spend one-third of their income on food. So the U.S. Census Bureau assumes that a six-member family in the United States will need about $1,270 per person each year—slightly over $100 per person per month—for an adequate diet under an economy food plan based on the "quantities and types of food compatible with the prefer-ence of United States families, as revealed in food consumption studies" (Orshansky 1965, p. 5).

Observe that the dollar allowance for food for an adequate diet in the U.S.—$1,270 per person in a household of six members—is about the same as the stated PPP income per capita in Ghana in 1989—$1,300. We already know that Ghanaians do *not* spend all their income for food. If we make the reasonable assumption that Ghanaians devote 60 percent of their incomes for food, that implies an expenditure of $780 per person per year, or about $65 per person per month—roughly two-thirds the U.S. allow-ance for an adequate diet.

At first blush, it might then appear that $1,300 per person per year is im-plausibly low, even for a nation as poor as Ghana. The reasoning is that if the American poor need $100 per month for an adequate diet, then Gha-naians must require an income figure of roughly the same magnitude. If the Ghanaian diet is adequate—which we assume it is, or severe malnutrition would prevail in Ghana—then the food consumed by Ghanaians must be worth substantially more than $65 per month in U.S. dollars. In other words, based solely on the value of the food consumed in Ghana, per cap-ita consumption in Ghana must be more than $1,300 per year. Otherwise the numbers don't add up: if the food consumed annually in Ghana is worth about $1,270 per person, where does the other 40 percent come from for nonfood expenditures?

The problem with this line of reasoning is that it fails to take into ac-count that Americans buy processed foods in retail stores whereas the vast majority of people in poor nations grow their own food or buy unpro-cessed food in open-air markets. The $100 per month standard set by the Census Bureau is based on retail food prices, and Ghanaians most often do not pay retail prices. This makes a huge difference, because a dollar on the farm buys much more food than a dollar at a retail grocery store. To ap-preciate the magnitude of the difference, consider these figures from the U.S. Department of Agriculture for farm price as share of retail price in 1999 (USDA, 2002): eggs, 47 percent (that is, a dozen eggs that cost $1.00 in a retail store would fetch $0.47 on the farm, on average); beef, 49 per-cent (allowing for waste); milk, 39 percent; oranges, 28 percent; dried beans, 25 percent; apples, 21 percent; rice, 20 percent; potatoes, 19 per-cent; corn, 24 percent (canned), 13 percent (frozen). Note that the ratio of retail price to farm price ranges from 2 to 1 for eggs to 5 to 1 for products such as rice and potatoes. When we realize that the retail price for pro-cessed foods is at least two to three times greater than the farm price for an equivalent quantity, then the $65 monthly food allowance for Ghanaians makes sense. In poor countries where a large fraction of the people either grow their own food or buy unprocessed food on the farm or in open-air markets, the farm price is the relevant price. It is quite plausible that the typical Ghanaian subsists on a market basket of foodstuffs whose on-the-farm value would be no more than $65 per month in the United States.

If we concede that $1,300 is a plausible figure for per capita income for poor nations such as Ghana, there is still the problem of nations with even lower PPP income estimates. For example, the PPP estimates indicate that per capita income in Chad was only one-half that of Ghana in 1989 (Table 3.1). Recall that the FX-based income estimates are on the order of $100–$200 *per year* for many poor nations, and we have already ruled out those estimates on the grounds that they are implausible. But what about the plausibility of the lowest PPP estimates?

DO CHADIANS REALLY LIVE ON $640 A YEAR?

There are two ways to approach the $640 question. The first way is to think about the production side. Is it reasonable that the annual production of the average person in Chad really would fetch only $640 if it were produced and sold elsewhere, such as in the United States? The answer is yes, it is reasonable. The key here is to realize that a large share of Chadian production consists of unprocessed farm goods consumed at home or sold in open-air markets. So the appropriate prices for valuing Chadian output are the on-the-farm prices—the prices that farmers in the United States would receive for the same unprocessed goods—not the retail prices that consumers pay in stores. And as we see below, production in Chad consists largely of inexpensive farm commodities such as sorghum.

The second approach to the $640 question is to think about the consumption side—can Chadians actually subsist on $640 a year (in 2000 U.S. dollars)? If we make the same assumptions about Chad that we did for Ghana—that the average household consists of six members, and that people in Chad devote 60 percent of their income to food—then we conclude that the on-the-farm value of the food consumed by the average person in Chad is only $30–$35 per month in 2000 U.S. dollars. That level is harder to reconcile with the Census Bureau's $100 per month allowance for an adequate diet, because if the average is $30–$35 per month then those below average are living on perhaps $20–$25 per month for food.

It does not necessarily follow, however, that the $640 figure is far off the mark. First, Chad really is poorer than Ghana.[5] In addition to the income estimates, there are other objective indicators that the citizens of Chad tend to be worse off than the citizens of Ghana (World Bank 1990, tables

1, 28, and 29). As of the late 1980s, the infant mortality rate was about 50 percent higher in Chad (13 percent versus 8.8 percent), life expectancy was eight years lower in Chad (forty-six years versus fifty-four years), adults in Chad were only one-half as likely to be literate as adults in Ghana were (25 percent adult literacy in Chad versus 53 percent in Ghana), and primary-school-age children in Chad were only 70 percent as likely to be enrolled in primary school as their counterparts in Ghana (51 percent enrollment rate versus 71 percent enrollment rate).

Second, staple foods in Chad are cheaper than the foods assumed by the USDA economy food plan. Sorghum—the mainstay of the Chadian diet—is a highly nutritious grain that is fed to cattle, not people, in the United States.[6] Millet—a common food for humans in Chad—is used in the United States in bird feed. The point is that the Chad diet is less expensive than the diet assumed by even the economy food plan for Americans. The same point applies to diets in many poor regions of Asia, where rice is the staple food. And it is important to stress again that the food consumed by the poor in poor nations should be valued at the farm price, because most grow their own food or purchase food at on-the-farm prices. Third, from estimates of daily calorie supply (Table 3.2), it appears that the average person in poor nations eats less than the average poor person in the United States does, since daily calorie supply in the United States is well above the average of 1,800–2,200 calories that prevails in very poor nations. The relative caloric shortfall in poor nations is not quite as stark as it first appears, since children constitute a higher percentage of the population in poor nations, and children require fewer calories than adults. Nonetheless a large disparity would remain even if we adjusted for the difference in the caloric requirements of children and adults (appendix to this chapter) and adjusted the calorie figure for the U.S. poor downward by assuming that in the United States the poor consume somewhat fewer calories than the nonpoor consume. It appears that, on average, people in very poor nations eat both cheaper food and less food than do the poor in the United States.

Fourth, incomes for a given year do not necessarily reflect permanent incomes, since incomes often fluctuate considerably from year to year in very poor nations, depending on rainfall during the growing season, political stability, and so on. That is why the list of very poorest nations changes from year to year. There is much more turnover in the list of the ten poorest nations than there is in the list of the ten richest nations. Nations that are in the bottom ten at a given point in time are typically there because they have had a bad year or a series of bad years. Chad and Ghana well illustrate this point. Both had higher per capita incomes in 1975 than they did in 1989. If we use the PPP estimates from the Penn World Table, we find that in 1975 Ghana's per capita income was $1,650 and Chad's was $1,030 (both expressed in 2000 dollars). Ghana's income declined after 1975 in part because of a disastrous dip in world prices for cocoa, Ghana's chief export. Chad's income fell because of droughts in 1984 and 1985, wars, and low prices for cotton. More recent data from the World Bank (2000b, tables 3 and 11) indicate that during the 1990s the economy grew faster than the population in Ghana but not in Chad.

The roller-coaster pattern of advance and decline among the world's very poor nations brings us to a key observation in our consideration of the plausibility of PPP income estimates: the poorest nations in the world are poor precisely because they have not shared significantly in the world's sustained economic growth over the past two hundred years. Although the Industrial Revolution of the past two centuries has raised incomes in most of the world, there are pockets of the world that have not benefited, or that have benefited relatively little. These are the nations that now make up the very poor. It is not that these nations were desperately poor before, and simply have not caught up. It is more accurate to say instead that they have been left behind, since in the case of the very poorest nations, living conditions today probably tend not to be radically different from living conditions of the past. And that is an important point to keep in mind. In the West, where rapid economic change is the norm, current generations can scarcely conceive of the world experienced by their ancestors of the nineteenth century. Meanwhile, subsistence farmers in Chad continue the practice of slash-and-burn agriculture while pastoralists continue traditional herding practices, and both groups live a life that in many ways is similar to the lives lived by their ancestors over a century ago.

Finally, households in poor nations such as Chad are substantially larger on average than households in rich nations. While the saying that "two can live as cheaply as one" is not entirely accurate, it is certainly the case that two living together can live more cheaply than two living separately. In other words, there are economies of scale in human habitation, and these economies help to explain how Chadians are able to survive on $640 a year. The point is important enough to merit separate discussion.

THE EQUIVALENT UNITS ISSUE

There is another way that families in poor nations make ends meet: more live under the same roof. In other words, families in poor nations tend to enjoy household economies that effectively raise their standard of living for a given level of per capita income. It is those household economies that we want to focus on here. There are two sources of household economies in poor nations. First, the average household in poor nations is more than twice as large as the average household in rich nations, so poor nations enjoy an economy-of-scale effect due to the collective use of resources at the household level. Second, children constitute a higher percentage of the population in poor nations, so poor nations require less food per capita than do rich nations. The lower caloric requirements for children can be quite consequential in very poor nations, since food constitutes such a large share of the household budget in that setting.

The appendix to this chapter quantifies the effect of greater household economies in poor nations. The conclusion is that, because of differences in household economies between poor nations and the United States, the effective PPP income of poor nations in U.S. dollars is 15 to 25 percent higher than their stated PPP income. In other words, solely because of differences in household size and age structure, a stated per capita income of $1,000 in a poor nation amounts to a per capita income of $1,150–$1,250 in the United States for an equivalent level of living. These increases are not insignificant. Even in Chad, the very poorest nation in Table 3.1, a 20 percent increase means that equivalent income per capita is estimated to be about $770 rather than $640—a boost of $130 per person (2000 U.S. dollars). For a typical Chad household of six members, this is an increase of about $780 per year in total "effective" household income.

Let us return then to the question that prompted this discussion, the question of whether it is plausible that Chadians in fact live on $640 a year. In very poor nations such as Chad most people are poor, and poor families in the poorest nations most often must devote one-half or more of their budgets to food, leaving little for nonfood items. The results are tangible—the poor in the West often own television sets and cars and most often live in dwellings with wood floors and indoor plumbing, while the poor in poor nations are more likely to have only transistor radios and bicycles and to live in dwellings with dirt floors and no plumbing. Moreover, adults and children in poor nations tend to eat less food, and cheaper foods, than do the poor in the West. Finally, the poor in poor nations are able to take advantage of household economies that might raise their effective incomes as much as 25 percent. Taken together, these considerations suggest that the PPP income estimates are credible for countries such as Chad.

Are the Historical Income Data Reliable Enough?

No one believes that the data are perfect, but are they reliable enough? That depends partly on what we want to use them for. Here we want to use the national income data to determine the general contours of income inequality for the world—whether between-nation inequality is rising or falling, whether global inequality is rising or falling, and whether the hypothesized inequality transition is taking place. (Since global income inequality is between-nation inequality plus within-nation inequality, we also want to know about the reliability of within-nation inequality data—but that issue is best treated separately, in Chapter 9.)

INCOME DATA SETS USED IN THIS STUDY

The historical record on national income is richer than some might think. Attempts to estimate national income date back to the seventeenth century, when Gregory King used a variety of evidence on income, expenditure, and production to estimate the English national income (Maddison 1995, p. 118). King's methods have been greatly refined over time and expanded to other nations. Michael Mulhall's *Industries and Wealth of Nations* (1896) used exchange rates to derive income estimates for nineteen nations. A half century later Colin Clark (1940) attempted to correct for differences in the purchasing power parity of currencies. His study of income levels in thirty nations represented a watershed in that it paved the way for the PPP income data that are the standard today. The present-day system of standardized national accounting schemes dates from the pioneering work of Simon Kuznets in the United States and Richard Stone in the United Kingdom (Perlman 1987). In 1932 the U.S. Senate passed a resolution requiring the secretary of commerce to report "estimates of the total national income of the United States for each of the calendar years of 1929, 1930, and 1931" (cited in ibid., p. 138). Kuznets, a professor of statistics at the University of Pennsylvania, was appointed to oversee the generation of those estimates. In the United Kingdom the impetus was World War II, and in 1941 James Meade and Richard Stone produced for Churchill's war cabinet an accounts system designed to reveal slack areas of the economy that could be tapped for the war effort. The detailed accounting schemes of the United States and the United Kingdom formed the model for a standardized national accounting scheme to measure national incomes worldwide. Owing to the data collection efforts of the United Nations, among others, we now have official estimates of income growth in nominal (FX-based) and real (PPP-based) terms for virtually all the world since 1960.

The analyses in this book are based on income and population data from three major sources: the 1960–1989 income series from the Penn World Table (version 5.6, from Summers et al. 1994), the 1980–1998 income series from the World Bank (1998, 2000a), and the 1820–1992 income series from Maddison (1995). Income is measured as GDP per capita. Aside from the years covered, the series differ somewhat in the data and methods they use to derive purchasing power parity. Nevertheless, the different data sets paint a fairly consistent picture about the overall trends in between-nation income inequality in the last decades of the twentieth century.

The Penn World Table (PWT) data set is an outgrowth of the International Comparison Project begun in the 1960s. The PWT data set has become the industry standard for comparative income analysis in economics. Because of the discontinuity caused by the breakup of the USSR into smaller nations, the analyses here supplement the PWT data with more recent data from the World Bank. The PWT data set used here ends in 1989 and includes the USSR as one nation (Summers et al. 1994). Following the recommendation of Summers and Heston (1991, p. 344) for trend analysis, analyses using the PWT data set are based on the variable RGDPCH ("real GDP, chain index") as the income measure, because RGDPCH is designed to "bring changing relative prices into the analysis explicitly through a chain index." The second income series uses World Bank data (1998, 2000a) to extend the analysis into the 1990s. The 1990s data set includes separate income estimates for the Soviet republics. Because the dissolution of the USSR boosts between-nation income inequality simply because of reclassification (what was formerly income inequality across the Soviet republics is reclassified as between-nation inequality), I treat the 1965–1989 and 1990s trends separately. Because the PWT income series is not updated as often as the World Bank income series, I rely on the World Bank data for the most recent years. To put our findings for the second half of the twentieth century in historical context, we need a third data set for the historical trend.

HISTORICAL DATA

Ideally we would like to have reliable data on per capita income for every nation, beginning with the first industrial revolution in the late 1700s. The closest to this ideal is Maddison's (1995) painstaking study, which provides PPP income data for 56 key nations—his "sample nations"—beginning with 1820 for most of them. Maddison (1995) is the standard source for income estimates for the nineteenth and early twentieth centuries. Because Maddison begins with 1820, that is my starting point as well. In addition to the 56 sample nations, Maddison provides PPP income estimates for 143 nonsample nations for 1950 and 1990, as well as aggregate yearly estimates for the 143 nations for 1950 to 1992. Together the 199 sample and nonsample nations constitute virtually the entire world population.

Although the 56 sample nations contain most of the world's population (about 90 percent in 1820 and 86.5 percent in 1992: Maddison 1995, table F-1) as well as most of the world's income (about 91 percent in 1820 and 93 percent in 1992: Maddison 1995, table F-3), there are important gaps (for example, there are no data before 1900 for sub-Saharan African nations). Included, nevertheless, are data for a range of nations—richer, poorer, and in the middle—sufficient to provide a good empirical base for reaching conclusions about the general patterns of income inequality across nations and across regions back into the early nineteenth century.

As a general rule the data for poorer regions such as Africa tend to be spottier and less reliable than the data for richer regions such as Western Europe. In addition, the data tend to become spottier and less reliable as we go back in time, so we are less confident about our estimates for 1820 than we are about our estimates for the late twentieth century. That said, Maddison's historical income series is quite adequate for determining the direction of the trend in between-nation income inequality during the period of Western industrialization. Importantly, Maddison adjusts the historical series for current territorial definitions, so observed changes are not artifacts of shifting national boundaries. As noted before, even if income estimates for poor nations are grossly understated for the early nineteenth century, we still conclude that the Western industrialization period was characterized by growing income inequality across nations.[7] Ironically, then, the conclusions in this book about the pre-1960 inequality trends promise to be less contentious than the conclusions about the post-1960 trends, even though the post-1960 data are better. As a result the reliability of the more recent data is likely to attract more attention than the reliability of the historical data.

Are the Contemporary Income Data Reliable Enough?

Although the PWT and World Bank income series used here represent a significant advance over the FX-based income series, no one claims that the income data are error free, and I will take pains to present results from alternative approaches designed to test the robustness of the book's major conclusions. It is useful first to distinguish two types of measurement error that could cause problems in this study. The first is the standard measurement imprecision reflected in this statement about the PWT income estimates: "A generous estimate of margins of uncertainty in the benchmark estimates might be 20–25 percent for low-income countries and 7 percent for high-income countries" (Kravis and Lipsey, 1990, abstract). This error is assumed to be random across countries but systematic over time within countries (because of the routinization of data collection in a country, the sorts of errors that result in inflated or deflated income estimates at time 1 are likely to be present at time 2 as well). The effects of this sort of measurement error can be studied using computer simulation, and I report the results of such simulations for the PWT and World Bank data. In effect the simulations bound the estimates of change in between-nation income inequality. In some instances we find that the bounds contain zero, indicating that there is insufficient evidence to rule out the hypothesis of no change in between-nation income inequality. In other instances the upper bound is less than zero, indicating that between-nation income inequality is declining. In no instance do we find evidence of growing income inequality across nations.

The second type of measurement error is error that is related to national income. We could conjecture (see note 7) that economic activity is more likely to be overlooked in poor agricultural nations because production for home use is harder to detect than market production. To gauge the severity of the problem, it is useful to compare national differences using two different methods for estimating living standards: the conventional income method based on production, and an alternative method based on surveys of household consumption.

PRODUCTION MEASURES VERSUS CONSUMPTION MEASURES

Although the PPP-based method provides more plausible estimates than the FX method does of income differences between rich and poor nations, PPP estimates might overstate the differences between rich and poor nations with regard to household disposable income or consumption. The issue turns on the likely understatement of income in poor nations. It could be hypothesized that economic activity in poor nations (relative to activity in rich nations) is likely to be understated in both urban and rural areas. Studies of the underground or informal economy find economic activity that is concealed in many urban areas in poor nations (for example, Funkhouser 1996; Portes and Schauffler 1993). Official statistics are less likely to capture this activity than the economic activity in the formal sector. Of course there is hidden economic activity in rich nations as well, but the problem generally is more acute in poor nations. Thus if underground market activity could be captured accurately for all nations, we would expect to observe some narrowing of the income gap between rich and poor nations.

A similar logic applies to rural production in poor nations. In general the poorer the nation, the higher the percentage of workers engaged in subsistence agriculture. In the case of subsistence agriculture, income estimates will be understated when the national account figures miss significant production for home use. Although the United Nations System of National Accounts (1993, para. 6.48) directs that "goods or services produced for their own final use are valued at the basic prices of similar products sold on the market," that directive might be more difficult to follow in the case of agricultural nations. The home consumption of goods and services is substantial in agricultural societies compared with industrial societies. Hence, to the extent that national accounts understate the value of goods and services produced for their own final use, this downward bias will tend to be more pronounced in poor agricultural nations than in rich industrial nations.

As expected, surveys of actual household expenditure find that differences in actual personal consumption between rich and poor nations are less pronounced than differences in GDP (or GNP, for that matter). But this finding does not necessarily imply that the data on production tend to understate economic productivity in poor nations, since the proportion of total production that is devoted to private consumption tends to be significantly higher in poor nations. Maddison (1995, p. 22) explains: "It should be remembered that changes in per capita GDP are not the same as changes in per capita private consumption. Over time, there have been substantial increases in the proportion of expenditure going to investment, and to government consumption." For example, in the United Kingdom private consumption as a percentage of GDP declined from 88 percent in 1820 to 64 percent in 1992 (ibid., pp. 25–26), and in general the share of total GDP devoted to private consumption declines with average income.

For our purposes, the important point is that the use of data on personal consumption in place of GDP results in lower estimates of inequality across nations. So if we define income in terms of consumption rather than in terms of production, we find lower levels of income inequality across nations. Thus, while Branko Milanovic's (2002) objective is to provide estimates of global income inequality in 1988 and 1993 using data from nationally representative household surveys (as opposed to standard GDP or GNP estimates),[8] his most interesting finding for us is that the consumption/GDP ratio is larger for poorer regions and declines monotonically with income. In 1988, for example, the consumption/GDP ratio (times 100) was 78.5 for Africa, 61.0 for Asia, 57.2 for Eastern Europe, 55.9 for Latin America, and 51.5 for Western Europe/North America (ibid., table 9). As a result, in 1988 the per capita income ratio between the world's richest continents (Western Europe and North America) and the world's poorest continent (Africa) was 11 to 1 based on per capita GDP but 7 to 1 based on per capita consumption (ibid., table 7).

In short, the findings from surveys of household expenditures suggest that inequality in per capita GDP across nations overstates inequality in living standards across nations, consistent with the hypothesis that economic activity is more likely to be underdetected in poor countries. Before accepting that conclusion, however, it is important to note that household expenditure surveys are not immune to underreporting bias either, since household expenditure surveys will miss much of the welfare effect of government expenditures. To the extent that rich nations have disproportionately higher public expenditures on health, education, and welfare, then household surveys of personal spending tend to understate the inequality in living standards across nations. Hence if it is true that economic activity is more likely to be overlooked in agricultural societies, then income estimates based on national account data and household survey data are biased in opposite directions. National account data tend to overstate inequality across nations by underestimating household production in poor nations, whereas household expenditure data tend to understate inequality across nations by missing the welfare effects of greater government welfare expenditures in richer nations. The findings of Summers and Heston (1999) suggest as much. Summers and Heston define consumption broadly to include government expenditures (Milanovic restricts his measure of consumption to personal consumption) and Summers and Heston's estimates are based on national account data (Milanovic's estimates are based on expenditure surveys). Consistent with Milanovic's key conclusion, Summers and Heston also observe that the consumption/GDP ratio tends to be larger for poorer nations—so inequality in per capita GDP across nations overstates somewhat inequality in living standards across nations. Importantly, though, the differences between rich and poor nations on the consumption/GDP ratio are not as pronounced in the Summers and Heston (1999, fig. 16.5) data as they were in the Milanovic data. This finding suggests that, by omitting the effects of government welfare expenditures, the household consumption data of Milanovic understate the actual inequality in living standards across nations.

The big picture, then, is as follows. Although there is enormous inequality in the distribution of income across nations, the FX estimates are simply off the chart: average incomes are *not* 200 to 300 times larger in rich countries than in poor countries. Based on the Milanovic household consumption surveys, even the PPP income estimates of a roughly 25-to-1 ratio in average incomes for the richest versus poorest countries might be slightly exaggerated. If we examine the ratios for continents instead of individual countries, the Milanovic data suggest a ratio on the order of 7 to 1 for the world's richest versus poorest continents if household expenditure surveys are used and a ratio of about 11 to 1 if standard PPP income data (from national accounts) are used. Quite clearly, results from the household survey data are much more consistent with the standard PPP income estimates than with the FX income estimates. In fact, Milanovic's results—which are based on a different type of data—independently confirm the credibility of the standard PPP-based estimates of between-nation income inequality. Because expenditure surveys understate somewhat the level of between-nation income inequality (by failing to capture the effect of greater government expenditures in richer nations), the true level of income inequality across nations should be somewhat higher than Milanovic's expenditure data suggest—right in line with the standard PPP income-inequality levels, which are in fact somewhat higher.

INSTALLING AN INCOME FLOOR

In the analyses reported later I experiment with an income floor for the poorest nations. Values of the floor are set as multiples of the World Bank poverty threshold for people in poor nations (for example, 1.5 times the threshold), so the poorer the nation the greater the income boost, in line with the conjecture that undetected economic activity is more prevalent in subsistence farming nations such as Chad. The experiments are designed to address the concern that better detection of economic activity in recent years would overstate the rate of growth (or understate the rate of decline) of income in the poorest nations, thereby exaggerating the rate of decline in inequality across nations (but see Nuxoll 1994, who concludes that the standard PPP data might understate the rate of income growth in poor nations). The experiments also address the possible suspicion among some that—arguments in this chapter notwithstanding—Chadians in fact cannot live on $640 per year. I find no basis for these concerns about possible bias in the results here, because installing an income floor (within limits) scarcely affects the between-nation trend. Declining income inequality is observed across nations whether the standard PPP income estimates for Chad and other very poor nations are used or whether those estimates are arbitrarily boosted to 50 percent above the World Bank poverty threshold.

OTHER RELIABILITY CHECKS

With rare exceptions (for example, the occasional use of FX income data) researchers use the same data sets, so the disagreement over whether income inequality is rising or falling across nations is not primarily a data reliability issue. Nonetheless, because of the widespread perception of growing inequality, some might conjecture that the finding of declining inequality reported here is fragile. Perhaps if the analysis had been different—a different measure of income inequality, or a somewhat different income measure, or slightly different end points—the trend would have been up instead of down. After all, cross-nation regression results are notoriously fragile (Levine and Renelt 1992), and some might suspect the same fragility for inequality trends based on national data. It is important, then, to test the results for robustness.

In addition to the income-floor robustness check already described, I tested the results in a number of other ways. These tests are described in detail later, so a list suffices here. To test the decline in between-nation income inequality, we examine the trend: using multiple inequality measures; measuring income by GNP as well as by GDP; employing per worker income as well as per capita income; weighting nations by population size as well as weighting nations equally; varying the weight given to income change at the lower end of the income distribution relative to change at the upper end of the distribution; removing key nations such as China; and juxtaposing the findings here with the findings from parallel studies. Moreover, the results for change in income inequality across nations are confirmed with supplementary analyses examining change in income inequality across major regions as well as analyses examining trends in inequality using the United Nation's Human Development Index.

Measuring Income over Time

We noted in Chapter 1 that world per capita income is about eight times greater today than it was in the early nineteenth century. In this section we examine the issues that arise when comparing material well-being over such a long time period. The measurement of income over time within a nation poses challenges that are similar to those we face when measuring income differences across nations. Although we are not faced with the challenge of converting currencies to a common currency, we are faced with the challenge of changing relative prices, because the relative prices of items vary over time within countries just like relative prices vary across countries at a given point in time. In addition, we are faced with the issue of changing options, since some items available today were not available historically at any price. By examining these issues we gain a better understanding of what it means to say that the income of the average person today is eight times greater than the income of the average person in the early nineteenth century. The key point to understand is that the past century has witnessed significant change in the relative prices of many goods. In some instances changes in relative prices within nations over the past century dwarf even the large differences in relative prices that prevail from nation to nation at a given point in time. To illustrate the point, we examine the twentieth-century change in relative prices for selected commodities in the United States. We find that the fivefold multiplication in living standards in the United States over the twentieth century (calculated using national account statistics) is an average that obscures major differences across commodities. Compared with the average U.S. income at the beginning of the twentieth century, the average U.S. income today could buy much more than five times the quantity of some items and much less than five times the quantity of some other items. In addition, there are other items that we take for granted today—from televisions to transatlantic flights—that could not be purchased a century ago.

The historical shift in relative prices does not mean that we cannot compare living standards across generations, but it does mean we must keep in mind that the comparison is based on average prices across commodities, and that those prices change over time. Recall the observation in Chapter 1 that growth in average world income masks the highly uneven nature of that growth across the world's regions. Our observation here is that gains in production efficiencies have been highly uneven across commodities as well, so the rise in average world income masks great unevenness not only in the growth of incomes across regions and nations but also in changing production costs across commodities. So when we say that the world's per capita income is eight times greater now than two centuries ago, we are referring to an eightfold increase for the average person based on prices for the average commodity.

SHIFTS IN RELATIVE PRICES

The shift in relative prices over time can be appreciated by comparing prices in the 1908 and 1990 catalogs of Sears, Roebuck and Company.[9] We begin with what Americans could purchase in 1908. According to the consumer price index (CPI; see U.S. Census Bureau 1999, p. 882), a dollar in 1908 on average would purchase about fourteen times as much as a dollar would in 1990.[10] Dividing $4,566 (the estimated average income in the United States in 1908 in 1990 dollars: Maddison 1995, table D-1) by 14 yields the result that the per capita income in the United States in 1908 was roughly $326, or about $27 a month, in 1908 dollars.

What could an American buy for $27—one month's average income—in 1908? Table 3.3 reports the prices for selected items from the Sears catalog. The catalog indicates that in 1908 a desk telephone and a slide trombone were in the same price range: a telephone could be purchased from Sears for $12 while a higher-quality B-flat slide trombone could be purchased for $13.75 and a less expensive B-flat slide trombone could be pur-

TABLE 3.3 Prices for selected commodities in the United States, 1908 versus 1990

Commodity	(1) Price 1908	(2) Price 1990	(3) 1908/1990 prices in constant $	(4) Multiplication of purchasing power, 1908–1990 (column 3 × 4.8)
Binoculars: 9-power (1908), 10-power (1990)	$33.50	$55	8.53	40.9
Desk telephone	$12	$20	8.40	40.3
Metal fan: 8″ (1908), 3-speed 12″ (1990)	$8.75	$22.36	5.48	26.3
Tennis balls	$0.34	$0.92	5.17	24.8
5-ft. retractable metal tape measure	$2.43	$6.66	5.11	24.5
Bicycle: one-speed (1908), ten-speed (1990)	$18	$110	2.27	10.9
House paint (one gallon, mixed)	$1.00	$12	1.17	5.6
26-inch handsaw	$1.27	$16.66	1.07	5.1
Rocking chair: oak (1908), hardwood (1990)	$3.85	$149	0.36	1.74
Two-blade pocket knife	$0.40	$17	0.33	1.58
Sterling silver teaspoon, medium weight	$0.79	$45[a]	0.25	1.18
Slide trombone: 7.5″ bell (1908), 8″ bell (1990)	$13.75	$600[b]	0.32	1.54
Slide trombone, less expensive	$7.95	$600	0.19	0.89
All items (based on the consumer price index)			1.00	4.8

Sources: For 1908 prices, Sears (1969 [1908]). For 1990 prices, relevant 1990 and 1991 Sears catalogs.

Note: Prices are in dollars unadjusted for inflation, that is, the 1908 prices are the actual prices in the 1908 catalog and the 1990 prices are the actual prices in the 1990 catalog. In unadjusted dollars, per capita income in the United States rose by a factor of 67 from 1908 to 1990, from $326 per person in 1908 to $21,866 per person in 1990 (based on Maddison 1995, table D-1). This 67-fold increase resulted from a 14-fold increase in the consumer price index and a 4.8-fold increase in real income (14 × 4.8 = 67). Put another way, on average Americans in 1990 had about $67 for every dollar they had in 1908, but the dollar in 1990 was worth only about one-fourteenth as much as the dollar in 1908 had been—so real purchasing power was multiplied by about 4.8.

a. Estimate based on JC Penney catalog, since the 1990 Sears catalog does not offer sterling silver eating utensils.

b. The 1990 Sears catalog does not offer trombones, so the price was estimated based on the typical retail price for a low-end brass B-flat tenor trombone listed on the Internet in 2001, adjusted to 1990 dollars.

chased for $7.95. So (ignoring the cost of shipping) for $27 an American in 1908 could purchase very roughly 2 telephones or 2 higher-quality trombones. For a month's income in 1908 an American could also purchase from Sears 1.5 bicycles (one-speed), 6 oak rocking chairs, 27 gallons of house paint, 44 solid silver teaspoons, or 79 tennis balls. Note the relative prices here: 1 telephone = 1 trombone = 3 rocking chairs = 13.5 gallons of paint = 22 sterling silver teaspoons = 39.5 tennis balls.

By contrast, in 1990 an American could purchase about 30 telephones for the price of 1 slide trombone—a number that is greater than the number of tennis balls (23) that one could purchase for the price of the less expensive Sears trombone in 1908. It is possible, of course, that a brass trombone made in 1990 is relatively more expensive because it truly is better, that is, the 1990 model is made out of better materials and produces a better sound than the one made in 1908. But the 1990 desk telephone probably also works better than the 1908 model did, so the relative price shift—from 1 trombone = 1 telephone to 1 trombone = 30 telephones—is not easy to explain away on the basis of changes in the relative quality of the two items. And it is not just telephones and trombones that shifted notably in their relative prices. Compare the 1990 equivalences with the 1908 equivalences using a bicycle as the standard. In 1908, 1 bicycle = 2.1 metal fans = 4.7 hardwood rocking chairs = 18 gallons of house paint = 53 tennis balls. In 1990, 1 bicycle = 4.9 metal fans = 0.7 rocking chairs = 9.2 gallons of paint = 120 tennis balls. So over the twentieth century bicycles in the United States became more expensive relative to tennis balls and metal fans but less expensive relative to wooden rocking chairs and house paint.

To facilitate these and other comparisons, Table 3.3 arranges a dozen items (including the higher- and lower-quality trombone) according to the ratio of their 1908 price to their 1990 price. The first two columns give the 1908 and 1990 prices, respectively, in dollars not adjusted for inflation, so the 1908 prices listed are the actual prices in the 1908 catalog and the 1990 prices listed are the actual prices in the 1990 catalog. Column 3 gives the ratio of the 1908 price to the 1990 price, multiplied by 14 to adjust for the fact that (following the consumer price index) a dollar in 1908 was worth fourteen times as much as a dollar was in 1990. So multiplication by 14 in effect norms the 1908/1990 price ratio to 1.0 for the average commodity. Two of the twelve items—house paint and hand saws—have ratios close to 1.0, indicating that their prices rose at about the same rate as the average item used to calculate the consumer price index. By contrast, the price of binoculars and telephones rose much more slowly than the rate of inflation, as indicated by a 1908/1990 price ratio substantially above 1.0 (that is, high 1908 prices relative to 1990 prices), while the price of hardwood rocking chairs, sterling silver eating utensils, and trombones rose faster than the consumer price index, as indicated by 1908/1990 price ratios well below 1.0 (low 1908 prices relative to 1990 prices). From these ratios we see immediately that relative prices have changed rather dramatically across items, since some of the ratios deviate markedly from 1.0.

AMERICANS IN 1990 VERSUS 1908

So how much better off was a typical American in 1990 than a typical American in 1908? From Table 3.3 it is clear that the answer varies considerably depending on what one wants to have. For those who want to watch birds and talk to their friends, life is good—binoculars and telephones are great bargains today compared with a century ago. From column 3 in Table 3.3 we see that in constant dollars an American could buy 8.5 binoculars in 1990 for the cost of 1 in 1908. As to quality of the 1908 and 1990 binoculars, possibly the 1908 product was made of heavier materials (which is not necessarily a good feature for binoculars) and was sturdier, but the 1990 binocular appears to be superior in performance. The 9-power binocular, which sold for $33.50 in the 1908 catalog (p. 190), had a "field of view at 1,000 yards [of] 240 feet," whereas the 10-power binocular sold for $54.96 in the 1990 Sears home and hardware catalog (p. 906) had a field of view of 367 feet at 1,000 yards and featured "zip focus." In any case, on the basis of the binoculars standard the average American in 1990 was 41 times as well off as the average American in 1908 (last column in Table 3.3), since in constant dollars the average American had 4.8 times more income in 1990 and each dollar had 8.5 times the "binoculars purchasing power" ($4.8 \times 8.5 = 41$).

For those who like to entertain their friends with musical concerts as they dine with sterling silver place settings, however, life is not so good. Judged on the basis of the sterling silver teaspoon standard, Americans are scarcely better off today than they were a century ago. In constant dollars a sterling silver teaspoon costs about four times as much today as it did in 1908 (column 3), so the average American income today can purchase only about 20 percent more sterling silver teaspoons than the average American income could have in 1908. The slide trombone standard is even more dramatic. By the slide trombone standard, Americans may be worse off today, depending on whether one uses the lower- or higher-quality 1908 trombone as the yardstick for comparison with the 1990 trombone. If the $7.95 B-flat tenor slide trombone offered by Sears in 1908 is of comparable quality to the lower-end B-flat tenor trombones on the market in 1990, then judging by the trombone standard Americans are worse off today than they were in 1908.

In sum, in terms of their ability to purchase hardwood rocking chairs, pocket knives, and (especially) silver teaspoons and trombones, Americans were not much better off in 1990 than in 1908. But in terms of their ability to purchase binoculars, telephones, fans, tennis balls, bicycles, retractable tape measures, paint, and handsaws, Americans were far better off at the end of the twentieth century than at the beginning. Over-time comparisons based on the rise in per capita incomes reflect a weighted average of these changes in living standards for specific items. So the approximately five-fold increase in average income in the United States over the twentieth century is precisely that—an average. Because of substantial shifts in the relative prices of commodities, the increase in per capita income understates how much better off most Americans are with respect to some goods and overstates how much better off Americans are with respect to other goods.

The same principles of course apply to the rest of the world as well. Calculated with PPP-adjusted dollars, average world income was roughly eight times higher at the end of the twentieth century than it was at the beginning of the nineteenth. This jump in average income, however, conceals the highly uneven nature of modern economic growth. That economic growth has been uneven in two senses: it has been uneven across the world's regions and nations, as noted in Chapter 1, and it has been uneven across commodities. This section has focused on the second type of unevenness, and warns us that the eightfold multiplication of the world's average income over the past two centuries does not mean that the purchasing power of the average person has increased eightfold for all commodities. Jumps in the standard of living have tended to be greatest for mass-manufactured goods and least for hand-crafted goods and for services. Bradford De Long (1995, pp. 9–10) notes, "To the extent that one's reference bundle of goods contains a large proportion of mass-produced manufactures, the eightfold multiplication in measured real GDP per worker [in the United States] since the mid-nineteenth century understates the growth of material wealth. To the extent that one's reference bundle of commodities is weighted toward services—measures wealth by how many butlers one can hire or by how many products made by skilled craftsmen one can buy—the eightfold multiplication overstates the growth of material wealth."

Finally, it is important to stress that we can compare relative prices over time only for items that were present earlier. The 1908 Sears catalog knows nothing of televisions, stereo systems, computers, microwave ovens, central air conditioners, chain saws, photocopiers, video cameras, video games, fax machines, and cordless telephones. After noting that a dollar in 1860 generally was worth much more than a dollar is today, De Long (1995, p. 7) points out that the dollar in 1860 actually had no worth at all regarding "entire classes of commodities we take for granted in day-to-day life," since those items were not available in 1860. Arguably, then, if we broaden the view of human welfare to include freedom of choice, the rise in human welfare over the last century might have been even greater than the income figures indicate, as we noted in Chapter 1.

Appendix A3: Adjusting for Household Economies in Poor Nations

Pronounced differences exist between rich and poor nations with regard to age structure and average household size. Age structure matters because children eat less than adults. Average household size matters because of household economies of scale. The objective here is to quantify the income implications of household differences between rich and poor nations by adjusting the per capita income in poor nations to an equivalent-adult, equivalent-household (EAEH) income based on average household size and percentage children in the United States. The United States is the appropriate standard to use for the EAEH adjustment, since national currencies are adjusted to the U.S. dollar. Because average household size and age structure are related phenomena—average household size tends to be larger in poor nations in large part because couples in poor nations tend to have more children—it is important to avoid double counting the effects. Observe that the economy-of-scale household effect bears primarily on nonfood items (shelter, consumer durables, and so on—items that yield economies of scale because their use can be shared) whereas the percentage-children effect bears primarily on food consumption. To avoid double counting, then, we apply the economy-of-scale adjustment only to nonfood expenditures and the percentage-children adjustment only to food expenditures. We calculate the adjustment for 1989, the endpoint of the Penn World Table income series used here.

ADJUSTING FOR PERCENTAGE CHILDREN

To adjust for percentage children, we follow the standard practice in the Penn World Table (for example, Summers and Heston 1999, p. 486) in weighting those age fourteen and under as 0.5 and those over fourteen as 1.0.[11] In the late 1980s the estimated percentage of the population aged fourteen and under was less than 20 percent in most rich countries (22 percent in the United States) and 40 to 50 percent in poor nations (World

Bank 1990, table 26).[12] Weighting those aged fourteen and under by 0.5 yields 89 adult equivalents per 100 people in the United States and 75–80 adult equivalents per 100 people in poor nations (75 adult equivalents based on 50 percent children and 80 adult equivalents based on 40 percent children). With respect to food expenditures, then, the equivalent income in poor nations is 11 to 19 percent higher per capita in poor nations relative to the United States (11 percent higher in the case of 40 percent children and 19 percent higher in the case of 50 percent children).

To illustrate the magnitude of the boost in equivalent income in a poor nation, consider the implications for Zambia, a landlocked nation in the southern part of Africa with an estimated 1989 per capita income of about $1,150 in 2000 U.S. dollars. Note that, with 22 percent children, the adult equivalent in the United States is $.78 + (.5)(.22) = .89$. With 49 percent children, the adult equivalent in Zambia is .755. In adult equivalents, then, the ratio for the United States to Zambia is $.89/.755 = 1.18$. In other words, in terms of food consumption where we assume that children eat half as much as adults do, 118 people in Zambia equals 100 people in the United States. The implicit boost in equivalent income in Zambia is .18 multiplied by .52 (food expenditures as a proportion of income in Zambia), or a boost of about 9 percent. So the equivalent-adult adjustment adds about 9 percent to Zambia's equivalent income, or roughly $100 per person ($.09 \times \$1,150$).

ADJUSTING FOR HOUSEHOLD SCALE ECONOMIES

Rich and poor nations also differ greatly with regard to average size of household. Average household size in most poor nations is between 5 and 6, which is twice as large as the United States average of about 2.6 persons per household. Because household members share resources such as shelter and consumer durables, the per capita income differences between rich and poor nations overstate the actual differences in living standards between rich and poor nations. So to get a better picture of the differences in equivalent income between rich and poor nations, we must adjust for differences in household scale economies. The idea here is to adjust households in poor nations to their "household equivalent" in the United States (again we standardize on the basis of household sizes in the United States, since national incomes are calibrated to the U.S. dollar). The issue can be posed this way: imagine that we subdivided the households to reduce average household size in poor nations from 6 persons per household down to the U.S. level of 2.6. How much would that reduction cost us in terms of household economy of scale, expressed as dollars per person? In other words, how much more per capita income would poor nations require in order to maintain a constant standard of living when average household size is cut from 6 down to 2.6?

To answer, we first need more precise data on household structure for the United States and for poor nations. Although the requisite data are readily available for the United States, they are harder to find for poor nations. For poor nations we use estimates based on a household survey conducted by the Central Statistical Office of Swaziland in 1995, the *Swaziland Household and Expenditures Survey* (Swaziland Statistical Office 1995). Although income estimates for Swaziland as a whole indicate that Swaziland is not as poor as the poorest nations in Africa and South Asia, the modestly higher per capita income in Swaziland appears to be largely an urban phenomenon, since incomes are nearly twice as high in its urban areas (ibid.). Rural residents tend to be poor, so it appears to be reasonable to use the household data for rural Swaziland as a first approximation to estimate the savings in poor nations due to their greater household scale economies vis-à-vis the United States.

Table A3.1 compares household sizes in the United States and rural Swaziland. In the United States in 1990 nearly a quarter of households consisted of a single person, whereas in rural Swaziland in 1995 fewer than 2 percent of households consisted of a single member. In the United States only about 10 percent of households had five or more members, whereas in rural Swaziland over 80 percent of households had five or more members. Differences of this magnitude are typical for poor nations compared with the United States, since the average household size for rural Swaziland is close to the average for poor nations as a whole.

Household scale economies are nonlinear functions of household size, since additional household members cost increasingly less. In other words, the first member of a household (hereafter called the *first-order member*) is the most costly, second-order members are the next most costly, and so on. This implies that costs per capita decline as the proportion of higher-order members increases, and costs per capita increase as the proportion of higher-order members declines. Higher-order household members constitute a much greater percentage of the population in poor nations. The bottom panel of Table A3.1 demonstrates that greater percentage in poor nations by translating the household size percentages into percentages of first-, second-, third-, fourth-, and fifth-order members in the United States versus rural Swaziland.[13]

Table A3.2 provides the next step for translating the differences in the household scale economies into increases in the effective incomes in poor nations. How much more income do poor nations effectively have because their households average 6.0 members rather than 2.6 members? The first

TABLE A3.1 Household size and position of household members: United States versus rural Swaziland (in percent)

	United States	Rural Swaziland
Household size[a]		
One member	24.7	1.4
Two members	32.3	2.8
Three members	17.3	6.1
Four members	15.5	7.7
Five or more members	10.3	82.1
Position of household members[b]		
First order	38.5	16.7
Second order	29.0	16.4
Third order	16.5	16.0
Fourth order	9.9	15.0
Fifth order or higher	6.2	36.0

a. *Sources:* U.S. Census Bureau, *Current Population Reports* (reported in *Statistical Abstract of the United States: 1998*, table 73) and Swaziland Central Statistical Office (1995), table 4.3.2.

b. See text for method of calculation.

column reports the proportional differences in first-order members, second-order members, and so on for the United States versus rural Swaziland. A higher proportion in rural Swaziland fall in the higher-order positions where household scale economies are greatest.

Poor nations enjoy household scale economies relative to the United States because their household structures look like the household structure of rural Swaziland, not like that of the United States. To translate the household structural differences of Table A3.2 into income effects, we must make assumptions about how scale economies increase with household size. If there were no scale economies, each additional member would increase a household's expenses by the factor $1/(N - 1)$ for $N \geq 2$. Scale economies occur to the extent that the actual increase is smaller than $1/(N - 1)$ when the Nth member is added. For example, when expenses increase by 60 percent (as opposed to 100 percent) when a second member is added, the second member is 40 percent less costly than the first member— a scale economy factor of .4. The scale economy factor is 1.0 in the case where the second member adds nothing to household costs and zero in the case where the second member adds 100 percent to household costs.

Although it is reasonable to assume that the scale economy factor for nonfood items is close to 1.0 for the second child and beyond (fourth- and

TABLE A3.2 Scale economy differentials, United States versus rural Swaziland

Position of household members	Swaziland minus U.S.[a]	Scale economy factor	
		Schedule 1	Schedule 2
First order	−.218	0	0
Second order	−.126	.74	.41
Third order	−.005	.85	.68
Fourth order	+.051	.95	.95
Fifth order or higher	+.298	.99	.99

a. Based on bottom panel of Table A3.1.

higher-order members) in very poor nations, the size of the scale economy factor is less clear for second-order and third-order members of a household (typically the second-order member is the spouse and the third-order member is the first child). Studies in rich nations provide only limited guidance, since estimates vary widely regarding the size of household scale economies in rich nations (Jencks 1987; Atkinson 1991).

Because the size of household scale economies is in doubt, the prudent strategy is to provide an interval estimate based on upper and lower estimates regarding the size of household economies. Table A3.2 presents the two scale economy schedules used here. The first is based on a scale economy factor of .74 for the second household member and the second schedule is based on a scale factor of .41 for the second member. The final section of this appendix explains how I used results from other studies to arrive at these scale factors. Aside from food, which is considered separately, fifth- and higher-order members add very little to household costs, so both schedules assume a scale economy of .99 for these members.

To estimate the total proportional savings resulting from the scale economies associated with the larger household sizes in poor nations, scale factors were multiplied by the proportional differences in the first column (Table A3.2) and summed. That calculation yields .29 for the first schedule and .25 for the second schedule. So the interval estimate is (.25, .29).

Putting it all together: The total EAEH adjustment adds 15 to 25 percent to equivalent income in poor nations, with the equivalent-household adjustment adding about 10 to 15 percent and the equivalent-adult adjustment adding about 5 to 10 percent. The size of the adjustment varies from nation to nation depending on the child-adult ratio and the ratio of nonfood expenditures to total expenditures. Recall that the percentage of the population under age fifteen ranges from 40 percent to 50 percent in poor nations, and that nonfood items typically constitute 40 to 50 percent of total expenditures in poor nations. In a nation where children make up one-half of the total population, and where one-half of total income is devoted to nonfood items, the total adjustment factor is:

EA adjustment + EH adjustment = .187(.5) + .27(.5) = .23,

where .27 is the midpoint of the interval estimate for household scale economies. In a nation where children constitute 40 percent of the total population, and where 40 percent of total income is devoted to nonfood items, the total adjustment factor is:

EA adjustment + EH adjustment = .113(.4) + .27(.4) = .15.

DERIVATION OF THE HOUSEHOLD SCALE ECONOMY SCHEDULES IN TABLE A3.2

It is reasonable to assume that household scale economies increase with additional household members. Hence I will assume modest scale economies for a spouse and more pronounced scale economies for children, especially higher-parity (higher-order) children.

The issue of household scale effects has been discussed in the literature on poverty in the West. Household scale economies are pertinent in that context because of the need to establish equivalent poverty lines for households of unequal size. This literature frames the issue in terms of the elasticity of household need with respect to household size, where an elasticity of 1.0 implies that needs increase at the same rate as household size (thus scale economy = 0) and an elasticity of zero implies that household needs do not increase at all with household size (scale economy = 1.0). A study that uses per capita income implicitly assumes an elasticity of 1.0.

Elasticity coefficients based on observed consumption patterns are on the order of .36; the elasticity coefficients used in setting the U.S. poverty line tend to be around .55; and the coefficients used in official studies in Western Europe are on the order of .72 (Atkinson 1991, p. 15). From these parameters I selected, for the second-order household member, elasticities of .33 (first schedule) and .67 (second schedule). To convert the elasticities to scale economies, I used the formula that adjusts total income to equivalent income (Buhmann et al. 1988):

Equivalent income = total income/n^s,

where n is the number of household members and s is the elasticity coefficient. From this formula we can calculate the costs added by the nth household member and from that result the scale economy factor follows immediately. To illustrate: for an elasticity of .33 for the second household member, equivalent income is total income divided by $(2)^{0.33} = 1.26$. For the first member ($n = 1$), income equals total income; thus to obtain an equivalent income when a second member is added, total income for the two-member household is multiplied by a factor of 1.26 as opposed to a factor of 2. So the scale economy for the second member is $2.0 - 1.26 = 0.74$.

4

Inequality: What It Is and How It Is Measured

THIS CHAPTER provides a compact statement of what inequality is and how inequality is measured. The literature on inequality and inequality measurement is lengthy and technical, and I do not attempt an exhaustive review. Instead I review what inequality means and explain the essential logic of inequality measurement. I begin by showing that inequality can be conceptualized as average disproportionality. Standard measures of inequality are congruent with this conceptualization, since we can express inequality indexes in a general form as disproportionality functions. The expression of inequality measures as disproportionality functions can help to demystify inequality indexes as well to unify and simplify the presentation of results. Instead of presenting a mishmash of inequality formulas that have no obvious connection, we can key the results to a single formula $\Sigma_i \, p_i \, f(r_i)$, where p_i is population share and r_i is income ratio as defined in this chapter.

The chapter begins by distinguishing inequality from related concepts such as equity. Inequality occurs when units possess disproportionate shares of some item of interest. The term "disproportionate share" is used here strictly in a mathematical sense, to mean a share that is bigger or smaller than the average share for all units. The equity question—is the share fair?—addresses a different issue, since a disproportionate share might or might not be perceived to be a fair share. To determine whether a given unit possesses a mathematically disproportionate share of some entity X, we can examine $X/\overline{X}$—the ratio of the unit's X to the average X for all units ($\overline{X}$ denotes the mean of X). For example, to determine whether an individual nation has a disproportionate income share, we examine the nation's "income ratio"—the ratio of the nation's per capita income to the average income for the world. The challenge is to figure out how to aggregate these unit disproportionalities to obtain a measure of overall inequality. We know that if the income ratios tend to cluster around 1.0 there is less inequality than if the ratios tend to deviate greatly from 1.0, so eyeballing the income ratios for all nations gives us some sense of the degree of between-nation income inequality.

In general, though, eyeballing is not a very reliable method for comparing the degree of inequality in different distributions, or even for determining whether inequality is increasing or declining over time. Social scientists have developed more formal indexes such as the Gini coefficient for summarizing the degree of inequality. These indexes are based on the principle that inequality increases as the income ratios increasingly deviate from 1.0—so the indexes in effect formalize the eyeballing principle just described. Different indexes yield somewhat different estimates of inequality, because they use different mathematical functions for determining "deviation" of income ratios from 1.0.

Defining Inequality

Inequality is the absence of equality. Equality exists when X (for example, income) is equally distributed across units, that is, when each unit possesses the same level of X. The units could be individuals or groups of individuals, such as households or counties or nations. In the case of groups, between-group equality exists when each group possesses the same *average* level of X.[1] Income inequality can occur at different levels of aggregation, that is, incomes can vary across individuals (individual-level inequality), across households (household-level inequality), across nations (between-nation inequality), and so on. Equality at a higher level of aggregation does not necessarily imply equality at a lower level; equality across nations, for example, does not imply equality across individuals. The term *global income inequality* refers to total income inequality for the world, which is the sum of between-nation income inequality and within-nation income inequality. As we shall see, two inequality indexes—the Theil index and the mean logarithmic deviation—are the best inequality measures to use when constructing total inequality from its within-group and between-group components (as here, where groups are nations).

Because perfect equality in incomes does not exist, the issue is not whether there is inequality but rather how much inequality there is. Hence the task is to devise summary measures of inequality that distinguish more inequality from less equality. A number of inequality measures have been suggested. Before examining some of the more common ones, it is important to take a closer look at the inequality concept itself, since some of the confusion over whether income inequality is growing reflects confusion over what the term *inequality* means.

INEQUALITY IS NOT SYNONYMOUS WITH INEQUITY

Inequality and inequity are often confused. Newspaper headlines trumpeting new findings about "pay inequity," for example, very often turn out to be articles describing differences in pay—pay inequality to be sure, but not necessarily pay inequity. Distinguishing inequality and inequity is not hairsplitting. The concept of inequity explicitly invokes norms—what ought to be; inequality does not. To infer wage inequity from wage inequality is to assume that perfect wage equality is the most just system. Whatever the philosophical merits of such an assumption, it is out of step with prevailing belief systems. Unless all work is equal, the widespread norm of "equal pay for equal work" is inconsistent with the notion that justice is best served by completely eliminating inequality in pay, and sociological studies of individuals' perceptions of justice consistently find that the vast majority of people—in the United States as well as in other nations—believe that equal pay for all jobs would *not* be fair (Kelley and Evans 1993).[2] For most individuals the issue of just rewards hinges on the source of inequality (do some get more because they work harder and contribute more?) as well as on the degree of inequality.[3] So the conflation of inequality and inequity is misleading. Authors who use the terms interchangeably should forewarn readers that by using the terms as synonyms they are implicitly assuming that justice is best served through perfect equality.

INEQUALITY IS BASED ON RATIOS, NOT GAPS

The simple mathematics of income growth and gaps dictates that income gaps widen between units as incomes change at the same rate $r > 0$ for all units and income gaps narrow between units as incomes change (decline) at the same rate $r < 0$ for all units. That law is obvious, but much mischief has resulted from ignoring it. The problem arises when articles on income inequality point to widening gaps as evidence of rising inequality, or vice versa. This problem is found in academic articles[4] as well as in more popular discussions, and it is not uncommon in analyses of inequality across nations, where researchers routinely find that income gaps between richer and poorer nations *are* widening (for example, from 1965 to 1989 the income *gap* between the United States and Taiwan widened by $600 [in 2000 U.S. dollars] even though the income *ratio* plummeted from 7 to 1 down to 2.3 to 1). Because we live in a world where average income has been doubling every half century or less, the gap between richer and poorer nations naturally will widen, quite apart from any change in the degree of inequality across nations.

It is important to note that the argument here is based on the standard disproportionality-based definition of income inequality—the view that income inequality refers to the relative magnitude of incomes. Thus at the individual level income inequality remains constant when income grows at the same rate for every individual. (The same principle holds for equal-sized aggregates.) To define inequality otherwise leads to conceptual and practical problems—including measurement problems, since inequality indexes are based on the standard view that inequality is unaffected by proportional increases or declines. Nonetheless some have argued that inequality increases when income increases at the same rate for everyone and declines when income declines at the same rate for each unit. This alternative conceptualization of inequality could be called *gap inequality*, because it combines the notion of widening gaps with the conventional notion of inequality. Interestingly, while Serge Christophe Kolm (1976) argues that proportional increases serve to increase inequality (gap inequality), Sen (1973) notes that one could argue the opposite, that proportional increases serve to reduce inequality.

Throughout this book the term *inequality* is used in the standard sense. To avoid confusion, when referring to the concept of changing absolute differences I will use the terms "widening gap" and "narrowing gap." Gaps and inequalities are best analyzed separately, since they address different issues. Because this book focuses on income inequality, we use standard measures of inequality such as the Gini. Inequality pertains to proportionate share of some item—not to size differences—and that is the conceptualization of inequality that underlies inequality measures, as we now see.

Income Ratios and Income Inequality

The income ratio for a nation is that nation's per capita income divided by the average income worldwide. For example, the United States had an income ratio of 4.14 in 1989, indicating that in 1989 the income of the average person in the United States was more than four times greater than the income of the average person in the world. We begin our discussion of inequality measures by examining income ratios for the world's richest and poorest nations in 1989, just before the USSR dissolved. This examination serves a dual purpose. First, by examining ratios for nations at either end of the income distribution we gain a sense of the magnitude of the disparity in incomes for the most extreme cases. Second, in examining an income ratio we are examining the essential datum for an inequality index, since inequality indexes condense the information contained in the income ra￫ tios into a single number. Thus income ratios form a natural point of departure for discussing inequality indexes.

The data from the national accounts indicate enormous income disparities across nations. To appreciate the magnitude of the differences, consider Table 4.1, which reports the income ratios for the ten richest and ten poorest nations in 1989 according to the Penn World Table estimates. Income ratios for the very poorest nations are on the order of 0.10 to 0.13, indicating that the average person in these nations has an income that is only 10 to 13 percent of the world average. Per capita incomes in the ten richest nations are roughly 30 times larger than those in the ten poorest nations (unweighted average). Inspection of Table 4.1 should help readers understand why prior research (Chapter 5) has concluded that the majority of the world's total income inequality lies between nations.

The degree of inequality depends on the average distance of the income ratios from 1.0, the point of equality. If the income ratio for the United States increased to 5.0 while other incomes remained constant, between-nation income inequality would increase. By the same token, if the income ratio for the United States declined to 3.0 while other incomes remained constant, between-nation income inequality would decline. But suppose other incomes also changed. Suppose, for example, that the income ratios

TABLE 4.1 Income ratios for ten richest and ten poorest nations in 1989

Richest	Income ratio (r_j)	Poorest	Income ratio (r_j)
United States	4.14	Central African Rep.	0.134
Canada	4.01	Comoros	0.134
Switzerland	3.73	Mali	0.127
Luxembourg	3.65	Uganda	0.126
Australia	3.40	Burundi	0.122
Sweden	3.36	Malawi	0.120
Norway	3.35	Burkina Faso	0.119
Hong Kong	3.27	Niger	0.116
Finland	3.26	Zaire (Dem. Rep. of Congo)	0.097
West Germany	3.17	Chad	0.094
Average	3.53		0.116

Data Source: Penn World Table, version 5.6 (Summers et al. 1994).
Note: Income ratios are based on gross domestic product per capita, adjusted for purchasing power parity.

for the poorest nations increased (reducing inequality) while the ratio for the United States also increased (increasing inequality). What would be the *net* effect—would these simultaneous changes increase or reduce between-nation income inequality? Or what if Switzerland's ratio increased from 3.7 to 4.0, Australia's ratio declined from 3.4 to 3.0, and Malawi's ratio doubled from 0.12 to 0.24—would between-nation income inequality go up or down?

These are pertinent questions, since income growth rates vary substantially from nation to nation over any given period of time. By simply eyeballing the income ratios in Table 4.1 we can see that rich nations are much richer than poor nations. To determine whether income inequality is rising or falling across nations, however, we need more precise methods for assessing degree of disproportionality. That is the purpose of inequality indexes—to reduce to a single number the degree of disproportionality represented by the income ratios. To reduce national income ratios to a single index measuring income inequality, we need two pieces of information—the income ratios themselves and the nations' population shares.

INEQUALITY AS AVERAGE DISPROPORTIONALITY

By definition a quantity X is equally distributed over the N units in a population when $X_j = \overline{X}$ (the mean of X) for all $j = 1, 2, \ldots, N$. Assuming X—a nonnegative quantity—exists in the population (so $\overline{X}$ is not zero), define the *income ratio* for unit j as the ratio of X for the jth unit to the average X for all units:

$$\text{income ratio:} \quad r_j = X_j/\overline{X}, \tag{4.1}$$

where X denotes income. Note that inequality is zero when and only when $r_j = 1.0$ for all j; otherwise, inequality is greater than zero. The ratio $r_j = X_j/\overline{X}$ reflects the extent to which the jth unit possesses a mathematically disproportionate share of income (a ratio greater than 1.0 indicates a disproportionately large income share; a ratio less than 1.0 indicates a disproportionately small share). We can conceptualize inequality as the average disproportionality across all units, that is, as the average distance of the r_j from 1.0, where "distance" is measured by some function f such that $f(1.0) = 0$.

Standard inequality indexes are measures of average disproportionality (Firebaugh 1998, 1999; Reardon and Firebaugh 2002). Because inequality indexes are measures of average disproportionality, they can be expressed in a common form:

$$I \text{ (Inequality Index)} = \sum_j f(r_j)/N, \tag{4.2}$$

where $\Sigma_j\, f(r_j) = f(r_1) + f(r_2) + \ldots + f(r_N)$ and N is the total number of cases. In the case of individuals, the units are the same size so they are weighted equally, as in equation 4.2. In the general case, however, units differ in size (for example, population varies across nations). In instances where the research calls for giving each nation equal weight, then between-nation inequality is a simple (or unweighted) average, in line with equation 4.2. In instances where the research calls for giving each *person* equal weight, however, then nations are weighted by their size, and between-nation inequality is a weighted average of the national disproportionalities. Hence a more general expression for inequality indexes is:

$$I = \sum_j p_j f(r_j), \tag{4.3}$$

where Σ denotes summation and f denotes the disproportionality function, as before, and p_j denotes *population share*, defined as n_j/N—the size of the *j*th unit as a proportion of the combined population of all units (note that the population shares sum to 1.0). Chad, the poorest nation in 1989, had a population share of .0011 (Table 3.1); the United States, the richest nation, had a population share of about .048 in 1989; and China, the world's most populous nation, had a population share of about .217. When each unit is weighted the same, then $p_j = 1/N$ and equation 4.3 reduces to equation 4.2. So in calculating between-nation income inequality we use equation 4.2 when we want nations to be weighted equally and equation 4.3 when we want individuals to be weighted equally. Because global income inequality is based on the equal weighting of individuals, this book focuses on between-nation income inequality as calculated by equation 4.3 ("weighted inequality").

COMMON DISPROPORTIONALITY FUNCTIONS

Table 4.2 gives the disproportionality functions for the five principal measures of inequality used in this study (see appendix to this chapter). Recall that disproportionality functions measure the distance of income ratios from 1.0. One obvious measure of distance of the income ratio from 1.0 is $|r_j - 1|$, linear distance. A measure of inequality called the mean relative deviation, or the Schutz coefficient, is based on this disproportionality function (Allison 1978). The Schutz coefficient is rarely used, however, and

TABLE 4.2 Disproportionality functions for inequality indexes used in this study

Index	Disproportionality function
Squared coefficient of variation (CV^2)	$(r_j - 1)^2$
Gini index (G)	Individual-level data: $\| r_i - r_j \| /2$ where $\| \bullet \|$ is the absolute value. Grouped data: $r_j(q_j - Q_j)$, where q_j is proportion of total population in units poorer than unit j, and Q_j is proportion of total population in units richer than unit j (so $p_j + q_j + Q_j = 1$).
Theil index (T)	$r_j \log(r_j)$
Mean logarithmic deviation (MLD)	$\log(1/r_j) = -\log(r_j)$
Variance of logged income (VarLog)	$[\log r_j - E(\log r_j)]^2$

Note: r_j is income ratio $(X_j\overline{X})$; p_j is population share; log is the natural logarithm; E is expected value.

it fails to satisfy key criteria for inequality measures, so we consider it no further. By squaring linear distance we obtain the disproportionality function used in the squared coefficient of variation (CV^2), a standard measure of inequality used in this study. The popular Gini index is based on the disproportionality function $|r_i - r_j|/2$, or one-half the distance between the income ratios for units i and j. In the case of complete equality, the distance between income ratios is zero for all pairs of units, so the Gini is zero. Otherwise the Gini is greater than zero. Another popular index, the Theil index, is based on the disproportionality function $r_j \log(r_j)$. The sum of this function is zero when and only when the income ratio is 1.0 for all j. The mean logarithmic deviation (MLD) is based on the disproportionality function $-\log(r_j)$. Obviously the sum of $\log(r_j)$ is zero when and only when the income ratio is 1.0 for all j. The fifth inequality index used in this study is the variance of logged incomes, abbreviated VarLog. VarLog is based on the disproportionality function $\log r_j - E(\log r_j)$, where $E(\log r_j)$ is the expected value (mean) of the log of the income ratios.

EXAMPLE: BETWEEN-NATION INCOME INEQUALITY IN 1989

From equation 4.3 and the disproportionality functions in Table 4.2, it is straightforward to calculate values for the five inequality indexes. Using

the Penn World Table income data, we obtain the following values for between-nation income inequality in 1989:

- Theil = 0.526
- MLD = 0.539
- Gini = 0.543
- VarLog = 0.964
- CV^2 = 1.337

So the index values are slightly above 0.50 for the Theil, the MLD, and
the Gini, and substantially larger for the two variance-based measures
(VarLog and the squared coefficient of variation). To provide perspective
on the magnitude of the inequality indicated by these values for between-
nation income inequality, income inequality within the average nation in
1989 was on the order of 0.20–0.22 for the Theil and the MLD (Chapter
9). It is also informative to compare the between-nation levels with the levels that prevail in the nations of Latin America, where income inequality is
notoriously high. The best evidence suggests that the level of income inequality in Latin American countries is very roughly 0.45–0.50 for the
Theil and the MLD. So it is fair to say that the degree of income inequality
found across nations is somewhat greater than the degree of within-nation
income inequality found within the region of the world (Latin America)
where income inequality is the most pronounced.

To further assist our intuition about the level of inequality reflected in
the inequality figures above, suppose we collapsed the 120 nations of the
Penn World Table into just two nations of equal size—nation Have and nation Have-Not—on the basis of average national income. We would find
that the one-half of the world's population living in Have would enjoy an
average income of about $11,600 in current (2000) U.S. dollars. The aver-
age income for the half of the world living in nation Have-Not would be
about $2,000 in current U.S. dollars. This approximately 6 to 1 ratio for
Have versus Have-Not is very roughly the same as the 1989 income ratio
for the United States versus Thailand. The 6 to 1 ratio understates the actual level of between-nation inequality in 1989, since it ignores income differences among the nations that make up Have and among the nations that
make up Have-Not. The exercise nonetheless is useful for helping readers
conceive in very general terms the magnitude of income differences between nations. If we did in fact collapse nations into two groups of equal
size on the basis of their per capita income, per capita income in the richer

group would be almost six times greater than per capita income in the poorer group.

Criteria for Inequality Indexes

Because inequality is ubiquitous, the challenge is not to distinguish inequality from equality but to distinguish more inequality from less inequality. Distinguishing more inequality from less inequality is not as easy as one might think, and a large technical literature has arisen around the issue.[5] To select appropriate summary measures of inequality from the assortment of measures that have been proposed, the first step is to specify criteria for evaluating inequality measures. An ideal measure of world income inequality would be scale-invariant, would be additively decomposable into between-nation and within-nation components, would obey the principle of transfers, and would be consistent with the welfare principle that income transfers among the poor are more consequential than income transfers among the rich.

• *Scale invariance.* Suppose all incomes were doubled for a fixed population. Then average income is also doubled, but income ratios remain the same, so income inequality is not affected. Hence inequality measures should not be affected when income is increased or reduced at the same rate for everyone. This property is known as scale invariance because the property ensures that the measurement of inequality does not depend on the scale used—whether dollars or francs or pesos or whatever. (The property is also called "mean independence" because the level of inequality is not dependent on the overall mean.) The scale invariance property distinguishes change in income inequality from change in income gaps. The point is important because, as noted above, inequality is based on shares, not gaps.

• *Additive decomposability.* Suppose everyone in the population is sorted into mutually exclusive groups, such as nations or households or age groups. An additively decomposable inequality index is one in which the index value for overall inequality is a weighted sum of the within-group index values and the between-group index value. Additive decomposability is not required for simply describing the trend in between-nation inequality, but the property is critical to analyses that construct the trend in global inequality by combining the within-nation and between-nation trends, as in this study. The analyses reported subsequently rely heavily on the Theil and the MLD because they have the property of additive decomposability.

• *Principle of transfers.* Inequality is reduced when $1 is transferred from a richer person to a poorer person and increased when $1 is transferred from a poorer person to a richer person. Not all inequality indexes obey this principle at all points on the income distribution. For example, the variance of the logarithm of income—a popular measure of income inequality—fails to obey the principle of transfers at high income levels (Allison 1978; Jenkins 1991).

Of the popular indexes of inequality, only the Theil and the mean logarithmic deviation satisfy these three criteria and also are consistent with the welfare principle that $100 means more to a poor person than to a rich person (so an income transfer at higher levels of income is less significant than the same transfer at lower levels of income). The Gini index of inequality is scale-invariant and obeys the principle of transfers, but the Gini is not additively decomposable (Bourguignon 1979; Cowell 1988; Reardon and Firebaugh 2002) nor is the Gini consistent with the welfare principle. The variance of the logarithm fails to obey the principle of transfers at some points on the income distribution, and the squared coefficient of variation is not consistent with the welfare principle.

Summary of Inequality Measurement

Equality exists when every unit has a mathematically proportional share of the item of interest. Because proportional share implies an income ratio of 1.0, departure from equality, or disproportionality, for a given unit is measured by distance of that unit's income ratio from 1.0. The purpose of a summary index of inequality is to replace the income ratios—reflecting the disproportionalities of individual units—with a single number reflecting the weighted average of the disproportionalities. Hence inequality indexes take the general form $I = \Sigma_j \, p_j \, f(r_j)$, where p_j is population share and $f(r_j)$ is a function measuring the distance of the income ratio from 1.0.

Of the five inequality measures I use, I rely most heavily on the MLD, the Theil, and the Gini. Albert Berry, François Bourguignon, and Christian Morrisson (1991) use the MLD as one of their two inequality measures in a study of global income inequality (their other measure is the Theil), and I will feature the MLD as well. Although not as well known as other inequality indexes, the MLD has attractive properties. It is scale-invariant and additively decomposable, and it satisfies the principle of transfers as well as the welfare principle. In addition, the MLD can be expressed as the logarithm of the ratio of the arithmetic mean to the geometric mean. That expression of the MLD reveals an interesting link between inequality and people's evaluations of justice, since studies find that perceived injustice is also a logarithmic function of a ratio, where the ratio is actual reward/just reward (Jasso 1999). The MLD is a nice complement to the Theil, since the MLD is affected more by populous nations whereas the Theil is affected more by rich nations. Thus the MLD is more sensitive than the Theil is to income change in nations such as China while the Theil is more sensitive than the MLD is to income change in nations such as Sweden.

As we shall see in this study, the relative sensitivities of the MLD and the Theil to population change and income change hold for within-nation inequality as well as for between-nation inequality. The within-nation component of global income inequality is a weighted average of the income inequalities of all nations. The Theil and the MLD use different weights (Chapter 9). The Theil weights by income share (a nation's total income expressed as the proportion of the world's total income) whereas the MLD weights by population share. Thus change in income distributions in Asian countries will have a greater effect on change in the MLD index than on change in the Theil index, since the population shares for Asia are twice as large as its income shares. On the other hand, distributional changes in Western industrialized nations will have a greater effect on change in the Theil, since the Western industrialized nations claim half the world's income while containing less than one-sixth of the world's population. In instances where the Theil and MLD results differ, it is useful to associate the Theil with the West and the MLD with Asia.

Although the Gini index is the most popular measure of inequality, it has shortcomings. Because the Gini is not based on the logarithm function, it is not consistent with the welfare principle that income transfers are more consequential among the poor than among the rich. In addition, the Gini is harder to calculate than most other measures and it does not have the property of additive decomposability. The latter is especially problematic in a study of global income inequality, where the data come in national chunks. However, the Gini trends provide nonredundant information about income inequality, since the Gini is relatively more sensitive to change around the median of the income distribution. Hence the Gini forms a nice complement to the Theil and the MLD. Of the three indexes, the Theil tends to be the most sensitive to income trends in large rich nations such as the United States and Japan, the MLD tends to be the most sensitive to income trends in populous nations such as China and India, and the Gini tends to be the most sensitive to income trends in middle-income nations.

Appendix A4: Five Inequality Indexes

Inequality indexes are distinguished by their disproportionality functions. Table 4.2 listed the disproportionality functions for the five principal inequality indexes used in this study. This appendix describes the indexes in more detail.

• *Theil index (T)*. This index was proposed by Henri Theil (1967, p. 102). Because the Theil index is based on the disproportionality function $r_j \log(r_j)$, the Theil index can be written:

$$T = \sum_j p_j r_j \log(r_j). \tag{A4.1}$$

Clearly the Theil is zero under perfect equality, since $\log(1) = 0$. Unless $r_j = 1$ for all units, T is a sum of positive and negative values, because $\log(r_j)$ is positive for $r_j > 1$ and negative for $r_j < 1$. The sum of the positive values is always greater (that is, $T > 0$), because the negative logarithms receive weights less than one ($r_j < 1$ when $\log[r_j]$ is negative) whereas the positive logarithms receive weights greater than one ($r_j > 1$ when $\log[r_j]$ is positive).[6]

The most important practical difference between the Theil and the other inequality indexes used here is the *relatively* greater sensitivity of the Theil to change at the upper end of the income distribution. Note that $\log(r_j)$ is weighted by $p_j r_j$ in the Theil. That point is significant, since $p_j r_j$ is equivalent to the total income in unit j divided by the total income for all units— that is, $p_j r_j$ is a unit's income share (for example, in 1990 the U.S. economy produced about 20 percent of the total world income, so the U.S. income share was about 0.20).

• *Mean logarithmic deviation (MLD)*. The mean logarithmic deviation is the logarithm of the mean of X minus the mean of the logarithm of X. This difference is positive, because the logarithm of the mean is always greater than or equal to the mean of the logarithm. In other words, when we first log the X's and then calculate the mean we obtain a smaller number than when we calculate the mean first and then log. The result will be the same when and only when X is the same for everyone. Hence the MLD is zero when and only when there is equality.

Simple algebra yields the disproportionality function for the MLD. The logarithm of the mean of X can be written $\log(\overline{X})\Sigma_j p_j$ (since $\Sigma_j p_j = 1$) and the mean of the logarithm of X can be written $\Sigma_j p_j \log(X_j)$. Hence the difference is $\log(\overline{X})\Sigma_j p_j - \Sigma_j p_j \log(X_j)$, or:

$$
\begin{aligned}
MLD &= \Sigma_j p_j \left[\log(\overline{X}) - \log(X_j)\right] \\
&= \Sigma_j p_j \log(\overline{X}/X_j) \\
&= \Sigma_j p_j \log(1/r_j). \tag{A4.2}
\end{aligned}
$$

Thus the disproportionality function for the MLD is $\log(1/r_j)$ or $-\log r_j$.

• *Gini index (G).* The Gini index is the best-known measure of inequality. For grouped data the disproportionality function for the Gini is $r_j(q_j - Q_j)$, where q_j is proportion of total population in units poorer than unit j and Q_j is proportion of total population in units richer than unit j. The Gini index is the population-weighted average of this disproportionality function. Hence the Gini for grouped data is (Allison 1978):

$$G = \sum_j p_j r_j (q_j - Q_j). \tag{A4.3}$$

When the income ratios are all 1.0, then $q_j = Q_j = 0$ for all j, and the Gini is zero, as it should be. When each unit is weighted equally (for example, when the units are individuals) then $p_j = 1/N$ and $G = \Sigma_j r_j(q_j - Q_j)/N$. In this case the upper limit of the Gini is $1 - (1/N)$, where N is the number of cases. Note that the upper limit of the Gini approaches 1.0 as N increases.

• *Squared coefficient of variation (CV²).* Although this study relies most heavily on the Theil, the MLD, and the Gini, there are instances where it is also useful to examine results for two variance-based measures, the squared coefficient of variation and the variance of the logarithm. The coefficient of variation is the standard deviation divided by the mean. The standard deviation (σ) is not an appropriate measure of inequality, because σ is not scale-invariant. Division by the mean produces scale invariance. The coefficient of variation is typically squared when used as a measure of inequality, since the squared form is easier to work with algebraically. The squared coefficient of variation is simply the average of the squared distance of the income ratios from 1.0:

$$CV^2 = \sum_j p_j (r_j - 1)^2. \tag{A4.4}$$

From equation A4.4 it is obvious that CV^2 is zero when and only when all units possess the same amount of X (so $r_j = 1$ for all units).

The squared coefficient of variation gives equal weight to income transfers at all levels (Schwartz and Winship 1979). Most other inequality measures compress incomes at the upper end, so that an income transfer at a lower level of income registers a greater effect on the index than does the same transfer at a higher level of income. The failure of the squared coefficient of variation to do likewise is problematic in the study of between-nation inequality, since most would agree that a $500 change in average income is much more significant for a nation with an average income of $1,000 than for a nation with an average income of $20,000. Nonetheless there are instances where CV^2 provides useful supplementary information about the nature of trends in income inequality.

• *Variance of the logarithm of X (VarLog).* The name describes the measure: take the logarithm of X, then take the variance of those logged values. That two-step process produces a scale-invariant measure that obeys the welfare principle but not the principle of transfers. The general formula for VarLog is:[7]

$$VarLog = \sum_j p_j (\log r_j - E[\log r_j])^2. \tag{A4.5}$$

PART III

EVIDENCE

CHAPTER 5

What We Already Know

GLOBAL INCOME INEQUALITY has been attracting intense interest. In the April 28, 2001, issue of *The Economist,* for example, the globalization scholar Robert Wade writes that "having ignored world income distribution for decades, international economics has lately seen a burst of interest" (p. 72). This renewed interest is well justified, as he explains:

> Anybody interested in the wealth and poverty of nations must be interested in what is happening to the global distribution of income, one would suppose. A lot turns on the question. If the world's income distribution has become more equal in the past few decades, this would be powerful evidence that globalisation works to the benefit of all. . . . And it would help to settle a crucial and long-standing disagreement in economic theory, between the orthodox view that economic growth naturally delivers 'convergence' of rich and poor countries, and alternative theories which, for one reason or another, say the opposite. (p. 72)

Wade is certainly right that "a lot turns on the question" of "what is happening to the global distribution of income." In this chapter and the four that follow, we will review the evidence. To set the stage, we begin with what most observers agree on with regard to global income inequality. The chapter is fairly short, because many features of global income inequality are the subject of debate—certainly there is not the degree of consensus that one would expect given the confident statements quoted in Chapter 2. One reason for the lack of consensus is that research on income inequality traditionally has focused elsewhere, so direct empirical evidence on global income inequality is surprisingly thin.

There is nonetheless consensus in the empirical literature on two key points: first, that income inequality across nations shot up over the nineteenth and early twentieth centuries and, second, that most of the world's total income inequality lies between, not within, nations. The points are related, of course, since between-nation inequality is the larger component of global inequality precisely because of the steep rise in between-nation inequality over the course of Western industrialization. In any case, the historical rise in between-nation income inequality is well established: there is no need to repeat the evidence reviewed earlier. The statement that between-nation inequality is the larger component of global income inequality is not especially controversial either, but the literature on this issue is less well known. We begin the chapter by reviewing the pertinent evidence in more detail. The second part of the chapter reviews the traditional economics literature on income inequality, and makes the point that we do not know as much as one might expect about the global distribution of income, because until recently studies of income inequality have focused primarily on the causes and consequences of income inequality within nations.

Most of the World's Total Income Inequality Is between Nations

Studies uniformly find that the between-nation component is larger than the within-nation component of world income inequality.[1] The key issues still open to debate involve the dominance of the between-nation component—is it larger by a factor of two, by a factor of three, or by a factor greater than three?—and the direction of change in the between/total ratio—is the prominence of the between-nation component increasing or receding? Table 5.1 summarizes the findings of key studies of the relative size of the between-nation and within-nation components of world income inequality. An early study by Henri Theil (1979) estimated that the between-nation component accounted for about 65 percent of the total inequality in 1970. Later studies have tended to yield higher estimates. These estimates are bounded on the lower end by Berry, Bourguignon, and Morrisson (1991), whose estimates range from 65 to 68 percent, and Roberto Korzeniewicz and Timothy Moran (1997) on the upper end, who find, in estimates based on the Theil index, that in 1992 the between-nation component was six times larger than the within-nation component.

The studies by Paul Schultz (1998), Brian Goesling (2001), and Milanovic (2002) provide estimates for recent years via three different methods. To estimate the between-nation component, Schultz uses data for 120 nations encompassing more than 90 percent of the world's population. To estimate the within-nation component, Schultz uses the Deininger-

Squire data supplemented by regression analysis of that data to impute inequality for 64 of the 120 nations (generally the smaller nations) with no data on income inequality. Using this method, Schultz (1998) estimates that the between-nation component made up 69 percent of the total world inequality in 1960 and 73 percent in 1970, 1980, and 1989 (MLD). Using the variance of the logged income to measure inequality yields similar but slightly lower estimates (Table 5.1). Goesling (2001) uses similar methods for the between-nation component, but bases his estimates of within-nation income inequality on nations with reported income inequality data. Because of these restrictions, Goesling's within-nation sample was smaller than Schultz's, consisting of 35 nations in 1980 and 60 nations in 1992. For both years, however, the Goesling sample represented all the world's geographic regions and the majority of the world's population, including China, India, Russia, the United States, and Indonesia. Using the Theil index, Goesling (2001, table 2) estimates that the between-nation component accounted for 78 percent of world income inequality in 1980 and 74 percent in 1992.

Milanovic's (2002) study stands out because it is the first to calculate world inequality directly from nationally representative survey data covering most of the world's population. To explain: calculations of the between/total ratio typically begin with data that are already aggregated to the national level, that is, the calculations begin with mean income for a nation (to estimate the between-nation component of world inequality) and the Theil or some other summary measure of income inequality for a nation (to estimate the within-nation component). Milanovic (2002) compiled income data from household surveys for a common group of 91 nations in 1988 and 1993, covering about 84 percent of the world's population. From this data compilation he constructed a data set based on income groups for each of the 91 nations. Because most nations' data are deciles, most nations had 10 data points, but some had fewer and some had more. From this data set of roughly 1,000 data points for each year, it is possible to estimate the world's total income inequality using the general inequality formula $I = \Sigma_j \, p_j \, f(r_j)$, where p_j is population share and r_j is income ratio (Chapter 4). Because j indexes a subnational income group, in this approach total world inequality is calculated as a weighted average of the disproportionalities (the $f[r_j]$) of the one thousand or so subnational income groups.

Milanovic (2002) estimates that between-nation income inequality accounted for 75 percent of the world total in 1988 and 74 percent of the total five years later. The consistency of these estimates with the Schultz and Goesling estimates is reassuring. Based on different sets of nations, differ-

TABLE 5.1 Estimates of between-nation versus within-nation components of global income inequality

Study	Inequality index	Description of sample	Year	Between-nation as % of total
Theil (1979)	MLD	N = 110 nonsocialist nations (for between component)	1970	65%
Whalley (1979), table 4	Gini	N = 80; excludes China and USSR	1972	Between = .667 Total = .740
Berry, Bourguignon, and Morrisson (1991), table 3.4	Theil	Socialist and nonsocialist nations; uses upper estimate of economic growth for China	1950 1960 1970 1977	67% 65% 66% 65%
	MLD		1950 1960 1970 1977	68% 66% 67% 67%
Korzeniewicz and Moran (1997), table 2	Theil	N = 46 nations, including China; income *not* adjusted for PPP	1965 1992	79% 86%
	Gini		1965	Between = .682 Total = .749
			1992	Between = .738 Total = .796
Schultz (1998), table 4	MLD	N = 120 nations, including most of world's population	1960 1970 1980 1989	69% 73% 73% 73%

Schultz (1998), table 2	VarLog	Same as above	1960	67%
			1970	71%
			1980	71%
			1989	70%
Goesling (2001), table 2	Theil	N varies for within-nation inequality	1980	78%
			1992	74%
Milanovic (2002), table 19	Theil	Household survey data for N = 91 nations, including all large nations and most former Soviet republics	1988	75%
			1993	74%

Note: Because the Gini does not decompose into between-nation and within-nation components, the ratio of the between to the total ($\times$ 100) is not a meaningful percentage. For the Gini, the table therefore simply presents the coefficients separately for between-nation and for total world inequality.

ent indexes of inequality, substantially different methods for estimating the within-nation component, and—in the case of Milanovic—a different sort of income measure (Milanovic's "income" measure is based not on output but on surveys of household expenditures), the three studies nonetheless all reach the conclusion that the between/within ratio is nearly 3:1. This sort of consensus is rarely seen in cross-national studies.

A notable exception to the 3:1 consensus appears in the Korzeniewicz and Moran (1997) study, where the authors conclude that the ratio in 1992 is 6:1, using the Theil, and 13:1, using the Gini. (At the other extreme, the Bourguignon-Morrisson 1999 estimates yield a 3:2 ratio for between-to-within inequality in recent decades, but those estimates are not cited in Table 5.1 because they are based on nation groups instead of on nations.) The Korzeniewicz-Moran estimates for between-nation income inequality are inflated because they do not adjust the national income data for purchasing power parity (PPP). Aside from that, the conclusion of Korzeniewicz and Moran that more than 90 percent of global income inequality is between-nation inequality is based on their interpretation of the between/total ratio for the Gini coefficients (.91 in 1965 and .93 in 1992) as "proportion of inequality accounted for by between-country inequality" (Korzeniewicz and Moran 1997, table 2)—but recall that the between-group Gini and within-group Gini do not sum to the total Gini (Chapter 4), so this ratio cannot be interpreted as a proportion or percentage in the case of the Gini.

Although the size of the between-nation component of global income inequality is not thirteen times the size of the within-nation component, it is as much as three times the size of the within-nation component. Traditionally, however, most research on income inequality has investigated the smaller component, as we now see.

A Note on the Traditional Literature on Income Inequality

One looks in vain for discussions of the inequality transition in the traditional sociology and economics literatures on income inequality. There are several reasons for this blind spot. One reason is that studies reporting declines in between-nation income inequality (Chapter 6) have been drowned out by more vocal and more visible proclamations of growing inequality. Another reason is that studies of income inequality traditionally have been preoccupied with other matters. Most studies of income inequality do not study global inequality or between-nation inequality at all but focus instead on inequality within a nation or a subset of nations. This other body of work focuses on the causes and consequences of income inequality within nations, which differs from the focus here on trends in global income inequality. Because academic studies traditionally have focused on income inequality within nations, most social scientists probably think first of this literature when they hear the term "income inequality." Because this literature is interested in the causes and consequences of income inequality within nations, the typical study of income inequality relies heavily on the standard statistical toolkit used by social scientists. This book does not; in fact, the book does not contain a single regression equation. Thus readers who are interested in global income inequality are not disadvantaged if they are unfamiliar with statistical methods. What is more important here is a willingness to consider the evidence wherever it leads.

Despite the difference in objectives between this study of global inequality and the larger body of work on inequality within particular nations, a selective overview of the larger body of work is appropriate for two reasons. First, it serves to orient readers, many of whom will be more familiar with the within-nation inequality literature than with the global inequality literature. Second, there may be a causal link between a nation's level of inequality and its growth rate. Indeed, orthodox economic arguments about inequality and growth imply that income inequality facilitates income growth, so the trend in within-nation income inequality could affect the trend in between-nation income inequality:

trend in within-nation income inequality → trend in between-nation income inequality

The conjectured causal effect of the within-nation inequality trend on the between-nation inequality trend is revealed when we juxtapose two prominent literatures in economics, the "trade-off" literature, which argues that reduction in inequality leads to slower economic growth (that is, there is a trade-off between equality and growth), and the Kuznets curve literature, which posits that reductions in inequality are more likely for rich industrialized nations than for nations in the earlier stages of industrialization. Together the trade-off and Kuznets curve literatures imply a growth disadvantage for richer nations and thus income convergence, as declining inequality in richer nations inhibits their income growth relative to the growth of poorer nations.

THE KUZNETS CURVE AND THE GREAT U-TURN

In his classic paper on economic growth and inequality, Simon Kuznets (1955) speculated that industrialization has a nonlinear effect on income inequality, with inequality increasing as nations begin to industrialize and then declining at later stages of industrialization. In the early stages of industrialization, most of a nation's labor force is still engaged in agriculture. As industrialization proceeds, workers move from the larger agricultural sector to the smaller industrial sector. Because wages are higher in the industrial sector, this migration from farm to factory boosts income inequality in the early stages of industrialization. The effect is a compositional one, that is, it occurs as an automatic numerical consequence of the increasing proportion of the labor force engaged in the higher-wage industrial sector (Kuznets 1955, p. 15). Eventually, as the agricultural sector shrinks and the industrial sector increases in size, further movement from agriculture to industry serves to reduce rather than to increase income inequality. Currently, though, the agricultural sector is the much larger sector in the world's poorer regions, so low-income nations presumably are still located on the part of the curve where farm out-migration boosts income inequality.

The sociological version of the Kuznets curve is found in Gerhard Lenski's *Power and Privilege* (1966). For Lenski, the source of the inverted U (rising inequality in the early stages of industrialization and falling inequality at later stages) is not labor migration but the interests of the powerful. As a general rule, "power will determine the distribution of nearly all of the surplus possessed by a society" (p. 44, emphasis omitted) so "the degree of inequality in distributive systems will vary directly with the size of a society's surplus" (p. 85, emphasis omitted). Because industrialization increases the surplus, inequality increases at early stages of industrialization. At later stages of industrialization, however, inequality ceases to grow, because it is in the best interests of the powerful to make concessions in relative terms in order to maintain political stability and ensure continued absolute gains in living standards (pp. 313–318).

The inverted-U hypothesis has been tested with cross-country data. Quantitative cross-country studies have been a staple of social science research at least since the 1960s, when economists and other social scientists began to assemble cross-sectional data to (among other things) look for the Kuznets curve. The first step is to use income data for individuals or households to calculate a measure of inequality (such as the Gini coefficient) for each nation. Hence the size of the sample is determined by the number of countries with data on income inequality, and the variance in inequality is based on the variance in the level of income inequality from nation to nation. (Note the contrast with global inequality and between-nation inequality, where at any point in time a single Gini summarizes global inequality and a single Gini summarizes between-nation inequality.) Next, income inequality is regressed on income level and its square, and perhaps some control variables, to determine if there is evidence for an inverted-U association between income inequality and level of income:

national per capita income → national income inequality (curvilinear pattern)

Empirical results have been mixed. Although Klaus Deininger and Lyn Squire (1998) find little support for the curve using their data on the evolution of income inequality within nations over time, Montek Singh Ahluwalia (1976a,b) finds strong support for the Kuznets curve in early analyses, as do François Nielsen and Arthur Alderson (1995, 1997) and Robert Barro (2000) in more recent longitudinal studies of inequality.

Subsequent analysis in this book provides evidence that is more consistent with the findings of Nielsen and Alderson and Barro than those of Deininger and Squire. In particular, we find evidence of rising income inequality in large industrializing nations in Asia, consistent with the Kuznets curve. But there is also evidence of rising income inequality in some (but not all) rich nations, such as the United States, contrary to expectation, since rich nations should be on the downward-sloping part of the Kuznets curve. Although this "great U-turn" (from declining income inequality in the industrial West during the early twentieth century to growing inequality more recently: Harrison, Tilly, and Bluestone 1986; Harrison and Bluestone 1988) was not anticipated by the Kuznets curve, the new pattern of growing inequality in some rich nations does not invalidate the Kuznets hypothesis, because his compositional argument applies to the effects of labor movement at early versus later stages of industrialization. The rich nations of the West are no longer industrializing and in fact some appear to be deindustrializing, in the sense that industrial production constitutes a shrinking share of their total output (Chapter 10). Nonetheless the U-turn in the inequality trend in some rich nations does complicate predictions about the effect of within-nation inequality trends on between-nation trends. If rising inequality boosts growth, and inequality is rising for both rich and poor nations, then it is not clear whether the within-nation trend overall is compressing or dilating between-nation income inequality. Most likely the recent effects of the within-nation trend on the between-nation trend have been minor.[2]

GROWTH VERSUS EQUITY: THE TRADE-OFF LITERATURE IN ECONOMICS
The foregoing discussion about the effects of within-nation inequality on between-nation inequality assumes a trade-off between equality and

growth. Because of the greater savings rate among the rich than among the poor, orthodox thinking in economics has held that inequality is more conducive to healthy economic growth, so there is a trade-off between equality and growth (Kaldor 1956). Egalitarian policies designed to compress income inequality will do so at the cost of a reduced rate of economic growth.

Recent research challenges that thinking, however. The availability of more and better data on inequality has opened the door to a new generation of cross-country studies where economic growth rate is regressed on measures of income inequality to test the model:

national income inequality → growth rate of per capita income
(positive effect?)

Although the conventional argument about the trade-off between equality and growth is based on wealth inequality, not income inequality, the use of income inequality as a proxy for wealth inequality is not considered to be a major problem in cross-country regressions, since "both measures of distribution generally vary together in cross-sections" (Aghion, Caroli and García-Peñalosa 1999, pp. 1617–18). The growth regressions consistently show that higher levels of inequality tend to produce *slower* rates of economic growth (Benabou 1996).[3] The divergent experiences of the Philippines and South Korea are instructive in this regard. In the early 1960s the two nations were roughly the same in terms of most indicators of economic development (for example, per capita GDP and per capita investment), but South Korea had a significantly lower level of income inequality. Since the early 1960s income growth in South Korea has far outstripped income growth in the Philippines—that is, growth has been slower in the more unequal nation, contrary to conventional arguments.

Several explanations have been offered for inequality's negative effect on growth. In his textbook on economic development, Michael Todaro (1981) cites four reasons why high levels of inequality might inhibit growth in poor nations. First, the wealthy in poor nations do not necessarily invest in productive resources that would benefit the domestic economy, but instead "rich elites are known to squander much of their incomes on imported luxury goods, expensive houses, foreign travel, and investment in gold, jewelry, and foreign banking accounts" (p. 138). Second, the very low income levels of the poor reduce their productivity, because of bad health, malnutrition, and low levels of education. Third, the low income levels of the poor reduce the effective size of the domestic market.

Raising the income levels of the poor would boost the aggregate demand for local products such as food and clothing. Finally, wide income disparities act as an economic disincentive to those at the bottom, and could lead to political instability. In a more formal treatment, Philippe Aghion, Eve Caroli, and Cecilia García-Peñalosa (1999) conclude that inequality reduces growth, first, because inequality reduces investment opportunities in an imperfect capital market (*"redistribution creates investment opportunities* in the absence of a well-functioning capital market," p. 1622); second, because inequality worsens the incentives for borrowers; and third, because inequality leads to macroeconomic volatility.

In short, recent scholarship casts doubt on the view that nations must choose between growth and equality. Contrary to the trade-off view, it appears to be the case that a high level of inequality undermines income growth rather than boosting it (Aghion, Caroli, and García-Peñalosa 1999). If so, and if the Kuznets curve no longer applies to nations at the upper end of the income distribution, then the larger literature on income inequality within nations in fact gives little guidance on the question of how change in income inequality within nations affects change in income inequality across nations. The relationship is not obvious. One must determine whether income inequality is changing at the same rate and in the same direction for rich and poor nations, and whether the effects of income inequality on income growth rate are the same for rich and poor nations. That is not the purpose of this book; our purpose is to document the trends themselves. Is income inequality growing across nations? Is income inequality growing within the average nation? And, on the basis of the answers to the first two questions, is income inequality growing globally?

Finally, this note on the traditional literature on income inequality began by observing that studies of income inequality most often have examined income inequality within nations rather than inequality across nations or inequality for the whole world. We end by asking why that has been the case. There are at least four reasons. The first reason is data availability. Estimates of global inequality require estimates of per capita income and income inequality for all regions of the world. Second, within-nation income inequality is more amenable to policy. There are no international agencies with the muscle to enact serious policies for redistributing income across nations. Third, it could be argued that the study of within-nation inequality is more relevant, since the psychic costs of local comparisons probably exceed the psychic costs of comparisons across nations. In other words, feelings of relative deprivation are based on one's peer group, and one's peers are local. As Karl Marx noted, "A house may be large or small; as long as the surrounding houses are equally small it satisfies all social demands for a dwelling. But if a palace rises beside the little house, the little house shrinks into a hut" (quoted in Lipset 1960, p. 63). Finally, as noted in Chapter 1, some may see no point in studying global inequality because they believe we already know the essential facts.

Whatever the reasons for scholars' past neglect of the between-nation trend in income inequality, the situation may be changing. Only studies of weighted between-nation income inequality pertain directly to global income inequality,[4] and studies of the weighted between-nation trend appeared in the *American Journal of Sociology* in 1997 and 1999 (Korzeniewicz and Moran 1997; Firebaugh 1999). The weighted trend also was the featured subject of Paul Schultz's 1998 presidential address delivered to the European Society of Population Economics (Schultz 1998). Two working papers by the economist Xavier Sala-i-Martin appeared in 2002. Public interest in the subject is growing as well, as evidenced by the feature article in *The Economist* entitled "Global Inequality: Winners and Losers" (Wade 2001) quoted at the beginning of this chapter. Research on the subject will no doubt escalate as more become aware of its import, and as demographers, economists, historians, political scientists, and sociologists continue to refine their tools for studying inequality. A new generation of studies linking between-nation to global inequality may be on the horizon. The next three chapters seek to set this new generation of studies on a firm footing, first, by making sure that researchers realize that the weighted trend is the one that bears on global inequality and, second, by getting the facts right about the weighted trend.

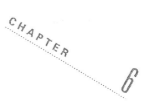

Income Inequality across Nations in the Late Twentieth Century

IT SEEMS THAT almost everyone believes that income inequality is growing across nations. In a recent review article on globalization, Mauro Guillén (2001, p. 247, emphasis in original) writes that "the evidence unambiguously indicates that there is today *more* inequality across countries than ten, twenty, fifty or even one hundred years ago." To support his claim of rising income inequality across nations, Guillén—like many others—notes the widening gap between richer and poorer nations. No one disputes that income *gaps* are increasing between nations. As we shall see in this chapter, however, growing inequality is not the culprit, since there is less income inequality across countries today than there was ten or twenty years ago. The widening of the income gaps has been caused by rising incomes, not by rising income inequality.[1]

This is the first of three empirical chapters on the between-nation trend. I begin with the trend in between-nation income inequality, because so much is riding on this trend. First, if it is true that between-nation inequality is declining, then alarm over widening income gaps across nations is misplaced. Widening gaps should be no cause for alarm when the widening of those gaps is the consequence of growing incomes. To be alarmed at rising gaps in such a case implicitly is to prefer lower national incomes, since that would mean narrower gaps. Second, declining between-nation inequality implies a historic shift in the direction of global income inequality. If inequality has ceased growing across nations, then most likely it has ceased growing globally as well. Growth in global income inequality over the past two centuries has been driven by growth in inequality across nations. Because between-nation income inequality is no longer growing, any further growth in global income inequality must be driven by growth in within-nation inequality. As we discover in subsequent analyses, current and future growth in within-nation inequality is unlikely to match current and future decline in inequality across nations, so global income inequality has most likely peaked, as least for the present historical epoch.

In this chapter we investigate the trend in between-nation income inequality beginning with the 1960s and ending with 1998 (the most recent data available at the time of the analysis). We find that income inequality across nations was relatively stable or declined slightly from the mid-1960s through the 1980s, and then declined more rapidly during the 1990s. Chapter 7 explains why the historic shift from rising to declining between-nation income inequality in the last half of the twentieth century has failed to attract much notice, and Chapter 8 focuses on the pivotal role played by Asia in the turnaround in the between-nation trend. Most of the analyses in these three chapters are based on PPP income data from the Penn World Table. The Penn income series is the standard data set for comparing national incomes, but it is spotty before 1960. After 1960 the series is fairly complete, covering over 90 percent of the world's population for the 1960s, 1970s, and 1980s. For the 1990s I use PPP income from the World Bank, since at the time of my analysis the Penn income series provided only limited data for the 1990s. The World Bank provided income estimates separately for the former Soviet republics; the available PWT data did not. Hence this chapter presents two sets of analyses, one based on the 1960–1989 Penn income series and the other based on 1990s income data from the World Bank.

Because of conflicting claims about the direction of the trend in between-nation income inequality since 1960, special attention is paid to key analytic issues. One analytic issue is the measurement of inequality, since findings might depend on the index used. To appreciate this concern, note that the Gini indicates that earnings inequality was stable from 1975 to 1985 in the United States (Blackburn and Bloom 1987) whereas the variance of logged income (VarLog) indicates growth in earnings inequality over that period (Harrison, Tilly, and Bluestone 1986; see Levy and Murnane 1992, p. 1351 and table 2). As this example illustrates, it is possible for different inequality indexes to point to different conclusions about trends. Hence this chapter reports results for the Theil, the MLD, and the Gini, supplemented as appropriate by the two variance-based indexes, the squared coefficient of variation and VarLog.

A second analytic issue is the reliability of the national income data. The reliability issue was discussed in Chapter 3. In addition, it is important to note that our analysis of the between-nation trends includes simulations designed to assess the sensitivity of the trends to the effect of measurement error in the income estimates. Note also that the data are relatively complete, since income estimates are readily available for recent decades for almost all nations. Data are more readily available for calculating between-nation income inequality than for calculating within-nation income inequality, and the recent trend in between-nation inequality is easier to examine than earlier trends, because national income data for the second half of the twentieth century are more reliable and complete than national income data for the nineteenth and early twentieth centuries. By starting with the trend in between-nation income inequality in recent decades, then, I begin where the data are the richest and the most reliable.

A third analytic issue is that income differences do not capture all material differences across nations. Perhaps the distribution of income is no longer worsening across nations, but other distributions are. Worsening distributions for other indicators of human welfare would undermine our reliance on income inequality as an all-purpose indicator of inequality in life conditions across nations. It is important, therefore, to validate the reversal of the between-nation trend in income inequality with evidence on trends in other between-nation inequalities. In that vein, this chapter compares the twentieth-century trend in income inequality across the world's regions with the twentieth-century trend in inequality based on the Human Development Index (HDI), a broader measure of welfare.

The Trend in Between-Nation Income Inequality since 1960

Unless we are prepared to dismiss the results of a global statistical system of national accounts expressly designed to produce national income estimates, we should be able to determine empirically the general level of income inequality across nations, and whether that inequality is growing or shrinking. The data suggest that between-nation income inequality declined in the last decades of the twentieth century. Table 6.1 reports those results for nations weighted by population size (as they must be to permit conclusions about global income inequality). To simplify the presentation, Table 6.1 lists the inequality coefficients at five-year intervals beginning with 1960. The basic patterns are these. First, between-nation income inequality increased in the early 1960s. This increase is evident in all three indexes of inequality. Second, between-nation income inequality peaked in the 1960s or the 1970s. This is apparent from examination of the data in five-year intervals, as well as from examination of the trend from annual data (Figure 6.1, based on Schultz 1998, table 1). Both data sets—the Penn data for 1960 to 1989 and World Bank data for 1990 to 1998—suggest

TABLE 6.1. Observed trends in between-nation income inequality, 1960–1998

Year	Penn PPP data			World Bank PPP data		
	Theil	MLD	Gini	Theil	MLD	Gini
1960	.517	.518	.540			
1965	.552	.577	.560			
1970	.548	.586	.558			
1975	.540	.592	.555			
1980	.531	.573	.550			
1985	.512	.531	.539			
1989	.526	.539	.543			
1990–GDP				.599	.638	.578
1998–GDP*				.531	.529	.541
1990–GNP				.606	.645	.583
1998–GNP				.537	.536	.546

Sources: Summers et al. (1994) for the Penn income series data, and World Bank (1998, 2000a) for the World Bank income data. The Penn PPP results for the Theil and the Gini were first reported in Firebaugh (1999), table 4, which also reports results for the squared coefficient of variation and VarLog. All the measures point to similar conclusions for 1960–1989 (Firebaugh 1999).

Note: The nations are weighted by population size, so each individual is given equal weight. All income measures are adjusted for purchasing power parity. For the World Bank income series, results are reported for both gross domestic product (GDP) and gross national product (GNP) per capita. The Penn World Table data set consists of 120 nations and the World Bank data set consists of 156 nations. Both data sets contain both capitalist and socialist nations and all populous nations, and both cover the vast majority (92 percent or more) of the world's population.

*With revised GDP estimates for Germany for the 1990s, the 1998 Theil increases from .531 to .535 and the 1998 MLD increases from .529 to .534.

that between-nation income inequality is declining. On the basis of the Penn data, all three indexes indicate that between-nation income inequality was lower in 1989 than it had been in 1965. Analysis of the World Bank data indicates that the decline in between-nation income inequality continued in the 1990s, with observed declines in the Theil, in the MLD, and in the Gini. Third, the decline in between-nation income inequality appears to have accelerated in the 1990s. For the period 1965 to 1989, the Theil index declined 4.7 percent, the MLD declined 6.6 percent, and the Gini declined 3.0 percent. For the period 1990 to 1998, the Theil index declined 11.4 percent, the MLD declined 17.1 percent, and the Gini declined 6.4 percent. Graphs presented in Melchior, Telle, and Wiig (2000, diagram 2.2), in Dowrick and Akmal (2001, fig. 1), and in Milanovic (2001, fig. 7) also indicate an accelerating decline in between-nation income inequality in the 1990s.

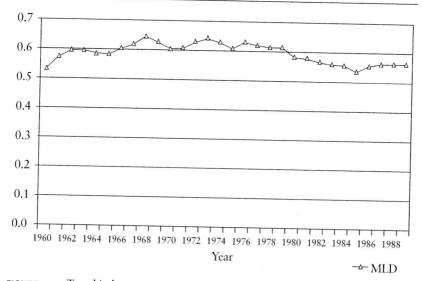

FIGURE 6.1 Trend in between-nation income inequality, 1960–1989. Based on
Schultz 1998, table 1.

Is the Decline Real?

As we saw in Chapter 2, income inequality across nations increased dramatically from the early nineteenth century to the mid-twentieth century. This increase, I hypothesize, constitutes the first phase of a global inequality transition, and we are currently at the beginning of the second phase, a period of declining inequality across nations. Because the thesis of a global inequality transition—with the late twentieth century as the turning point—is a new proposition, it is important to verify that the observed decline is not an artifact of the data or methods used here. To find out how much confidence we can place in the conclusion that between-nation inequality has declined in recent decades, this section reports the findings of several tests for robustness.

FIRST ROBUSTNESS CHECK: OTHER STUDIES

The most obvious test of robustness is to compare the findings of this study with those of other studies of the between-nation trend over the same period. Because we want to look at the sort of between-nation inequality that bears on global inequality, we restrict our review to studies that weight nations by population size. Table 6.2 reports the results for six recent studies (including Firebaugh 1999, the predecessor to this study) of change in income inequality across nations in the 1970s and 1980s where nations are

TABLE 6.2   Estimated change in between-nation income inequality over the 1970s and 1980s

Study	Inequality index	1970	1980	1989	% change 1970–1989
Schultz (1998, table 1)	MLD	.603	.582	.563	−6.6%
	Gini	.565	.553	.552	−2.3%
	VarLog	1.11	1.09	1.01	−9.0%
Firebaugh (1999, table 4)	Theil	.548	.531	.526	−4.0%
	MLD*	.586	.573	.539	−8.0%
	Gini	.558	.550	.543	−2.7%
	VarLog	1.08	1.07	.960	−11.2%
	CV²	1.36	1.29	1.34	−1.5%
Summers and Heston (1999, fig. 16.3)	Gini	.558	.552	.547	−2.0%
Boltho and Toniolo (1999)	Gini	.539	.544	.526	−2.4%
Melchior, Telle, and Wiig (2000, diagram 2.2)	Gini	.58	.57	.56	−3.6%
Milanovic (2001, fig. 7)	Gini	.545	.538	.525	−3.7%

Note: Nations are weighted by population size. All studies use income adjusted for purchasing power parity. Most studies conclude with 1989, because the dissolution of the Soviet Union interrupted the income time series in the 1990s. Two other studies that appeared in 2002 reinforce the findings above. Saurav Dev Bhatta (2002, table 2) reports between-nation Ginis that exactly replicate those in Firebaugh (1999), and Xavier Sala-i-Martin (2002b, tables 1 and 2) finds that between-nation income inequality—as measured by the Gini, VarLog, Atkinson, Theil, MLD, and CV²—has declined since the late 1970s.

*Added here (not reported in original study).

weighted, where the income data are adjusted for PPP, and where the entire income distribution is used, not just the tails. Surprisingly few studies meet these criteria, and to increase the coverage I use 1970 as the starting point (some studies begin with 1970 instead of 1960). Most studies use the Gini coefficient to measure inequality, but some studies supplement the results for the Gini with other inequality measures. In all six studies, for all twelve coefficients reported, between-nation income inequality declined from 1970 to 1989. What is impressive about the results of these studies is their consistency. Consistent results like these are the exception rather than the rule in cross-nation research, and it is noteworthy that the studies reach the same conclusion despite analytic differences—the studies are based on somewhat different samples of nations, they use different data sets in some instances, and they measure income inequality with different measures. We find the same downward trend whether we use the Gini, the

Theil, the MLD, the variance of logged income, or the squared coefficient of variation.

Contrary to conventional wisdom, then, the evidence strongly suggests that between-nation income inequality declined over the 1970s and 1980s. Moreover, there is evidence that the decline may have accelerated in the 1990s. This result is not reported in Table 6.2, because the dissolution of the Soviet Union in 1989 means that the post-1990 trend is based on a different list of nations. However, studies that use a constant or nearly constant sample of nations spanning the 1980s and 1990s find that the decline continued, and perhaps accelerated, in the 1990s (Dowrick and Akmal 2001, fig. 1; Goesling 2001, table 2; Melchior and Telle 2001, diagram 1; Milanovic 2001, fig. 7). We examine the 1990s trend in between-nation income inequality in more detail subsequently.

SECOND ROBUSTNESS CHECK: GDP VERSUS GNP

One criticism sometimes raised against the Penn income series is that its income estimates are based on output produced within a nation's borders (gross domestic product) rather than on output claimed by a nation's residents (gross national product). The usual concern is that GDP could inflate the income level of the residents of a poor nation in instances where a nontrivial portion of the total GDP accrues to multinational corporations. In practice, though, per capita output differences are so large across nations that GDP versus GNP is a nonissue. As researchers soon find out in cross-nation research, for a wide cross-section of the world's nations—like the one we have here—the correlation between per capita GDP and per capita GNP approaches $r = 1.0$. The GNP versus GDP issue pales in comparison with the purchasing power parity issue.

Nonetheless the suspicion persists that GDP-based measures might understate income inequality across nations. A test is possible here because the World Bank provides parallel estimates for the 1990s for GDP per capita and GNP per capita. The results are reported in Table 6.1. For 1990, the GNP estimate of between-nation income inequality is 1.2 percent higher than the GDP estimate for the Theil (.606 for GNP versus .599 for GDP), 1.1 percent higher for the MLD (.645 versus .638), and 0.9 percent higher for the Gini (.583 versus .578). The 1998 estimates give similar results. So inequality based on GNP in fact is higher, but the differences are very small. Not surprisingly, the rate of decline in between-nation income inequality calculated on the basis of GNP is indistinguishable from the rate of decline calculated on the basis of GDP. Between-nation income inequality declines by 11.4 percent for both GDP and GNP measured by the Theil index, by 17.1 percent for GDP and 16.9 percent for GNP as measured by the MLD, and by 6.4 percent for GDP and 6.3 percent for GNP as measured by the Gini. So there are more significant issues to worry about than the GDP versus GNP difference.

One worrisome issue is what to do about changing national lists as nations come and go. The changing-nations issue is especially critical with the dissolution of the USSR in 1991. The results in Table 6.1 bear on that issue as well. Note that there the estimated level of between-nation income inequality is higher when based on the World Bank data than on the Penn data—compare the 1989 and the 1990 estimates. (This difference is much larger than the GDP versus GNP difference.) The Penn versus World Bank difference is due in part to the fact that the 1960–1989 Penn data set treats the USSR as a single nation (as it was in that period) whereas the 1990s World Bank data set treats the former Soviet republics as separate nations. Thus we expect higher between-nation inequality in the 1990s merely because some of the within-USSR income inequality is reclassified as between-nation income inequality.[2] This difference explains why we examine the 1990s trend separately.

THIRD ROBUSTNESS TEST: INSTALLING AN INCOME FLOOR

We also check the possibility that the observed decline in between-nation income inequality is due to a change in the degree of underreporting of economic activity in poor nations. Recall the argument that economic activity is less likely to be reported in subsistence agricultural societies. If so, and if that underreporting bias declines as subsistence agriculture declines, then part of what appears to be income growth in the very poorest nations could instead reflect the more accurate detection of income. Thus some of the observed decline in between-nation inequality could be due to the overstatement of growth rates in poor nations where subsistence agriculture is prevalent but declining.

To address this issue I experimented with different income floors. Table 6.3 reports results for the between-nation trend where the income floor is set at 50 percent higher than the World Bank poverty threshold for poor nations. (Other income floors yield similar results, unless the floor is set so high that it results in obvious counterfactuals, such as sluggish income growth in China.) Because average income in some poor nations is close to the World Bank poverty threshold, the introduction of this 150 percent poverty floor does in fact change the income estimates in some instances. But the estimates for change in between-nation inequality barely change. With or without the income floor, our estimates indicate that between-nation income inequality has declined since the 1960s.

TABLE 6.3   Observed change in between-nation income inequality, 1965–1989 and 1990–1998: Theil, MLD, and Gini

	Theil	MLD	Gini
Without income floor			
1965–1989	− 4.7%	−6.6%	−3.0%
1990–1998	−11.4%	−17.1%	−6.4%
With income floor			
1965–1989	−4.5%	−6.3%	−2.3%
1990–1998	−11.7%	−18.2%	−6.6%

Source: Based on the Penn PPP data, from Summers et al. (1994). N = 120 nations.
Note: The income floor used here is $655 GDP per capita in 1990 U.S. dollars and $855 GDP per capita in 1998 dollars. This floor is based on 1.5 times the World Bank (1990) poverty threshold for people in poor nations.

The introduction of an income floor also bears on the contention, addressed earlier, that even the PPP income estimates for poor nations are implausibly low. Although Chapter 3 makes the case for the plausibility of the PPP-based incomes used here, the results in Table 6.3 further address the issue by demonstrating that the observed change in between-nation inequality is not dependent solely on income figures for poor nations that some might find hard to believe. Even when we arbitrarily boost average income figures to levels that are 50 percent above an established poverty threshold for poor nations, we still find declining income inequality across nations.

POINT ESTIMATES INDICATE THAT BETWEEN-NATION INCOME INEQUALITY IS DECLINING

Much of the analysis in this chapter is motivated by a concern about whether the decline in between-nation income inequality observed in this (and other studies) is real, or whether it can be explained away as an artifact of the type of data used to measure income (GDP versus GNP), or of the inequality index used, or of the improved measurement of income in poor nations. There is still one robustness check to be done—a check for the effect of measurement error—but that check yields interval estimates instead of point estimates. Before examining those results, it is useful to pause to reflect on what the point estimates tell us. In sum, the point estimates uniformly indicate declining between-nation income inequality over recent decades. It is important to stress that the declines are not dramatic, and that the decline in between-nation inequality is occurring in the context of income disparities across nations that are enormous. Nonetheless the finding that weighted inequality across nations is no longer growing is big news, because it indicates the arrest of the historical upward trend.

For scholars the challenge will be to adjust theories to the new reality of declining income inequality across nations. An overarching issue is to what extent the reversal of growth in between-nation inequality reflects a sharp break with the past—a new world order—as opposed to reflecting the evolutionary outcome of the spread of industrialization to all regions of the world. My view, elaborated in Chapters 10 and 11, is that the change is evolutionary, more closely tied to spreading industrialization than to a new information age. A more specific issue for scholars to debate is the status of world system, dependency, and other polarization theories that posit the increased segmentation of the world into distinct income groups as richer regions gain at the expense of poorer regions. In this context the term *polarization* must mean more than widening income gaps between nations or regions of the world, since income growth itself leads to wider gaps. On the one hand, then, polarization theories are trivial if they are referring merely to widening gaps, since everyone concedes that gaps widen as national incomes grow. On the other hand, if polarization theories are referring to increasing segmentation of the world into income groups on the basis of growing between-nation income inequality, they appear to have little current relevance for the world as a whole (though there are particular instances of polarization in this sense, such as sub-Saharan Africa versus the rest of the world). The findings here call for a rethinking of the relevance of general polarization theories to today's world.[3]

Interval Estimates

Studies based on PPP income data uniformly find that weighted between-nation income inequality has declined over recent decades. If we could assume that the income data were perfect, that would be the end of the story, and we could proceed to the question of why conventional wisdom about between-nation inequality is lagging so far behind the research literature. But the income data are far from perfect, so it is important to assess the uncertainty attached to our estimates of change in inequality. Uncertainty about change in between-nation inequality arises not from sampling error (since the data here constitute virtually the entire population) but from measurement error. In the absence of well-developed theory on the sensitivity of inequality indexes to measurement error, I use Monte Carlo computer simulation. This section reports the results of a simulation analysis designed to bound the estimates of the 1965–1989 and 1990–1998 changes in between-nation inequality. Because they are based on measurement error instead of sampling error, the bounds are not confidence intervals in the usual sense. Nonetheless the notions are similar, and I treat the intervals that contain zero as grounds for concluding that there is insufficient evidence in the data to reject the proposition that between-nation income inequality failed to change over the time interval.

ASSUMPTIONS ABOUT THE NATURE OF MEASUREMENT ERROR

The estimation of national income is vexed by measurement error. Even in rich nations, where we expect the data on income generally to be of high quality, official estimates of income growth are often adjusted later, and the question of exactly how fast an economy is growing is often the topic of some dispute among experts. So estimates of national income undeniably are imprecise. The question is whether that imprecision is sufficient to rule out definitive conclusions about the direction of change in between-nation income inequality over recent decades. If we placed bounds around the observed percentage changes in the inequality indexes reported in Table 6.1, would those bounds include zero (no change)?

To establish bounds, we need to make assumptions about the nature of measurement error on income. Previously we have examined arguments about systematic bias *across* nations (for example, the notion that income is more likely to be underreported in agricultural nations). The simulations are designed to test a different type of systematic bias, that of error *within* nations that is correlated over time. The premise is that, for reasons that are specific to individual nations, income estimates will be overstated for some nations and understated for others. Those reasons—whatever they are—tend to persist over time. Thus nations that overstate income at one point in time will tend to overstate income at a later point in time, and nations that understate income at one point in time will also tend to understate income at a later point in time.

There are good reasons for expecting such systematic bias in the estimation of national income over time. In the first place, estimates of national product are based on production statistics that are collected by accounting offices in each nation. Despite the efforts of international agencies to promote uniformity in the collection and manipulation of these data, inevitably there are procedural differences from nation to nation. Raymond Vernon (1987, p. 67) notes, "The general rules that international agencies lay down . . . are fairly specific. . . . But the rules are likely to be differently applied in different countries." If—as it is reasonable to assume—nations tend to be relatively consistent in the procedures they use over time, then we expect the direction of the bias to be consistent for a nation over time, with consistently understated production for some nations and consistently overstated production for other nations.

Even if national production were measured without error, national income would tend to be consistently overstated (or understated) for a given nation over time because mispricing will tend to be correlated over time, as the overvaluation or undervaluation of goods and services also tends to persist over time within nations. To cite one example, Korzeniewicz and Moran (2000) argue that PPP estimates of income in China are inflated because the value of medical services has been routinely overstated for China. If so, then the error in the PPP estimates of China's income will be strongly positively correlated (China's income will tend to be consistently overstated)—which has much less impact on the trend in between-nation income inequality than would random measurement error for China. With respect to estimating change in between-nation income inequality, systematic within-nation measurement error is less harmful than random within-nation measurement error, as we verify in the simulations. (Note that measurement error is a problem whether incomes are based on exchange rates or on purchasing power parity. The problem is magnified for exchange-rate data, however, because the volatility of exchange rates tends to inflate the random component of measurement error, resulting in greater uncertainty about change in between-nation income inequality in the case of exchange-rate-based income, aside from all the other problems inherent in the use of exchange rates to measure national income.)

MODELING UNCERTAINTY

The systematic nature of the error just described implies that measurement error will be positively correlated over time within nations. The effects of this correlated measurement error can be simulated using Monte Carlo techniques to generate bounded estimates of change in between-nation income inequality for 1965–1989 and for 1990–1998. The first step is to use a random number generator to add measurement error to the income figures for the 120 nations. This creates a new data set or a new "sample." Changes in the Theil, the MLD, and the Gini are calculated for this new sample. The process is repeated N times, that is, N samples are generated and measures of inequality are calculated in each of the N samples or trials. Here I used $N = 100$ trials, so the process I used yields 100 estimates of the percentage change in between-nation inequality for each of the inequality measures (Theil, MLD, and Gini). Because they are based on different samples, the 100 estimates vary, and this variance is the key to bounding the estimates. The intervals for percentage change are given by this formula:

$$\text{Interval estimate} = \mu \pm z\sigma \qquad (6.1)$$

where μ is the mean percentage change for the 100 trials, σ is the standard deviation of the 100 estimates of the percentage change, and z is the z-score.[4] To generate a 95 percent "confidence interval" I used the value $z = 2.0$ (I rounded $z = 1.96$ off to 2.0 to be conservative).

In short, I simulate the effects of measurement error by adding an error component to the income estimates and reestimating the inequality indexes. By doing this repeatedly I obtain interval estimates in place of the point estimates reported earlier. The variance of the error component was not decided arbitrarily, but used the assessments of those who are in the best position to judge the quality of the income estimates—those most directly involved in the data collection. Fortunately, the researchers involved in generating the Penn income estimates for 1960–1989 have graded the quality of the estimates for each country by assigning letter grades ranging from "A" to "D," where "D in our minds means the real GDP estimate could well be 30 percent higher or lower, and an A, 5–10 percent in either direction" (Summers et al. 1994, app., first paragraph under "Grading of PWT Country Estimates"). Similarly, two of the architects of the PPP project—Irving Kravis and Robert Lipsey—write that "a generous estimate of margins of uncertainty in the benchmark estimates might be 20–25 percent for low-income countries and 7 percent for high-income countries. The errors in extrapolations to countries not covered by the surveys could go as high as 30–35 percent" (Kravis and Lipsey, 1990, abstract).[5] I interpret these comments to mean that we can be fairly confident that the real incomes are within ±5–10 percent of the estimated incomes for the nations graded A and within ±30 percent of the estimated incomes for the nations graded D. For the simulations I have quantified "fairly confident" as $p = .95$, so that 95 percent of the time the real income is within the margin of error, where the margin of error follows a schedule based on the A to D reliability grades provided in Summers and Heston (1991, app. A.2) as updated in Summers et al. (1994, app.).[6] There is no reliability grade for the several dozen (typically small) nations that are in the 1990–1998 World Bank data but not in the 1965–1989 Penn data. To be conservative, I assigned a grade of D to those nations in the simulations for 1990–1998.

China is a special case. Although all agree that China's income has shot up in recent decades, there is disagreement over the rate of increase, and the version of the Penn income data I use here (version 5.6) relies on downwardly revised estimates of income growth for China (Summers et al. 1994, app.). Because income estimates for China vary, it might be tempting to remove China from the analysis. One person in five lives in China, however, so removing it would mean that we could no longer talk about global inequality in a meaningful way. A better strategy is to model the measurement error for China, which I did in two ways. First, I ran China-only measurement error simulations where I specified zero measurement error for all nations except China, but with a huge margin of error (± 50 percent) for China's income. I report those results below to underscore the importance of China: as we shall see, in some instances the assumption of ± 50 percent error for China alone produces intervals that are as wide as those produced by the baseline measurement error model where error is added to all nations. Second, I ran simulations that combined the baseline model with the China-error model. In this highest-error model, I use the margins of error from the baseline model—these range from ± 9 percent for nations with the most reliable income data to ± 30 percent for nations with the least reliable income data—for all nations except China, where I use the margin of error of ± 50 percent.

RESULTS FOR 1965–1989 CHANGE

Figures 6.2 to 6.4 depict the interval estimates for 1965—1989 change in between-nation income inequality. We note immediately that one's conclusion about change in between-nation income inequality over this period depends on one's assumption about the strength of the within-nation error correlation. As noted above, there is good reason to expect a high level of consistency in the level and direction of error in national income estimates over time. If the consistency were great enough to generate a correlation of $r = 0.90$ for the 1965 and 1989 within-nation errors, then the evidence strongly suggests that income inequality in fact declined across nations because the intervals fail to include zero for $r = 0.90$ for any of the inequality measures (Figures 6.2 to 6.4).

In the case where $r = 0.80$ for the error in measured income over time within nations, we conclude that income inequality declined across nations on the basis of the Gini and the MLD but not the Theil. In the case of the Theil, the interval includes zero (barely) for all three error models (baseline model, China-only model, and highest-error model). Finally, where $r = 0.70$ in the error in measured income over time within nations—a reasonable lower bound for this correlation—there is insufficient evidence to reject the proposition that the observed decline in the inequality indexes was

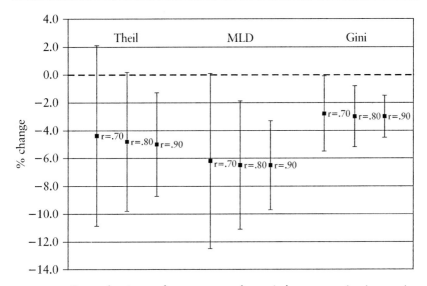

FIGURE 6.2 Interval estimates for percentage change in between-nation income inequality, 1965–1989: Simulation results for Theil, MLD, and Gini (baseline error model).

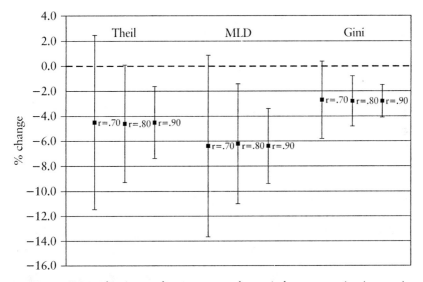

FIGURE 6.3 Interval estimates for percentage change in between-nation income inequality, 1965–1989: Simulation results for Theil, MLD, and Gini (China-only error model).

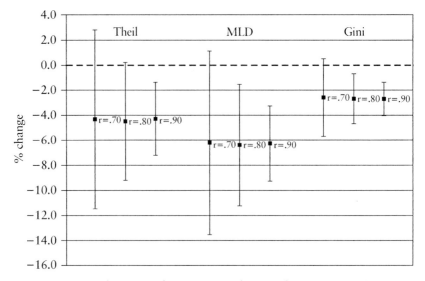

FIGURE 6.4 Interval estimates for percentage change in between-nation income inequality, 1965–1989: Simulation results for Theil, MLD, and Gini (highest-error model).

due merely to measurement error. In all instances but one (change in the Gini index in the baseline model) the interval includes zero in the simulations based on $r = 0.70$.

A second finding that stands out in these figures is that the Gini estimates are the least affected by measurement error. Thus while the Gini index yields the most conservative point estimates of the decline in between-nation income inequality—an estimated decline of 2–3 percent based on the Gini versus a decline of 4–5 percent based on the Theil and 6–7 percent based on the MLD—the interval estimates for the Gini are no more likely to contain zero than are the interval estimates for the Theil and the MLD, reflecting the greater stability of the Gini estimates. Hence one is just as likely to conclude that inequality declined when using the Gini as when using the Theil or the MLD, but the estimated magnitude of the decline is smaller based on the Gini. Because the Gini is based on units' income rankings as well as units' income ratios, income changes tend to affect the Gini less than other inequality indexes. As a result the Gini tends to change more slowly over time than the other indexes do, as we saw in Tables 6.1 and 6.2 and as we will see in subsequent tables. It also appears to be the case that the Gini tends to be less affected by fluctuating incomes where the fluctuations are due to measurement error rather than to real change. So the Gini tends to provide more cautious but also less variable estimates of the change in income inequality over time.

In the final analysis, though, it is not the inequality index that determines our conclusion about whether between-nation income inequality declined between 1965 to 1989, since measurement error affects all the indexes the same way (note the similarity in the patterns in Figures 6.2–6.4). What matters is the nature and amount of the measurement error on income. The nature of the measurement error matters as much as the amount of measurement error. The simulations in Figures 6.2–6.4 assume massive levels of measurement error—as much as ±30 percent for many poor nations and as much as ±50 percent for China—yet our bounded estimates of change fail to include zero when $r = 0.90$ as well as when $r = 0.80$ for the Gini and the MLD. However, when we assume less systematic measurement error—that is, $r = 0.70$ over time within nations—the bounded estimates include zero. The simulations, in short, introduce some doubt about whether income inequality has in fact been declining across nations. Rising inequality is not one of the possibilities indicated by the data. But stable inequality is a possibility. If we think that there is enough random error in the national income estimates to produce a within-nation error correlation of $r = 0.70$ or less, then on the basis of the simulations there is insufficient evidence to reject the hypothesis that between-nation income inequality was at the same level in 1989 as it had been twenty-five years earlier. So perhaps between-nation income inequality leveled off but did not decline in the last part of the twentieth century. The situation is clarified by considering data for the 1990s, as we now see.

RESULTS FOR CHANGE IN THE 1990s

The evidence we have just reviewed indicates that between-nation inequality either declined or did not change over the twenty-five-year period before the fall of communism. In this section we discover that the results for the 1990s are in even sharper contrast to the popular view of rising inequality across nations, since income inequality across nations clearly declined over the 1990s. Combining the results for the 1990s with the results for 1965 to 1989 we conclude that between-nation inequality declined over the last third of the twentieth century. On the basis of point estimates, the Theil index declined by 11.4 percent from 1990 to 1998, the MLD declined by 17.1 percent, and the Gini declined by 6.4 percent. Figures 6.5 to 6.7 present the corresponding interval estimates for 1990–1998 change in between-nation inequality. The interval estimates were gener-

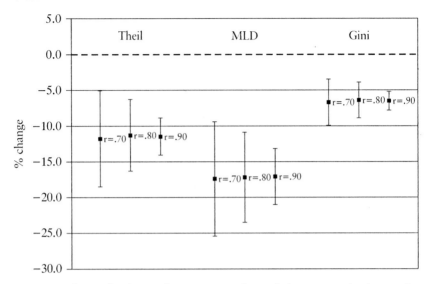

FIGURE 6.5 Interval estimates for percentage change in between-nation income inequality, 1990–1998: Simulation results for Theil, MLD, and Gini (baseline error model).

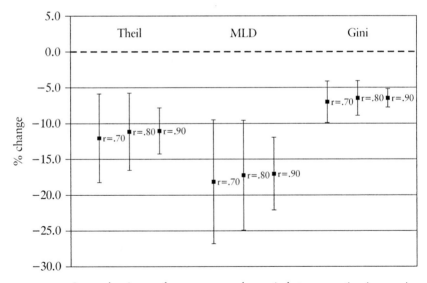

FIGURE 6.6 Interval estimates for percentage change in between-nation income inequality, 1990–1998: Simulation results for Theil, MLD, and Gini (China-only error model).

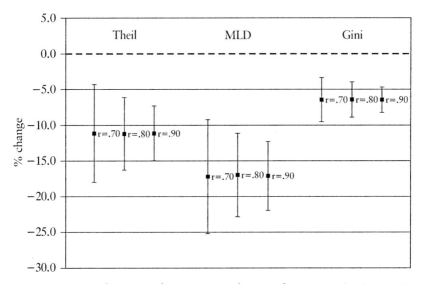

FIGURE 6.7 Interval estimates for percentage change in between-nation income inequality, 1990–1998: Simulation results for Theil, MLD, and Gini (highest-error model).

ated following the same simulation methods used for the 1965–1989 data. The patterns in Figures 6.5 to 6.7 are similar to the patterns for the 1965–1989 simulations, with the Gini giving the most conservative but also the smallest-variance estimates of the decline in between-nation income inequality and the MLD yielding the steepest estimates of the decline. However, unlike the results for 1965 to 1989, the results for the 1990s are quite clear-cut: inequality declined across nations. The declines observed in the point estimates are highly unlikely to be due to measurement error, because of the twenty-seven interval estimates depicted in Figures 6.5 to 6.7, not a single interval contains zero. Thus we conclude that between-nation income inequality declined over the 1990s whether we use the Theil or the MLD or the Gini; whether we use the baseline error model or the China-only error model or the highest-error model; and whether we assume that the within-nation error correlation is $r = 0.70$ or 0.80 or 0.90.

The decline in between-nation income inequality implies that if global income inequality is growing, the source of the growth lies within, not between, nations. Chapter 11 addresses the question of whether inequality is worsening globally; it adds the within-nation trend to the between-nation trend to estimate the change in global income inequality.

Other Between-Nation Inequalities

The claim of declining between-nation income inequality is likely to be contentious despite the story told by the income data, so it is important to determine whether we find similar results using measures of welfare other than income. This section examines change in the United Nations' Human Development Index (HDI) from 1913 to 1950 versus change from 1950 to 1995. The use of 1913, 1950, and 1995 is dictated by data availability. The HDI is an obvious choice because it has been widely promoted by the United Nations and others as a useful supplement or alternative to per capita income (Streeten 1995; Bennett and Roche 2000) and is probably second only to per capita income in popularity as an indicator of level of national welfare or economic development. The HDI is a simple average of indicators of longevity (life expectancy at birth), PPP income (as adjusted in a formula using the logarithm of per capita GDP, converted to U.S. dollars), and education (measured by a weighted average of adult literacy and school enrollment rates). The HDI tries to tap current views of economic development as involving more than income growth—views that have been influenced heavily by the arguments of Amartya Sen (for example, Sen 1999).

The United Nations has computed the index back to 1960, and Crafts (2000) has extended the estimates back to the 1950s for many nations and back to 1870 for some industrial nations. Because estimates of HDI are not available for many nations before 1950, we must use between-region inequality as a proxy for between-nation inequality. The nineteenth century "trifurcation" of the world noted in Chapter 1 created a world of enormous regional disparities, and as we see later (Chapter 8), these regional disparities account for a major portion of between-nation inequality, so a between-regional strategy has merit.

The left side of Figure 6.8 depicts change in between-region inequality in the HDI for the first and second halves of the twentieth century, and the right side depicts the change in between-region income inequality for the same periods. Regional inequality in the HDI declined sharply in the first half of the twentieth century, and then declined even more dramatically in the second half. The picture painted by the HDI is thus one of rapidly declining regional inequality over the twentieth century, as Crafts (2000) also found. In the case of income inequality, we find rising regional inequality over the first half of the twentieth century, as expected, and declining inequality over the second half of the twentieth century, again as expected.

The accelerating decline in inequality indicated by the HDI is precisely what we would expect given the turnaround in income inequality from ris-

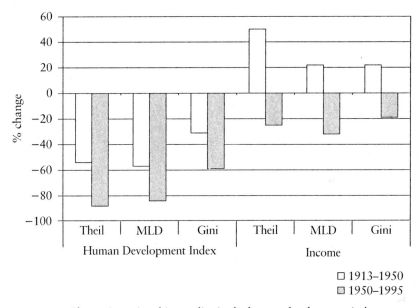

FIGURE 6.8   Change in regional inequality in the human development index versus change in regional income inequality: 1913–1950 and 1950–1995.

ing to declining inequality. Since income is one of the components of the HDI, the decline in between-region HDI inequality was slowed by the rise in between-region income inequality over the first half of the twentieth century and then accelerated by the decline in between-region income over the second half of the twentieth century. It would be difficult to dismiss this finding as reflecting merely the effect of measurement error. Although income is a component of the HDI (so measurement error on income would affect the HDI as well), the kind of measurement error on income that could most seriously affect estimates of the inequality trends— random measurement error over time—is not likely to bias the income inequality trends in opposite directions before and after midcentury. Moreover, since the nonincome components of the HDI—increasing life expectancy and rising education level—are strongly positively related to national income growth (for example, Firebaugh and Beck 1994), it is unlikely that inequality in HDI would have declined so rapidly across regions in the second half of the twentieth century absent any decline in income inequality across regions and nations also. In short, the finding of an accelerated decline in regional inequality in the HDI in the second half of the twentieth century is consistent with the claim that income inequality has declined across regions and nations in recent decades.

Persistence of the Myth of Growing Inequality:
Where Analyses Go Wrong

Income inequality is thought to be growing globally because it is thought to be growing across nations. Yet a downward trend in between-nation income inequality is so consistently observed that among researchers in the field there is a new emerging orthodoxy—the view that global income inequality in fact is declining (Dowrick and Akmal 2001). How are we to account for the persistence of the belief in rising between-nation and global inequality in the face of contrary findings in the research literature? Aside from simple inertia—for most of the past two centuries between-nation inequality did rise, and it takes time for perceptions to adjust to new realities—there are three key reasons why the myth of growing income inequality persists. The first reason is the confusion of growing income gaps with growing income inequality. The second reason is that many widely cited findings are not based on an actual examination of the entire income distribution, but instead are inferred on the basis of income growth only for nations at the tails of the income distribution. The third reason is that the cross-country correlation between income and income growth rate is often misinterpreted.

CONFUSION OF GROWING INCOME GAPS WITH GROWING INCOME INEQUALITY

It is uneven income growth—not income growth per se—that leads to growing income inequality. Because income growth per se results in bigger gaps but not greater inequality, it is a logical fallacy to infer growing income inequality from growing income gaps. The myth of growing global income inequality persists in part because of studies that make that illogical leap.

To appreciate the importance of distinguishing widening gaps from rising inequality in the study of global income inequality,[7] consider the 1950–1990 income growth in China versus the rest of Asia (India excluded). On the basis of the Maddison data (Table 1.1), the income gap more than quadrupled (China's average income was $467 less than the rest of Asia in 1950 and $2,045 less in 1990, in constant dollars). Yet the level of income inequality as conventionally measured did not change, since the income ratio for China to the rest of Asia was 0.57 both in 1950 and in 1990. Now consider the common claim that between-nation income inequality is growing because income gaps are growing between nations. By that logic, inequality between China and the rest of Asia skyrocketed from 1950 to 1990. (Note that by the same logic economic collapse is the best way to reduce inequality.) It is easy to see then why the confusion of growing gaps with growing inequality leads to the conclusion that global inequality is still growing. In a world where average income is doubling every half century or less, it is virtually inevitable that income gaps will grow. Hence the terminological brew that equates growing income gaps with growing income inequality cooks up growing global income inequality virtually by definition.

GENERALIZATION OF "TAILS ONLY" STUDIES TO WORLDWIDE INCOME INEQUALITY

The myth of growing global income inequality is also fueled by accounts based on comparisons of income growth for nations at the tails of the income distribution. Box 3.3 of the *World Development Report 2000/2001* (World Bank 2000b, p. 51) provides a typical example. Under the heading "Widening gaps between rich and poor countries account for much of the increase in worldwide income inequality across individuals over the past 40 years," a bar graph depicts the relative sizes of average incomes in the richest and poorest 20 countries in 1960 versus 1995. "In 1960 per capita GDP in the richest 20 countries was 18 times that in the poorest 20 countries. By 1995 this gap had widened to 37 times" (ibid.). Similarly, under the heading "Inequality has worsened both globally and within countries," the UN's *Human Development Report 1999* (UN Development Program 1999, pp. 38–39) notes that the income ratio for the richest versus poorest countries shot up from about 44 to 1 in 1973 to 72 to 1 in 1992. It is easy to see how widely reported figures such as these foster the belief in growing global income inequality, especially when these reports use headings explicitly stating that growing income inequality between the richest and poorest nations accounts for "much of the increase in worldwide income inequality across individuals."

As we have seen, income inequality across nations is not growing when we examine the entire distribution instead of examining just the nations at the tails. Focusing on the nations at the tails leads to the appearance of growing inequality because—in contrast to most other nations—the very poorest nations have experienced little if any income growth in recent decades, and some have experienced declines. But the very poorest nations are home to only a small fraction of the world's population, with the five poorest nations accounting for only about 1.3 percent of the world's people (Table 3.1) and the twenty poorest nations accounting for only about 5 percent of the world's people (World Bank 2000b, p. 51). With regard to global income inequality, the telling observation is not that incomes have been growing more slowly in the twenty poorest nations than in the twenty richest nations, but rather that more people live in poor nations with above-average income growth than in poor nations with below-average income growth. The myth of growing global income inequality persists in part because the literature focuses on the wrong facts.

MISINTERPRETATION OF THE CROSS-COUNTRY CORRELATION OF INCOME AND INCOME GROWTH

Finally, the notion that income inequality is worsening across nations is based on a misinterpretation of the well-known finding that income growth has tended to be slower in poorer nations than in richer ones: "On average, initially poor countries have grown more slowly than rich countries" (World Bank 2000b, p. 50). This positive cross-country association between income level and income growth rate is easy to misinterpret with regard to global inequality. Because the association is not weighted by population size, it conceals the critical fact that many more people live in poor nations that are catching up (largely in Asia) than in the poor nations that are falling farther behind. If we want to draw conclusions about global inequality then the weighting issue is paramount, as we now see.

CHAPTER 7

Weighted versus Unweighted Inequality:
Key to the Divergence Debate

WHY IS THE DECLINE in income inequality across nations one of the best-kept secrets in the social sciences? To address that question, this chapter takes up where Chapter 6 ended, with the observation that studies often fail to weight nations by population size. By failing to weight, researchers have missed the historic turnaround in inequality in the late twentieth century. Note that four decisions are consequential in the analysis of between-nation income inequality: the decision whether to adjust the income data for purchasing power, the decision whether to use income per capita or income per worker, the decision whether to weight nations by population size, and (assuming nations are weighted by population) the decision whether to include China in the analysis. Of the four decisions, three require minimal discussion, since virtually everyone agrees that China should be included in the study of global inequality, that incomes should be adjusted for purchasing power differences when making cross-country comparisons of living standards, and that income per capita should be used to compare living standards. Thus the only real issue is whether or not to weight, and that is the issue emphasized in this chapter. Because nations must be weighted by population size in the estimation of global income inequality, one cannot draw inferences about global income inequality from studies of between-nation income inequality that fail to weight. Much confusion about global income inequality has resulted from the failure to realize that results for unweighted between-nation income inequality do not bear directly on global income inequality in the late twentieth century.

Trends with and without Adjustment for Purchasing Power Parity

There are several ways to analyze income data to obtain the result that be-tween-nation income inequality rose over recent decades. One way is to use income data that are based on foreign exchange rates rather than on the principle of purchasing power parity (see the findings in Korzeniewicz and Moran 1997). We now verify earlier claims (Chapter 3) that FX data tend to exaggerate the income differences between richer and poorer nations and that FX data present a different picture of the trend in between-nation income inequality. Figure 7.1 shows the inequality trends for 1965 to 1989. If we use income data adjusted for purchasing power, the Theil, the MLD, and the Gini indexes all have values between 0.50 and 0.60, and the index values decline slightly from 1965 to 1989 for all three indices. In contrast, when unadjusted (that is, FX) data are used, the index values are higher—the initial 1965 index values range from 0.66 for the Gini to 0.89 for the MLD—and they increase over time. The Theil index begins at 0.82 in 1965 and increases to 1.08 in 1989, the MLD index increases from 0.89

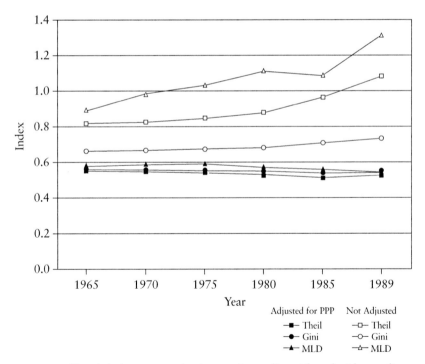

FIGURE 7.1 Trends in between-nation income inequality with and without adjust-ment for PPP. Based on Firebaugh (1999), table 3, and additional calculations.

to 1.31, and the Gini index increases from 0.66 to 0.73.[1] Lest some argue that the conflicting results in Figure 7.1 simply indicate that we cannot determine the direction of the trend in between-nation income inequality, it is important to recall the implausibility of the FX estimates noted in Chapter 3 (for example, the $100 average annual income for Ethiopia). Virtually all recent studies of between-nation income inequality follow the advice of the current United Nations System of National Accounts (1993, para. 1.38) that national currencies be converted into a common currency based on purchasing power parities and not exchange rates.

Trends in Weighted versus Unweighted Income Inequality

In an earlier study I demonstrated that the direction of the trend in between-nation income inequality depends on whether nations or individuals are weighted equally (Firebaugh 1999, Table 2). Nevertheless, "in typical analyses, economic trends in Luxembourg count just as much as economic trends in China, even though China has nearly 3,000 times more people" (Firebaugh 1999, p. 1605), and this failure to appreciate the importance of nations' population size has led to faulty inferences about the global trend in inequality. Two unpublished papers by Sala-i-Martin (2002a, 2002b) replicate the finding of diverging weighted and unweighted trends, and Sala-i-Martin (2002b, p. 29) echoes my warning that inferences about global inequality should not be based on unweighted trends because "the unweighted measures give a Chinese citizen . . . 1/3000th the weight [they give] a citizen of Luxembourg."

Much of the confusion over whether or not income inequality is growing across nations, then, stems from the fact that we obtain different answers depending on whether we weight. If nations are weighted equally (the *unweighted* trend), we conclude that income inequality across nations is growing. Figure 7.2 depicts the change in between-nation income inequality over the period 1965 to 1989 with and without weighting for population size. Note that unweighted inequality is lower in 1965 for all three indexes. But then the weighted and unweighted trends move in opposite directions. Although the weighted indexes all decline somewhat, the unweighted indexes all increase, with the unweighted Theil rising by 42 percent, the unweighted MLD by 12 percent, and the unweighted Gini by 7 percent. These findings are in line with the findings of other studies of falling inequality when nations are weighted and growing inequality when nations are not.

Because weighting is the central story here, one expects the weighting issue to be a focal point of discussions of the trend in between-nation in-

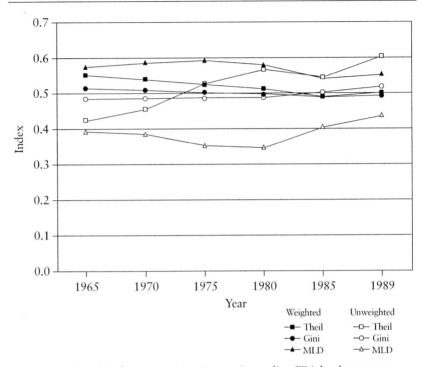

FIGURE 7.2 Trends in between-nation income inequality: Weighted versus unweighted.

come inequality. The outpouring of empirical work on growth theory over the past decade, however, largely overlooks the weighting issue, even when global income inequality is clearly the focus. Although it is commonplace to observe that poor nations are not, on average, catching up with rich nations, this observation has no direct relevance to global inequality since, as noted earlier, more poor people are living in poor nations where incomes are growing faster than the world average than in poor nations where incomes are not. The failure to stress the most telling empirical fact about the recent trend in income inequality across nations—that the weighted and unweighted trends are going in different directions—results in confusion about change in the global income distribution, as we now verify.

To Weight or Not to Weight?

Should one weight nations by their population size in studies of between-nation inequality? The answer depends on the goal. If the goal is to test a theory of how national economies work—so each nation can be viewed as a separate realization of some underlying economic processes—then each nation would be weighted the same. But if the goal is to calculate the average disproportionality of individuals' income ratios—that is, to make inferences about global income inequality—there is no reason why citizens of large countries should carry less weight than citizens of small countries, as an unweighted index gives us. People in China and Chad should have equal value in the analysis.

WEIGHTED BETWEEN-NATION INEQUALITY AS A COMPONENT OF GLOBAL INEQUALITY

Global income inequality can be expressed as the sum of between- and within-nation income inequality:

$$I = I_B + I_W, \tag{7.1}$$

where I is an additively decomposable inequality index such as the Theil or the MLD. This section verifies that the term I_B in equation 7.1 in fact is the term for weighted between-nation income inequality.

Suppose we had income data for every individual in the world. Then we could calculate the level of global income inequality using the Theil index (the same conclusions hold for the MLD):

$$T = \sum_i p_i r_i \log(r_i), \tag{7.2}$$

where the subscript i is used to underscore that these are individual-level data. Here $p_i = (1/N)$, where N is the world's total population, and r_i is the income ratio for individual i (i's income divided by the mean income for the world). Theil (1967, chap. 4) demonstrates that T can be decomposed into independent between-group and within-group components as follows:

$$T = \sum_j y_j \log(y_j/p_j) + \sum_j y_j T_j, \tag{7.3}$$

where j indexes population group (for example, nation), y_j is income *share* (group j's total income as a proportion of total income for the entire population), and T_j is the level of inequality in group j as measured by the Theil index. Here j indexes nation, so y_j is nation j's income as a proportion of total world income, p_j is nation j's population share, and T_j is the level of inequality in nation j as measured by the Theil index. Equation 7.3 states that total world income inequality can be calculated by adding between-nation income inequality—$\Sigma_j y_j \log(y_j/p_j)$—to within-nation income inequality, where within-nation inequality is a weighted-average of within-nation inequalities T_j.

The key point here is that the between-nation component in equation 7.3 is between-nation income inequality weighted by population size. To verify, note that income share is the product of income ratio and population share ($y_j = p_j r_j$, where the denominator for r_j is world mean income). Substituting $p_j r_j$ for y_j in equation 7.3 gives:

$$T = \sum_j p_j r_j \log(r_j) + \sum_j p_j r_j T_j. \tag{7.4}$$

Because $\Sigma_j p_j r_j \log(r_j)$ is the general formula given in Chapter 4 (equation A4.1) for the Theil index, we see immediately that the first sum in equation 7.4 is the result we obtain by calculating the Theil index for nations where each nation is weighted by its population. Note that we can calculate the between-nation component of global inequality without individual-level data since the between-nation component of the global Theil is the Theil that we obtain with national-level income data alone. Importantly, though, to calculate the between-nation component we must use the population-weighted Theil, which brings us to perhaps the most serious problem with the global inequality literature: results for unweighted between-nation inequality are used to draw inferences about global income inequality. That strategy leads to misleading inferences about global inequality when the unweighted and weighted trends diverge, as they have in recent decades.

ANOTHER WAY TO CONCEPTUALIZE THE WEIGHTING ISSUE

One way to think about income inequality is to think of the degree of inequality as reflecting the average distance between the income ratios for all pairs of individual units in a population. That is the conceptualization that underlies the Gini index, as we see when we write the Gini in this form:

$$G = (1/N^2) \sum_i \sum_j |r_i - r_j|/2, \tag{7.5}$$

where r_i is the income ratio for unit i, r_j is the income ratio for unit j, and $|\bullet|$ is the absolute value. From equation 7.5 it is clear that the Gini is simply one-half of the average distance between the income ratios for all pairs of cases in the population. Hence one way to estimate the Gini for between-nation income inequality is to randomly select (with replacement) two nations from the population, calculate one-half the distance between the nations' income ratios, repeat M times, and take the average. The way we select the nations determines whether we estimate the weighted Gini or the unweighted Gini. Suppose we selected nations at random. Then each nation would have probability $1/N$ of being selected, and we would be estimating the unweighted Gini. Alternatively, suppose we selected our pairs of nations by selecting two individuals at random, and calculated $|r_i - r_j|$ based on where the individuals live. Then each nation would have probability p_j of being selected, and we would be estimating the weighted Gini. So the issue of unweighted versus weighted between-nation inequality reduces to this question: are we interested in between-nation income inequality because of what it tells us about the average difference between nations' income ratios, or because of what it tells us about the average difference between individuals' income ratios? If our purpose is to examine global income inequality, then we are interested in between-nation inequality because of what it tells us about the average difference between individuals' income ratios.

Why the Weighted and Unweighted Trends Differ

GROWTH AMONG POOR NATIONS: LARGE NATIONS ARE DOING BETTER

All our inequality measures indicate that between-nation income inequality increased from 1965 to 1989 when nations are equally weighted but declined when nations are weighted by population size (Figure 7.2). In accounting for this difference, note that the weighted trend declined even though nations on average moved away from the overall income mean (as indicated by the rise in the unweighted trend). It follows that larger nations tended to move toward the world income mean while smaller nations tended to move away from the mean. Because there are more small nations than large nations, the trend is upward when nations are weighted equally.

If large nations have tended to move toward the overall income mean in recent decades, then incomes in large *poor* nations have tended to grow faster than the world average and/or incomes in large rich nations have tended to grow more slowly than the world average. The former appears to be the more important factor in recent decades, since incomes of large rich nations on balance have not grown notably slower than the world average. Per capita income in some large rich nations such as Japan and West Germany grew faster than the world average from 1965 to 1989; per capita income grew somewhat more slowly than the world average in the United States. By contrast, among poor nations there was clear movement toward the world income mean among larger nations, led by China and other nations of East Asia. The importance of China by itself to the weighted trend is evident when we remove China from the analysis: without China, between-nation income inequality was about the same at the end of the 1990s as it was in 1960 (Milanovic 2001, fig. 9). (The pivotal role of Asia in general is described in more detail in the next chapter.)

So the divergence in the weighted and unweighted trends is based largely on the differences in growth rates for large and small poor nations. The poorer nations that are doing well are disproportionately Asian nations with large populations; the poorer nations that are faring poorly tend to be small nations in Africa. Because there are many more small nations in sub-Saharan Africa than there are large nations in Asia, the unweighted trend rises, and because the population of Asia is much larger than the population of sub-Saharan Africa, the weighted trend declines.

EFFECTS OF CHANGING POPULATION SIZE

As we have just seen, a positive association between population size and income growth rate among poor nations over recent decades has produced declining weighted between-nation inequality in the face of rising unweighted inequality. It is also the case that in recent decades populations have grown faster in poorer nations than in richer nations, so a larger proportion of the world's population today lives in poorer nations. This faster population growth experienced by poor nations alters the weights used in the inequality formulas (the p_j) for the weighted trend only, since p_j is a constant $(1/N)$ for the unweighted trend. This section asks whether, in addition to the population-size phenomenon just described, *changing* population size might also have played a role in the decline in the weighted trend (and thus a role in the divergence of the weighted and unweighted inequality trends, since population changes alter the inequality calculations only in the weighted case).

To identify more precisely how changing population size relates to the difference between weighted and unweighted trends, consider the difference in the formulas for weighted and unweighted income inequality. Recall (Chapter 4) that inequality measures are weighted averages of disproportionality functions, so they have the general form:

$$I = \sum_j w_j \, f(r_j), \tag{7.6}$$

where w denotes weight, r denotes income ratio, and $f(r)$ denotes disproportionality function—the function that measures the distance of the income ratios from 1.0, the point of equality.

There are two differences between weighted and unweighted measures of inequality, one obvious and one hidden. The obvious difference involves the weights used—unweighted inequality is the simple average of the $f(r_j)$ whereas weighted inequality is the population-weighted average of the $f(r_j)$. Hence:

$$w_j = 1/N \quad \text{for unweighted index}$$
$$w_j = p_j \quad \text{for weighted index} \tag{7.7}$$

where N denotes number of nations and p_j denotes population share for nation j.

The other difference is hidden in the income ratio. An income ratio in the unweighted case is calculated by dividing a nation's per capita income by the simple average (mean) of the national per capita incomes, that is, by dividing by $\Sigma_j X_j/N$:

$$\text{Unweighted } r_j = X_j \Big/ \left(\sum_j X_j / N \right). \tag{7.8}$$

An income ratio in the weighted case is calculated by dividing by the average world income, which is the population-weighted average of national per capita incomes:

$$\text{Weighted } r_j = X_j \Big/ \sum_j p_j X_j. \tag{7.9}$$

Because average world income generally is not the same as the simple average income for nations, the weighted and unweighted income ratios generally are based on different denominators. In other words, r_j equals 1.0 at different income levels for the weighted and unweighted formulas, so weighted and unweighted inequality measures are based on different points of equality. In the weighted case, between-nation income inequality declines as national incomes move toward the world mean income. In the unweighted case, between-nation income inequality declines as national incomes move toward the mean income for nations.

Now we come to the critical point: unless population growth rates are independent of nations' economic level, change in population shares will change the point of equality in the weighted case. The world mean income is pulled up by faster population growth in richer nations and pulled down by faster population growth in poorer nations. (Note that change in the population shares of rich and poor nations does not affect the point of equality for unweighted income inequality.) In recent decades, populations have been growing more rapidly in poor nations than in rich nations. This more rapid population growth in poor nations has altered the point of equality for the weighted trend substantially, as Table 7.1 shows. Table 7.1 reports the points of equality for the weighted and unweighted trend from 1960 to 1989. In 1960, the points of equality were virtually the same for weighted and unweighted inequality, indicating a lack of association between population size and per capita income across nations in 1960. Since 1960, the faster population growth in poorer nations has reduced the point of equality in the weighted case relative to the unweighted case. By 1989 the point of equality in the weighted case was about 10 percent lower than the point of equality in the unweighted case.

Change in population shares could, by moving the point of equality, produce change in the index measures for weighted income inequality. This effect of changing population share would be independent of the effect of differences in the income growth rates of large and small nations. For example, faster-than-world-average population growth in a poor nation would reduce weighted inequality in an index that is especially sensitive to income differences at the lower end of the income distribution, since the faster population growth moves the world mean closer to the poor nation. By the same logic, faster-than-world-average population growth in a rich nation would reduce weighted inequality in an index that is sensitive to income differences at the upper end, by moving the world mean closer to rich nations. Hence it is the case that both faster-than-world-average income growth and faster-than-world-average population growth in a poor

TABLE 7.1   Points of equality for weighted and unweighted between-nation income inequality, 1960–1989

	Point of equality		Weighted/
	Weighted	Unweighted	Unweighted
1960	$2,277	$2,294	0.99
1965	2,660	2,729	0.97
1970	3,118	3,266	0.95
1975	3,426	3,761	0.91
1980	3,835	4,303	0.89
1985	4,059	4,421	0.92
1989	4,367	4,826	0.90

Source: Based on Summers et al. (1994) income data (in 1985 U.S. dollars). N = 120 nations.

nation would reduce weighted inequality in an index that is especially sensitive to income differences at the lower end of the income distribution, since the faster income growth moves the poor nation closer to the world income mean and the faster population growth moves the world income mean closer to the poor nation. By the same logic, slower-than-world-average income growth and faster-than-world-average population growth in a rich nation would reduce weighted inequality in an index that is especially sensitive to income differences at the upper end. In short, differential income growth rates move nations toward or away from the world income mean while differential population growth rates move the mean itself. The former clearly affects measures of weighted income inequality. The latter might or might not affect measures of weighted income inequality, depending on the index used.

It is not straightforward to disentangle empirically the effect of different rates of population growth (changing population shares) from the effect of different rates of income growth. One difficulty is that income ratios are functions of the population shares in the weighted case, so it is problematic to "hold the income ratios constant" while varying the population shares. Note that if we assume the same income growth rate for all nations, faster population growth in poorer nations will move the point of equality down, closer to poor nations and away from rich nations. Since most inequality measures are designed to give more weight to income differences at the lower end (in line with the welfare principle), this downward movement of the point of equality might tend to register as a decline in income inequality. In this way changing population shares might also have contributed somewhat to the observed decline in between-nation income inequality in the last part of the twentieth century independent of the effect of different rates of income growth across nations. The next section examines relevant evidence for this type of measurement artifact.

Trends Based on Fixed Population Shares

Assume a uniform growth rate for per capita income across all nations. Our measures of weighted between-nation income inequality could nonetheless decline over time, on the basis of changing population shares alone. This decline could occur in one of two ways. First, as just described, there could be faster population growth in poorer nations that moves the point of equality closer to poor nations, thereby reducing inequality as measured by indexes that conform to the welfare principle. Second, there could be faster population growth in middle-income nations, thereby reducing inequality (without moving the point of equality) by shrinking the tails of the income distribution. The second possibility is irrelevant here, since it did not occur. The first did occur, however, and this section examines the effect of the change in the equality point resulting from the faster population growth in poorer nations.

To isolate the effect of changing population shares, suppose per capita incomes had grown at the observed rates from 1965 to 1989 but that population shares had remained constant—that is, assume a uniform rate of population growth across nations from 1965 to 1989. (We use 1965 as the starting point because that is where the weighted inequality trend began to level off and turned downward for some of the indexes.) Then we calculate the world's mean income in 1989 as $5,038 instead of the observed mean of $4,367 (Table 7.2). Or, to view it another way, one could say that faster population growth in the poorer nations reduced the 1965–1989 increase in the world's mean income by about $671. Recall that in 1960 the weighted and unweighted means were virtually the same, so the weighted and unweighted measures were centered on approximately the same point of equality in 1960. The faster population growth of poor nations in recent decades has changed that. Instead of having indexes that are centered on $5,038 in 1989, as they would be if population shares had remained at their 1965 levels, between-nation inequality measures are centered on $4,367. As a result poor nations are $671 closer to the point of equality and rich nations are $671 farther away.

By moving the world income mean closer to poor nations and further from rich nations, we expect the 1965–1989 change in population shares to affect some inequality indexes more than others, and in different directions in some instances. Moving the world mean closer to poor nations should reduce 1989 between-nation inequality as measured by VarLog

TABLE 7.2 Points of equality for weighted indexes based on actual population versus fixed (1965) population shares, 1965–1989

	Point of equality based on		Actual/fixed pop. share
	Actual p_j	1965 p_j	
1965	$2,660	$2,660	1.00
1970	3,118	3,223	0.97
1975	3,426	3,639	0.94
1980	3,835	4,180	0.92
1985	4,059	4,553	0.89
1989	4,367	5,038	0.87

Source: Based on Summers et al. (1994) income data (in 1985 U.S. dollars). N = 120 nations.

(since VarLog compresses upper incomes with the logarithm function) and increase 1989 between-nation inequality as measured by the CV^2 (since CV^2 is based on squared distances from the mean). The other inequality measures should be less affected by shifts in the point of equality. Because the Gini is median-based, it should be the least affected by change in the mean caused by changing population shares, so the Gini is the most immune to this type of measurement artifact.

To test those expectations we compare the measured 1965–1989 change in weighted between-nation income inequality with the projected change in weighted inequality, assuming that population shares had remained at their 1965 levels (Figure 7.3). The squared coefficient of variation and the VarLog were the most affected by changing population shares, and in opposite directions, as expected. Note the difference in the dashed (actual trend) and solid lines (projected trend assuming 1965 population shares) for CV^2 and VarLog in Figure 7.3. For CV^2 the cumulated effect of faster population growth in poor nations from 1965 to 1989 served to increase the level of 1989 between-nation inequality, so that the actual value of CV^2 is higher than the projected value had population shares remained fixed. The actual value is higher because the faster population growth in poor nations pulled the point of equality down, further away from the incomes of richer nations, and CV^2 is more sensitive than the other indexes to income difference at the upper end of the distribution. VarLog, by contrast, is the most sensitive to income difference at the lower end, so pulling the point of equality toward poor nations reduces inequality as measured by VarLog. Hence in Figure 7.3 actual inequality is less than projected inequality in the case of VarLog.

Dashed lines are not given for the Theil, MLD, and Gini indexes because the trends based on fixed population shares (Figure 7.3) are virtually identical to the actual trends (Figure 7.1). Contrary to the conclusion of Firebaugh (1999),[2] we rule out changing population shares across nations as a principal source of the recent decline in weighted between-nation income inequality, since between-nation income inequality as measured by the Theil, the MLD, and the Gini declines just about as much when we fix the nations' population shares at their 1965 levels as it does when we do not hold the population shares constant. (The squared coefficient of variation declines *more* when we hold the population shares constant: Figure 7.3.) On the basis of this reworking of Firebaugh (1999) it appears that, *independent of income growth rates*,[3] changing population distribution across nations played a limited role in producing the decline in weighted between-nation inequality in the last part of the twentieth century. Independent of income growth rates, changes in the population distribution over the last

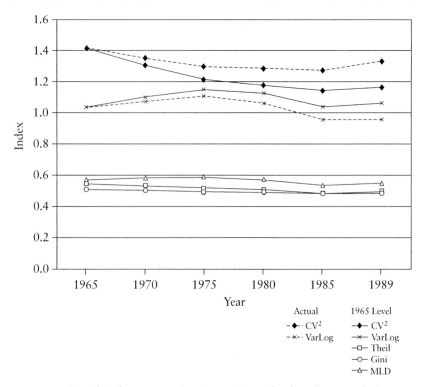

FIGURE 7.3 Trends in between-nation income inequality based on population shares fixed at 1965 level.

part of the twentieth century affected the weighted inequality trend only to the extent that faster population growth in poor nations pulled the weighted world income mean closer to poor nations. This downward shifting of the 1989 point of equality reduced 1989 between-nation inequality as measured by VarLog and increased 1989 inequality as measured by the squared coefficient of variation, but had little effect on the other inequality measures.

Trends Based on Overweighting of Poor Nations

Because an inequality index is an average (average disproportionality), the trend in an inequality index might miss offsetting changes in different regions in an income distribution. When there is income convergence in some regions of the income distribution and income divergence in other regions, one's conclusion about between-nation inequality might depend on the weight given to the different regions of the income distribution. Hence to further substantiate the decline in income inequality across nations, this section demonstrates that we obtain the same results for the 1965–1989 trend when poorer nations are given even more weight than usual in calculating inequality. (This type of weighting should not be confused with the weighted versus unweighted trend issue discussed earlier, since here the weighting is based on income rather than on population.) The decision to give more weight to poorer nations is dictated by the welfare principle—the principle that income increases at the upper end of the income distribution realize smaller welfare benefits than do income increases at the lower end of the income distribution. With some exceptions (for example, the squared coefficient of variation), inequality indexes are based on logarithms or some other type of function that compresses the upper end of the income distribution, so most inequality indexes are consistent with the welfare principle.

What is new here is that we use the Atkinson index, which permits one to vary the weight given to the lower end of the income distribution. Atkinson (1970) demonstrates that the index A is consistent with the welfare principle:

$$A = 1 - \left[\sum_j p_j r_j^{1-\epsilon} \right]^{1/|1-\epsilon|}, \qquad \epsilon > 0 \tag{7.10}$$

where (as before) p_j is the population share and r_j is the income ratio. The larger the ϵ, the greater the weight given the lower end of the income distribution and the lower the weight given to the upper end of the income distribution. Consider two nations of equal population where per capita income in the richer nation R is ten times the per capita income in the poorer nation P. Suppose we want to reduce the income inequality by transferring income from R to P. By varying ϵ we specify our aversion to inequality, with a higher value for ϵ indicating greater aversion. In this instance, where the per capita incomes of R and P vary by a factor of 10, it follows from equation 7.10 that we are willing to sacrifice up to $\$10^\epsilon$ income per capita in R in order to add $1 to the per capita income of P (Cowell 1977, p. 45). For example, $\epsilon = 0$ implies a willingness to take $1 from R to enrich P by $1, that is, we believe that total welfare is increased when income is transferred from a richer to a poorer unit. Values of $\epsilon > 0$ imply a stronger aversion to inequality, since $\epsilon > 0$ implies a willingness to accept a net income loss in order to reduce inequality; for example, $\epsilon = 1.0$ implies a willingness to accept a loss of $9 ($10 from R, $1 to P).

Table 7.3 reports results for ϵ for 0.1, 0.6, 1.1, and 1.5. Results are re-

TABLE 7.3   Change in between-nation income inequality, 1965–1989: Results for Atkinson index

Year	Relative weighting of lower end of distribution			
	$\epsilon = 0.1$	$\epsilon = 0.6$	$\epsilon = 1.1$	$\epsilon = 1.5$
1965	.055	.296	.466	.552
1989	.052	.282	.444	.528
1965–1989 change	−5.5%	−4.7%	−4.7%	−4.3%

Source of Estimates: Calculated from Firebaugh (1999), table 6, based on Summers et al. (1994) income data. N = 120 nations.

Note: The larger the ϵ, the greater the weight given the lower end of the income distribution. Larger values of ϵ reflect greater aversion to inequality (see text).

ported for a broad range for ϵ to demonstrate the robustness of the results. Note that $\epsilon = 1.5$ represents a fairly extreme reweighting in favor of the lower end of the distribution, since $\epsilon = 1.5$ implies the willingness to accept a net income loss of about $31 to enrich the poorer nation by $1 in the case where the two nations differ by a factor of 10. For all four values of ϵ, the observed value of A is lower in 1989 than it was in 1965, ranging from a 5.5 percent decline for $\epsilon = 0.1$ to a 4.3 percent decline for $\epsilon = 1.5$. The direction of the trend in between-nation income inequality, then, does not appear to be sensitive to the weight given to the different regions of the income distribution (see Firebaugh 1999, table 6, for additional results pointing to the same conclusion).

Summary: What Affects Findings

We can now take stock of what affects and what does not affect conclusions about the trend in between-nation income inequality over recent decades. Table 7.4 summarizes the key findings. The table lists eight choices that researchers face when studying between-nation income inequality—four that matter and four that might be expected to matter but do not. Consider first the choices that do not affect the between-nation inequality trend. GDP and GNP give the same results. The imposition of an income floor does not substantially affect the results, unless the floor is so high as to produce obvious counterfactuals. The choice of inequality index generally does not affect conclusions about the direction of the trend.[4] And, as we have just seen, overweighting low-income nations does not affect the direction of the trend.

Table 7.4 lists four other choices that do affect conclusions about the trend. One critical decision is whether to adjust the income estimates to re-

TABLE 7.4 Summary: What affects findings about the trend in between-nation income inequality in the late twentieth century

	How the findings differ for recent trends
Choices that matter	
. Adjusting for purchasing power (this chapter; Schultz 1998; Firebaugh 1999)	Adjusted: decline in inequality since 1960s Unadjusted: growth in inequality since 1960s
. Including China* (this chapter; Melchior, Telle, and Wiig 2000; Milanovic 2001)	Included: decline in inequality since 1960s Excluded: no substantial change since 1960s
. Weighting nations by population size (this chapter; Firebaugh 1999; Milanovic 2001)	Weighted: decline in inequality since 1960s Unweighted: growth in inequality since 1960s
. Per capita versus per worker income (Chapter 11)	Per capita: decline in inequality since 1960s Per worker: sharp decline in inequality since 1960s
Choices that matter very little for trends in between-nation income inequality	
. Use of gross domestic product or gross national product as income measure (Chapter 6)	
. Imposing a floor on estimates of per capita income—unless the floor is well above the World Bank threshold for poverty in low-income nations (Chapter 6)	
. Choice of inequality measure (Theil versus MLD versus Gini) does not matter in most instances (Chapter 6)	
. Overweighting of low-income nations (this chapter)	

Note: This table is based on findings reported in this chapter and in other chapters, as noted in parentheses.

*Assumes weighted data and PPP income. China is important only in the case of size-weighted inequality; when nations are weighted equally, the exclusion of China does not matter.

flect actual purchasing power differences across nations. Because almost all studies of between-nation income inequality use PPP data, however, this finding is not a central issue in the divergence debate. A second critical decision is whether or not to include China. China is significant for the between-nation trend in inequality not only because China has so many people, but also because China's faster-than-world-average income growth over the past half century means that China's income has been moving up toward the world mean. The result is that the income trend in China has worked to compress income inequality across nations. An early study (Berry, Bourguignon, and Morrisson 1983b) concludes that economic growth in China was the most important force equalizing world incomes from 1950 to 1977, and more recent studies echo this finding. For example, Arne Melchior, Kjetil Telle, and Henrik Wiig (2000) conclude that when China is included, between-nation income inequality clearly declined from the 1960s to 1997; however, "if we remove China from our sample, international inequality between countries has not changed substantially from 1965 to 1997" (p. 1). Milanovic (2001) reports similar results.

That said, it is important to note the dangers of dismissing the decline in between-nation income inequality on the basis that the decline is "due only to China." One person in five lives in China, and by playing the "let's remove some nation" game we can arrive at virtually any conclusion we want. If we removed Japan and the Soviet Union instead of China, for example, we would conclude that from 1965 to 1989 income inequality across nations declined twice as fast as reported in Table 6.1. If we removed the nations of sub-Saharan Africa—whose combined population is roughly one-half that of China—we would further accelerate the pace of the decline in between-nation income inequality. Yet why should we be removing nations at all? If we want to know the effect on between-nation inequality of the faster-than-world-average income growth in China, a better strategy is to recalculate between-nation inequality under the assumption that China's income growth has matched the world average. Using that strategy we find that income growth in China accounts for much but not all of the decline in income inequality across nations over recent decades (Sala-i-Martin 2002b).

A third decision that matters is whether to use income per capita or income per worker. Because nations vary so much in size, from over a billion people to a few hundred thousand, income figures for nations must be normalized in some way before they can be compared. Most often incomes are normalized by dividing by total population, but they can also be normalized by dividing by number of workers. The first measure—income per capita—is generally viewed as a measure of living standard or welfare, whereas income per worker captures worker productivity. As we shall see in Chapter 11, the decline in between-nation income inequality is more rapid for income per worker than it is for income per capita. So the choice of how to normalize does matter.

Because virtually all studies now use PPP measures of per capita income and include China, the dispute over whether between-nation income inequality is rising or falling does not turn on whether to include China or whether to use PPP income or whether to use per capita income. (If studies used income per worker in place of income per capita, they would find faster decline in between-nation inequality.) So, as the chapter's title suggests, the divergence debate distills to the issue of whether to weight. The conclusion is clear: if the results are to be applied to global income inequality, nations must be weighted by their population size.

Continental Divides: Asia, Africa, and the Reversal of the Trend

THE MESSAGE of this chapter is that the recent economic resurgence of Asia is behind the turnaround in the trend in between-nation income inequality. In recent decades East Asia in particular has experienced robust economic growth while sub-Saharan Africa has languished. The previous chapter argued that this growth difference between Asia and sub-Saharan Africa accounts for the difference in the weighted and unweighted between-nation inequality trends. The current chapter focuses on the weighted trend, and simulates the trend under the counterfactual assumption that per capita incomes in Asia grew at the same rate as per capita incomes in Africa did in recent decades. The conclusion is that between-nation income inequality would have continued to worsen if economic performance in Asia had paralleled the economic performance in Africa over the last decades of the twentieth century. In that sense, then, we can say that it was the resurgent economic growth in Asia that caused the turnaround in the between-nation inequality trend.

The pattern of thriving Asia/languishing Africa is a relatively recent historical phenomenon. Throughout most of the Western industrialization period, per capita income rose somewhat faster in Africa than it did in Asia. Over the nineteenth and early twentieth centuries it was Asia—not Africa—that lagged furthest behind the rest of the world. This point can be inferred from the income estimates presented in Chapter 1 (from Maddison 1995), which indicate that from 1820 to 1950 the average income in Africa rose by 80 percent while rising only 10 percent in India, 20 percent in China, and 70 percent in the rest of Asia (Table 1.1). Because most of the world's people live in Asia, income growth in Asia is pivotal.

Between-nation income inequality rose over the period of Western industrialization in large part because average income in Asia began below the world average in 1820 and slipped further behind over the next 130 years. In recent decades income growth in Asia has exceeded the world average, thereby working to compress between-nation income inequality.

In short, income trends in Asia have gone from exacerbating global income inequality to serving as a brake on the growth of that inequality—as Asia has gone, so has gone regional and between-nation income inequality over the past two centuries. This chapter revisits the issue of regional differences in income growth rates since 1820, a topic that was introduced in Chapter 1. The purpose here is to compare the historical data on regional and national growth rates in the nineteenth and early twentieth centuries with data since 1960. This comparison makes clear that the economic turnaround in Asia in the last half of the twentieth century was the single most important factor halting the centuries-old trend of economic divergence across regions and across nations.

Regional Growth Rates during Western Industrialization

DATA

As noted earlier, Maddison (1995) is the standard source for income estimates for the nineteenth and early twentieth centuries. It is the Maddison data set that Lant Pritchett (1996, p. 40) used as the basis for his claim that "the overwhelming feature of modern economic history is a massive divergence in per capita incomes between rich and poor countries." (Pritchett's study looks at the unweighted trend.) It is the Maddison data set that Bourguignon and Morrisson (1999) used in their study of the trend in total world income inequality since 1820. It is the Maddison data set that Boltho and Toniolo (1999) used in their assessment of the "achievements, failures, and lessons" of the twentieth century. It is the Maddison data set that I use here to examine differences in regional growth rates from 1820 to 1960.

In view of the declining reliability of income estimates as we go further back in time, for the pre-1960 data I follow Maddison's lead in reporting two sets of estimates—one set for the 56 sample nations and one set for the 199 sample and nonsample nations combined. The 56 sample nations accounted for 93 percent of the world's total output and 87 percent of the world's population in 1992 (Maddison 1995, p. 17). The 56 nations are those for which there is sufficient historical information to make reasonable estimates of per capita income. The term "nonsample nations" refers to numerous small nations for which the historical materials are sparse, and incomes are best estimated by comparisons with similar nations. Because the nonsample nations account for only about 7 percent of the world's output and about 13 percent of the world population, we reach the same conclusions whether we use the 56 sample nations or all 199 nations.

FINDINGS

The nineteenth and early twentieth centuries were characterized by unprecedented economic divergence of the world's major regions as the world polarized into a Western camp, consisting of Western Europe and the Western offshoots, an Asian-African camp that lagged seriously behind, and a Latin American and Eastern European camp that was somewhere in the middle (Chapter 1). The highly uneven nature of regional income growth over the Western industrialization period is obvious even from the most cursory examination of the data. According to the Maddison data, from 1820 to 1960 per capita incomes rose sixfold in Western Europe and ninefold in the Western offshoots. Strikingly, over this 140-year period of Western-led industrialization, income in China rose a meager 68 percent and income in India rose an even more sluggish 38 percent. Table 8.1 reports percentage change in per capita income, 1820–1960, for the world's geographical regions using Maddison's data for the 199 sample and nonsample nations combined. Results for the sample nations alone (reported in Table 8.2) are virtually equivalent, and to avoid redundancy I focus on the results for all 199 nations.

The 1820–1960 period was an era of growing global and regional income inequality, because the slowest income gains occurred in the regions that were already below the world mean at the outset of Western industrialization. Estimated incomes in 1820 are lowest in Africa ($450) and Asia ($550) and highest in Western Europe ($1,292) and the Western offshoots ($1,205). From this higher base, average incomes grew by about 500 percent in Western Europe and by about 800 percent in the Western offshoots. At the same time average incomes grew only about 125 percent in Africa and even more slowly in Asia. Clearly the period of Western industrialization was an era of the rich regions getting richer and the poor regions falling farther behind.

To gauge the rough magnitude of the increase in between-region inequality from 1820 to 1960, compare the change in the relative incomes for the rich and poor regions. We find from the Maddison data that in 1820 the average income in the world's richest regions—Western Europe and the Western offshoots—was less than three times larger than average income in Africa, the poorest region. By 1960 that ratio had ballooned from less than 3 to 1 to over 10 to 1 for the Western offshoots and over 7

TABLE 8.1 Change in per capita income from 1820 to 1960, by major regions of the world: Sample and nonsample nations (*n* = 199)

Region	Per capita income 1820	1960	Change
High-income group			
Western Europe (23 nations)	$1,292	$7,676	+494%
Western offshoots (4 nations)	1,205	10,813	+797%
Middle-income group			
Southern Europe (7 nations)	804	2,820	+251%
Eastern Europe (9 nations)	772	3,705	+380%
Latin America (44 nations)	679	3,077	+353%
Low-income group			
Asia (56 nations)	550	1,088	+98%
China	523	878	+68%
India	531	735	+38%
Africa (56 nations)	450	1,006	+124%
World totals (199 nations)	651	2,792	+329%

Source: Maddison (1995), table G-3 for regional income data and table D-1e for income data for China and India. The regional categories follow the classification in Maddison.
Note: Regional incomes are population-weighted averages, in 1990 U.S. dollars. "Western offshoots" refers to Australia, Canada, New Zealand, and the United States. "Asia" includes Oceania.

to 1 for Western Europe, as average income grew to $10,800 in the Western offshoots and to $7,700 in Western Europe while average income in Africa and Asia was barely over $1,000. So the nineteenth and early twentieth centuries witnessed the global income fracturing emphasized in Chapter 1, as Western Europe and the Western offshoot nations surged ahead and Africa and Asia lagged behind. Latin America played little direct role in this bifurcation, since income growth in Latin America roughly matched the growth for the world as a whole.

This historical evidence for regional divergence fits well with the evidence reviewed earlier regarding the historical divergence of incomes across nations. Of course, between-nation inequality and between-region inequality are not the same, and income inequality across nations in theory could decline despite growing inequality across regions (because national incomes can converge within regions). That theoretical possibility is implausible here, however, since it would be hard for nations to converge fast enough within regions to overcome the effects of the world's income fracturing from 1820 to 1960, which saw incomes grow three to four times

TABLE 8.2 Change in per capita income from 1820 to 1960, by major regions of the world: Sample nations only (*n* = 56)

| | Per capita income | | |
Region	1820	1960	Change
High-income group			
Western Europe (12 nations)	$1,292	$7,675	+494%
Western offshoots (4 nations)	1,205	10,813	+797%
Middle-income group			
Southern Europe (5 nations)	806	2,828	+251%
Eastern Europe (7 nations)	750	3,670	+389%
Latin America (7 nations)	715	3,302	+362%
Low-income group			
Asia (11 nations)	550	1,041	+89%
China	523	878	+68%
India	531	735	+38%
Africa (10 nations)	450	933	+107%
Average (56 nations)	661	2,931	+343%

Source: Maddison (1995), table E-3 for regional income data and table D-1e for income data for China and India. The regional categories follow the classification in Maddison.

Note: Regional incomes are population-weighted averages, in 1990 U.S. dollars. "Western offshoots" refers to Australia, Canada, New Zealand, and the United States. "Asia" includes Oceania.

faster in the world's richest regions than in the world's poorest regions. In any case, there is more direct evidence of rising income inequality across nations over this period, as noted in earlier discussion of the Bourguignon-Morrisson (1999) study of 33 nation groups. The findings of Andrea Boltho and Gianni Toniolo (1999) for the twentieth century generally support those of Bourguignon and Morrisson. Using PPP income data for 49 nations covering 80 percent of the world's population, Boltho and Toniolo conclude that between-nation income inequality rose over most of the century. For the 49 nations, the Gini coefficient grew from .393 in 1900 to .544 in 1980 and then fell to .496 by 1998.

As this brief review of the record indicates, there is a strong historical link between income inequality across nations and income inequality across regions. And it has been the divergence in incomes across regions that has largely driven the divergence in incomes across nations over the past two centuries. Between-nation income inequality shot up primarily because incomes diverged across the world's major regions or continents, not because incomes diverged across nations within major regions or continents. (Indeed, some studies find that national incomes have tended to converge historically within regions or income groups: Abramovitz, 1986; Baumol 1986; Baumol and Wolff 1988; Quah 1996; see also De Long 1988.) Clearly between-nation income inequality would not have shot up so rapidly—or perhaps would not have shot up at all—over the period of Western industrialization had there been no regional divergence in incomes over that period. If regional divergence is the engine driving between-nation divergence, then when income inequality stops growing across regions we expect income inequality to stop growing across nations as well. And that is precisely what happened in the last decades of the twentieth century, as we now see.

Regional Growth Rates since 1960

One theme of this book is that there is plenty of evidence to support Pritchett's (1996, 1997) claim that "big time" between-nation divergence has been the order of the day throughout most of the industrial era. Yet big-time divergence has not been the order of the day in the last decades of the twentieth century. What accounts for this reversal? In a word, Asia. Because Asia is the world's most populous region, it has been the Asian turnaround from growth laggard to growth leader that has halted the divergence in per capita incomes across regions and across nations. We begin by examining regional differences in income growth rates since 1960. For the 199 nations in the Maddison data set, constituting virtually all of the world's population, the world's average income increased by 86 percent from 1960 to 1990 in constant dollars (Table 8.3). Critically, though, this overall growth masks significant regional differences. While incomes shot up by 179 percent in Asia (due in large part to the tripling of per capita income in China), incomes in Africa increased by only 33 percent—and incomes in some African nations fell. Growth in per capita incomes in Latin America also lagged significantly behind growth in the world average over the combined decades of the 1960s, 1970s, and 1980s. Income growth in Western Europe, Southern Europe, and (of course) Asia significantly exceeded the world average over this period. Growth in Eastern Europe and the Western offshoots (Australia, Canada, New Zealand, and the United States) was similar to the world average, with Eastern Europe exhibiting growth that was slightly below the world average and the Western offshoots exhibiting growth that was slightly above the world average.

To gauge the impact of this tangle of regional differences on the trends in between-region and between-nation income inequality, we must consider the relative sizes of the regions. Table 8.3 reports that data in the last col-

TABLE 8.3   Change in per capita income from 1960 to 1990, by major regions of the world (*n* = 199 nations)

Region	Per capita income			% of world's population in 1990
	1960	1990	Change	
High-income group				
Western Europe (23 nations)	$7,676	$17,272	+125%	5.7%
Western offshoots (4 nations)	10,813	21,261	+97%	5.6%
Middle-income group				
Southern Europe (7 nations)	2,820	8,092	+187%	2.3%
Eastern Europe (9 nations)	3,705	6,397	+73%	8.2%
Latin America (44 nations)	3,077	4,735	+54%	8.5%
Low-income group				
Asia (56 nations)	1,088	3,031	+179%	58.0%
China	878	2,700	+208%	21.6%
India	735	1,316	+79%	16.1%
Africa (56 nations)	1,006	1,336	+33%	11.8%
World totals (199 nations)	2,792	5,204	+86%	100.0%

Source: Maddison (1995), tables G-1 (population) and G-3 (income) for regional data, and tables A-3e (population) and D-1e (income) for data for China and India.

Note: Regional incomes are population-weighted averages, in 1990 U.S. dollars. The regional categories follow the classification in Maddison (1995). "Western offshoots" refers to Australia, Canada, New Zealand, and the United States. "Eastern Europe" includes the former Soviet Union. "Asia" includes Oceania.

umn. Income trends in Asia will be critical, since the 56 nations of Asia contain more than half of the world's people, while income trends in Latin America will have less impact, since the 44 nations of Latin America are home to less than 10 percent of the world's population. Incomes grew fastest in the seven nations of Southern Europe, but this should have little impact on the overall trend since these nations constitute less than 3 percent of the world's population. On the other hand, China alone has great impact on the between-nation trend since China contains one-fifth of the world's people and China's per capita income roughly tripled from 1960 to 1990. The inequality-compressing effect of China's faster-than-world-average income growth will be tempered by the inequality-enhancing effect of the (slightly) slower-than-world-average income growth of India. The net result is a narrowing of regional inequality, as we shall see.

One reaches the same conclusions using other data sets, or other ways of dividing the world into geographical regions, or somewhat different starting and ending points. For example, Ronald Sprout and James Weaver

(1992) estimated the 1961–1987 rate of growth of per capita income for industrial market countries versus less-developed countries (LDCs). Their results are summarized in Table 8.4. For the 127 nations in the study, representing about 97 percent of the world's population, Sprout and Weaver found that the world's per capita income has been growing at a healthy rate over recent decades. This finding is consistent with other studies of world income growth in the last half of the twentieth century. The industrial market countries grew at an annual rate of 2.9 percent and the less developed countries grew at an annual rate of 3.2 percent, suggesting some narrowing of between-nation inequality over the period. When China is removed, however, the annual rate of income growth for LDCs falls to 2.3 percent, which is lower than the growth rate for industrial market nations—again pointing to the importance of China in determining the direction of the trend in between-nation income inequality.

There are, in short, clear continental divides in the pattern of world income growth since mid-century. Although the statistics on overall world income growth are encouraging, the aggregate picture conceals huge regional differences in the economic performance of nations. For low-income nations, income growth has varied substantially across regions. In East Asia per capita incomes have been doubling every fifteen years, while other regions have been bypassed by the growth phenomenon. Sub-Saharan Africa in particular has lagged badly behind. As Boltho and Toniolo (1999, p. 3) observe, "From 1950 to today, out of 48 sub-Saharan African countries for which data are available, 11 recorded negative per capita

TABLE 8.4 Annual growth rates in per capita income from 1961 to 1987, by major regions of the world

Region	Annual growth rate
Industrial market economies	+2.9%
Less-developed countries	+3.2%
Less-developed countries without China	+2.3%
Among less-developed countries:	
South Asia	+1.5%
East Asia	+5.1%
Middle East, N. Africa, S. Europe	+2.7%
Sub-Saharan Africa	+0.1%
Latin America and Caribbean	+2.3%

Source: Sprout and Weaver (1992), table 4, based on PPP income data from Summers and Heston (1988).

Note: Growth rates are population-weighted averages.

growth and a further 18 had annual growth of less than 1 per cent." The regional differences reported by Sprout and Weaver reinforce the point. By their calculations, from 1961 to 1987 per capita income grew at an annual rate of 5.1 percent in East Asia (by 4.4 percent excluding China) but only by 0.1 percent in sub-Saharan Africa.

As we saw earlier, the present-day pattern of "Asia catching up, Africa lagging behind" has not been characteristic of income growth over most of the past two centuries. Until recently the general pattern has been "Asia lagging, Africa lagging," resulting in an unprecedented increase in be-tween-nation income inequality over the nineteenth and early twentieth centuries. The hypothesis of this chapter is that the shift from "Asia lag-ging" to "Asia catching up" is responsible for the leveling off of the trend in between-nation income inequality. The next section tests the hypothesis by projecting the 1960–1990 change in between-region income inequality under the assumption that incomes grew in Asia at the same rate as they did in Africa over that period.

Asian Turnaround and the Reversal of the Trend

There are two striking findings in the historical data of Tables 8.1 and 8.2. The first is the great continental income divides of the nineteenth and early twentieth centuries as the world split decisively into a Western income camp (Western Europe and Western offshoots), a middle-income camp that subsumed Latin America and Southern and Eastern Europe, and an Asian/African camp. The second striking finding is that it was Asia—not Africa—that most lagged behind the rest of the world on income growth over the nineteenth century and the first half of the twentieth century. From 1820 to 1960, per capita income increased by an estimated 98 per-cent in Asia and by an estimated 124 percent in Africa. So both regions lagged behind over the period of Western industrialization, but Asia lagged behind further than Africa did. This underperformance in Asia is key to the nineteenth- and early-twentieth-century trend in between-nation in-equality. Lagging economic growth in Asia was the force driving the sharp rise in between-nation inequality from 1820 to 1960. As Bourguignon and Morrisson (1999, p. 12) put it, "the dominant unequalizing force through-out the nineteenth century and the first half of the twentieth century is the relatively slow economic growth of the Asian region, the most populated area of the world." Now it is the economic turnaround in Asia that holds the key to the reversal of the world's economic divergence. Asia has been catching up economically since the middle of the twentieth century, and it is this economic resurgence that accounts for the leveling off and decline of the post-1960 trend in between-nation income inequality and hence the stabilization and decline of global income inequality as well.

To appreciate Asia's pivotal role, consider first the actual 1960–1990 change in income inequality across regions as based on the income data reported in Table 8.3. Regional inequality declined from 1960 to 1990 by 15 percent as measured by the Theil, by 21 percent as measured by the MLD, and by 12 percent as measured by the Gini (Table 8.5). These results are consistent with the findings of Duangkamon Chotikapanich, Rebecca Valenzuela, and Prasada Rao (1997) for 1980 to 1990. A decline of this magnitude occurred because the rate of income growth in Asia over this period was about double the rate for the world as a whole (Table 8.3) and because Asia is the world's most populous region. Economic resurgence in Africa would have packed much less punch. To confirm that it was Asia's economic turnaround that caused this turnaround from regional divergence to regional convergence, I recalculated the inequality indexes using the 1990 level of income for Asia if per capita income in Asia had grown at the same rate as it did in Africa from 1960 to 1990. In other words, we suppose that income growth in Asia had lagged behind the rest of the world in the last part of the twentieth century as it had over the nineteenth and early twentieth centuries. In that case, world income would have been nearly $1,000 less per person in 1990, and regional income inequality would have increased substantially, not declined (Table 8.5).

These results underscore the profound effect of resurgent economic

TABLE 8.5 Change in regional income inequality: Actual change versus change assuming income had grown in Asia at the same rate as it did in Africa from 1960 to 1990

Inequality measure	1960	1990	Actual % change	Simulated 1990 results	
				1990	% change
Theil index	.417	.354	−15%	.595	+43%
MLD index	.390	.308	−21%	.542	+39%
Gini index	.469	.413	−12%	.543	+16%

Source: Calculated from regional income and population data, using the regional categories of Maddison (1995). See Table 8.3 for 1960 and 1990 income data and 1990 population data. These data are from Maddison (1995), tables G-3 (income) and G-1 (population) for regional data.

Note: Income growth in Asia and Africa lagged significantly behind the rest of the world over the period of Western industrialization (Tables 8.1 and 8.2). The simulated results here assume that this growth pattern had continued after 1960, with 1960–1990 growth rates in Asia matching the growth rates in Africa over this period.

growth in Asia on the distribution of world income. If income growth in Asia had continued to lag behind the rest of the world over the second half of the twentieth century, then there would be no new geography of global income inequality and we would be witnessing the continuation of between-nation, between-region, and global income divergence. Yet a new geography of inequality has emerged as Asia's economic resurgence has reversed the trend toward worsening income inequality across regions, and that, in turn, has reversed the trend toward worsening between-nation and global income inequality. In contrast to the world of the nineteenth and early twentieth centuries, in today's world regional differences in income growth serve to compress global income inequality.

Summary: The Trend in Between-Nation Income Inequality

Although this study is not the first to observe stable or declining between-nation income inequality in recent decades (see Schultz 1998; Firebaugh 1999; Melchior, Telle, and Wiig 2000), the decline is not well known, so we have devoted three chapters to it. Chapter 6 presented estimates of the change in between-nation income inequality for the quarter century before the collapse of communism, and then the change over the 1990s. When the two results are put together it is clear that income inequality across nations declined in the last decades of the twentieth century. With that result, and the results of Chapter 7 on weighted versus unweighted inequality and of this chapter on regional inequality, we now have a more complete picture of between-nation income inequality over the past two centuries. Divergence ruled the day over the period of Western industrialization that extended through the first half of the twentieth century. Between-nation income inequality increased, because the world's major regions diverged as the West surged ahead and Africa and Asia lagged behind. In recent decades, however, income per capita has grown more rapidly in Asia than in the rest of the world, and between-nation income inequality has declined as a result.

CHAPTER

9

Change in Income Inequality within Nations

THIS CHAPTER tries to determine whether income inequality has been rising, falling, or remaining the same in the average nation in recent decades. Earlier studies are inconclusive. Deininger and Squire (1996, table 5) report average Gini coefficients by region for the 1960s, 1970s, 1980s, and 1990s, but the averages are unweighted. Of the studies that examine weighted averages, Goesling (2000, 2001) reports rising within-nation inequality whereas Schultz (1998) reports declining within-nation inequality. Melchior, Telle, and Wiig (2000, diagram 3.1) collapse the national data into regions and examine regional change from decade to decade, beginning with the 1960s. There is no clear direction in the trend for within-nation income inequality for these regions—inequality is increasing in some and declining in others—and the authors conclude that "the picture is confusing—with few simple regularities" (p. 20).

The conventional view is that this finding of few regularities in the change in within-nation income inequality is to be expected, since the level of income inequality in a nation is a composite of many different forces—historical, economic, demographic, institutional, cultural, political, technological. Hence, as Jeffrey Williamson (1998) notes, one should not expect to find uniform changes in income inequality from nation to nation. Because change in within-nation income inequality is generally not reducible to a single set of causes that move in the same direction in all nations, increases in some nations are likely to be offset by declines in other nations, and average change most often is minimal.

In the late twentieth century, however, significant disequilibrating forces—including industrial expansion in the world's most populous region, and the dramatic fall of communism in Eastern Europe—overcame the typically offsetting composite effects noted by Williamson, and led to a rise in income inequality in the average nation. Although the claim of rising within-nation income inequality is likely to be controversial, I believe it is supported by the weight of the evidence. I have a longer and a shorter empirical defense for this claim. The shorter defense is that there is evidence that income inequality has risen in the four most populous nations of the world—China, India, the former USSR, and the United States. In the case of China, India, and the former USSR, the growth in income inequality followed economic liberalization (Lindert and Williamson 2000); in the case of the United States, the cause of the rise is more enigmatic (Levy and Murnane 1992; Morris and Western 1999). Because these four giants contain nearly half the world's population, rising income inequality in these nations implies rising income inequality for the average nation unless there is a commensurate decline in income inequality in the remaining nations of the world. Such a decline is highly unlikely, especially in light of the rise in income inequality in some (but not all) Western industrialized nations besides the United States in the 1970s and 1980s and the sharp rise in income inequality in Eastern Europe after the collapse of communism.

The longer defense is that, even though we do not have reliable data for all nations, we have enough reliable data for all regions except sub-Saharan Africa to draw at least tentative conclusions about the direction of regional change since 1980. These data suggest that income inequality has been growing—or at least not declining—since 1980 in all the world's major regions (except sub-Saharan Africa's status is unknown). On the basis of this region-by-region analysis, we conclude that income inequality most likely has been rising for the (weighted) average nation in the world. This chapter provides the region-by-region analysis.

Historical Trends in Income Inequality Revisited

It is useful first to place current patterns in historical context. Recall that Bourguignon and Morrisson (1999) collapse the 199 nations of the Maddison (1995) data set into 33 homogeneous nation groups and provide estimates of income inequality in those nation groups since 1820. Because the estimates are based on nation groups, not nations, the Bourguignon-Morrisson results are inflated estimates of within-nation income inequality; some of the income inequality within the nation groups actually is between-nation inequality, as noted earlier. For example, while the Bourguignon-Morrisson estimate of within-nation income inequality circa 1990 is 0.36 (MLD) based on nation groups, the MLD estimate based on nations is 0.21 for Schultz (1998, table A-3) and 0.20 for Goesling (2001, table 2). Thus the Bourguignon-Morrisson results should be interpreted as very rough and upwardly biased estimates of within-nation income inequality at a given point in time. These results nonetheless should paint a fairly reliable picture of the broad patterns of change in income inequality over the past two centuries.

We reviewed the Bourguignon-Morrisson results in Chapter 2 with an eye for what they would tell us about the transition from within-nation to between-nation inequality, phase 1 of the inequality transition. We saw very different patterns for the within- and between-nation-group trends over the past two centuries, with between-group inequality growing dramatically from 1820 to 1950 and inequality within the nation groups increasing slowly over the nineteenth century before declining more rapidly over the first half of the twentieth. Here we want to consider what the Bourguignon-Morrisson results suggest for the trend in global income inequality itself. Although the data are far from perfect, the results of the Bourguignon-Morrisson analysis are so strong that it is possible to state three general conclusions regarding the historical contours of global income inequality. First, global income inequality is higher now than it was at the beginning of the Western industrial period. Bourguignon and Morrisson (1999, p. 18) summarize their findings by saying that "world income inequalities have truly exploded since the early nineteenth century," and there is substantial evidence that they are right (Pritchett 1996, 1997). Second, the explosive growth in global income inequality over the course of Western industrialization was caused by ballooning income inequality across nations, not by rising inequality within nations. Had between-nation inequality remained constant, world inequality would have declined over the past two centuries, since within-nation inequality is lower now than it was in 1820. Indeed, calculated on the basis of the Bourguignon-Morrisson estimates, the current level of within-nation inequality falls below the level of within-nation inequality at any point in the nineteenth century. These results are consistent with conventional accounts that describe the preindustrial era as a period characterized by bimodal societies where the elite extracted a disproportionate share of the surplus, and the early industrial era as one where inequality typically worsened before succumbing to the inequality-compressing effects of the growth of the middle classes. So Bourguignon and Morrison's finding of increasing within-nation income inequality over the nineteenth century followed by declining inequality over the first part of the twentieth provides global quantitative evidence bearing on an influential account of recent history.

The final inference about global income inequality from the Bourguignon-Morrisson study is that the locus of the world's income inequality changed over the course of the Western industrial period, from inequality within nations to inequality across nations. This change in the locus of inequality is the result of rising inequality across nations and falling inequality within nations. Whereas the Bourguignon-Morrisson estimates indicate that the greatest income disparities at the early stages of world industrialization in the nineteenth century were found within nations, today the situation is the reverse, with between-nation income inequality being the larger component of world income inequality by a factor of nearly 3. Even making generous allowances for the imprecision of the nineteenth-century data, the signal here is too strong to be ignored. On the basis of findings for the late twentieth century, the thesis of this book is that the trends uncovered by Bourguignon and Morrisson are in the process of being reversed—that we are now entering a second stage of the global inequality transition, as between-nation inequality recedes and within-nation inequality worsens. We turn now to evidence on the recent within-nation trend.

Data and Methods

Unlike between-nation inequality—which can be calculated from national income means—within-nation inequality requires information on national income distributions. Here we rely on income quintile data from individual nations to estimate within-nation income inequality in the average nation circa 1980, 1989, and 1995. We face a trade-off between data coverage and aggregation bias, since the finer the data categories, the more nations that are excluded. By using income data aggregated into quintiles, it is possible to include data covering about 80 percent of the world's population. The general strategy is to calculate the level of income inequality in the average nation by calculating regional averages and aggregating. As in earlier chapters, I use Maddison's seven world regions. By examining the regional trends in within-nation income inequality before aggregating, we can identify the regions of the world where average within-nation income inequality is growing the fastest and the regions where it is growing the slowest (or declining the fastest). In addition, by examining the trend region by region we can identify the regions with the biggest data gaps, and qualify our conclusions accordingly.

CALCULATION OF WITHIN-NATION INCOME INEQUALITY

The calculation of within-nation income inequality involves two steps. The first step is to compute the within-nation average for each of the seven regions. The second step is to average those regional averages using the proper weights (income shares in the case of the Theil and population shares in the case of the MLD) to obtain within-nation income inequality for the entire world. Data limitations dictate a starting point of 1980 and an ending point of about 1995. We use the Theil and MLD indexes because they can be partitioned into a within-group (for example, within-nation) component and a between-group (for example, between nation) component. Previous chapters have examined the between-nation component of world income inequality, and this section focuses on how to calculate the within-nation component.

For the world as a whole, the within-nation component of total inequality is a weighted average of the level of income inequality within nations. Because the MLD index weights nations by their population shares whereas the Theil index weights nations by their income shares, the MLD will be relatively more sensitive to change in income inequality in large nations while the Theil will be relatively more sensitive to change in income inequality in rich nations. From equation 7.3, average within-nation income inequality as measured by the Theil is:

$$T_W = \sum_j y_j T_j, \tag{9.1}$$

where y_j is income share for the jth nation and T_j is the level of income inequality for the jth nation as measured by the Theil index. Similarly, average within-nation income inequality as measured by the MLD is:

$$MLD_W = \sum_j p_j MLD_j, \tag{9.2}$$

where p_j is population share for the jth nation and MLD_j is the level of income inequality for the jth nation as measured by the MLD index.

The inequality data for nations are reported by quintiles, so we need to rewrite the formulas in those terms. The Theil index can be expressed in general form as $\Sigma_i y_i \log(y_i/p_i)$ and the MLD index as $\Sigma_i p_i \log(p_i/y_i)$, where y_i is income share and p_i is population share for the ith unit (these are the same expressions as those given in Chapter 4, except that we substitute y_i for $p_i r_i$). Here the units are quintiles ($q = 1, 2, 3, 4, 5$), so we substitute $y_q \log(y_q/p_q)$ for T_j (the value of Theil for the jth nation) in the Theil index and $p_q \log(p_q/y_q)$ for MLD_j in the MLD index. Thus average within-nation Theil and MLD are:

$$T_W = \sum_j y_j T_j$$

$$= \sum_j y_j \sum_q y_{jq} \log(y_{jq} / p_{jq}) \tag{9.3}$$

and

$$MLD_W = \sum_j p_j MLD_j$$

$$= \sum_j p_j \sum_q p_{jq} \log(p_{jq} / y_{jq}), \tag{9.4}$$

where j indexes nation and q indexes quintile within a nation. It is important to note that y_j denotes the share of the world's total income that is held by nation j, whereas y_{jq} denotes the share of nation j's income that is held by the qth quintile in nation j. Similarly, p_j is the fraction of the world's population living in nation j, whereas p_{jq} is the fraction of nation j's population who are in quintile q. Because $p_{jq} = .2$ for all quintiles in all nations, we can express equations 9.3 and 9.4 more simply as:

$$T_W = \sum_j y_j \sum_q y_{jq} \log(5 y_{jq}) \tag{9.5}$$

and

$$MLD_W = \sum_j p_j \left[-.2 \sum_q \log(5 y_{jq}) \right]. \tag{9.6}$$

Because they are additively decomposable indexes, we can add between-nation income inequality to within-nation income inequality to obtain the global Theil and the global MLD:

Global Theil = between-nation Theil + within-nation Theil

$$= \sum_j y_j \log(r_j) + \sum_j y_j \sum_q y_{jq} \log(5 y_{jq}). \tag{9.7}$$

Global MLD = between-nation MLD + within-nation MLD

$$= \sum_{j} p_j \log(1/r_j) + \sum_{j} p_j \left[-.2 \sum_{q} \log(5y_{jq}) \right]. \qquad (9.8)$$

DATA COVERAGE

For data on within-nation income distributions I rely on the data compilation of Deininger and Squire (1996), with supplementary data from the United Nations University/World Institute for Development Economic Research (UNU/WIDER 2000) and World Bank (2000a). Data on national income distributions are spotty, with more complete data for some world regions than others. The Deininger and Squire compilation includes fairly complete and comparable data for Western Europe but includes limited data for Africa. Distributional data by quintile are available for all the world's large nations except Japan. Fortunately we have distributional data for poor nations such as China, India, Bangladesh, and Pakistan, so even without Japan the data set used here includes four-fifths of the world's people.[1] Insisting on more highly disaggregated data (finer than quintiles) would rule out many nations. Although quintile data tend to understate the level of within-nation inequality by ignoring variance in income within quintiles, it is unlikely that such aggregation bias has much effect on the trend in within-nation inequality (Bourguignon and Morrisson 1999). To include as many nations as possible, then, I base the within-nation estimates on quintile data.

Table 9.1 summarizes the data coverage by region. Although there are only 57 nations in the sample, 80 percent of the world's people live in the 57 nations. This 80 percent figure conceals important differences across regions, however. In the case of Western and Southern Europe the data coverage is close to 100 percent, and the coverage is 100 percent in the case of the Western offshoots. The coverage is about 88 percent for Asia and about 75 percent for Eastern Europe and Latin America. Africa is an outlier, with a coverage of only about 28 percent. This limited coverage would be less problematic if we could assume that the ten nations in the sample are representative of the whole of Africa, but that assumption is dubious (see the list of nations in Table 9.1). Hence the results for Africa should be seen as very tentative until better data are available. In view of the data problems for Africa, I report the world totals with and without Africa. (Excluding Africa, the remaining nations still encompass well over 75 percent of the world's population.) To jump ahead a bit, it turns out that the world results are the same with and without Africa.

TABLE 9.1 Data coverage for 1980–1995 within-nation income inequality: Population of 57 sample nations as percentage of regional totals

Region	Population
Western Europe	98%
Nations in sample (n = 10): Belgium, Denmark, Finland, France, Germany, Italy, Netherlands, Norway, Sweden, U.K.	
Western offshoots	100%
Nations in sample (n = 4): Australia, Canada, New Zealand, U.S.	
Southern Europe	96%
Nations in sample (n = 4): Greece, Portugal, Spain, Turkey	
Eastern Europe	75%
Nations in sample (n = 9): Armenia, Bulgaria, Czech Republic, Hungary, Poland, Romania, Russia, Slovak Republic, Ukraine	
Latin America	74%
Nations in sample (n = 8): Brazil, Colombia, Costa Rica, Jamaica, Mexico, Panama, Peru, Venezuela	
Asia	88%
Nations in sample (n = 12): Bangladesh, China, Hong Kong, India, Indonesia, Jordan, Pakistan, Philippines, Singapore, South Korea, Sri Lanka, Thailand	
Africa	28%
Nations in sample (n = 10): Algeria, Ghana, Guinea, Kenya, Mauritania, Niger, Nigeria, Uganda, South Africa, Zambia	
World	80%

Note: N = 57 nations, each with quintile income data (for computing within-nation income inequality). Numerator for percentage is 1990 total population of sample nations (from Deininger and Squire 1996) and denominator is 1990 total population for all nations in the region (from Maddison 1995, table G.1). Percentage of world's population in the 57 nations is the weighted average of the regional percentages.

Change in Within-Nation Income Inequality by Region

The first step is to use equations 9.5 and 9.6 to calculate weighted-average within-nation income inequality for each of the seven regions. Table 9.2 reports those results. In 1989 the lowest levels of income inequality were found in Eastern Europe, but by 1995 income inequality in Eastern Europe had surpassed the level in Western Europe and roughly matched the level in Southern Europe (Greece, Portugal, Spain, and Turkey). In 1995 the lowest levels of inequality were found among the nations of Western Europe (Theils and MLDs of roughly 0.14) followed by the other European nations and by Asian nations (Theils ranging from 0.17 to 0.19, MLDs ranging from 0.18 to 0.23). Asian and European nations tend to exhibit somewhat lower levels of income inequality than do the Western offshoot nations (Theil = 0.23 in 1995, MLD = 0.26). On the basis of these data, it would appear that African nations tend to have higher levels of income inequality than do the Western offshoot nations, but we can have little confidence in this result since the African data are so spotty. Income inequality tends to be far greater in Latin American nations than in European and Asian nations. In 1995, for example, the weighted-average nation in Latin America had an estimated Theil index value of 0.46 and an estimated MLD value of 0.51. To put these values into perspective, recall that the Theil and MLD values for between-nation income inequality are on the order of 0.50–0.60 for recent decades. So in the average nation in Latin America income is almost as unequally distributed across individuals as average income is across the nations of the world.

The most remarkable finding in Table 9.2 is that within-nation income inequality grew from 1980 to 1995 for all regions except Africa (and recall that the African data are the least reliable). This regional consistency in the trend in within-nation inequality was not anticipated, and is all the more remarkable in light of the magnitude of the regional differences in income growth rates noted in Table 8.3. The greatest gains in inequality were recorded in Eastern Europe, where within-nation income inequality almost doubled from 1989 to 1995. Although it is not surprising that income inequality would rise after the fall of communism, an increase of this magnitude over such a short period of time might be unprecedented. Income inequality also rose, though less dramatically, in the average nation in Western Europe, in the Western offshoots, in Southern Europe, in Latin America, and in Asia. These averages mask significant differences between nations, however. Not all Western European nations exhibited growth in income inequality, for example, but quite a few did, and in some nations (the United Kingdom, for example) the increase was fairly substantial. Based on the results here, income inequality rose on average about 8–10 percent in Western European nations from 1980 to 1995. Inequality grew more rapidly in the Western offshoot nations than in the nations of Western Europe (20 percent based on the Theil and 18 percent based on the MLD), with virtually all of that growth in the Western offshoots occurring in the 1980s. Inequality also grew fairly rapidly in Asian nations (13 percent increase based on the Theil, 23 percent based on the MLD), with most of that growth occurring in the 1980s. Finally, inequality in Latin American nations rose by about 10 percent on average over the 1980s, then leveled off in the 1990s.

TABLE 9.2 Estimated change in average within-nation income inequality for the seven regions, 1980–1995

| Region | Regional within-nation inequality | | | 1980–95 change[a] |
	1980	1989	1995	
Western Europe				
Theil	.130	.136	.140	+7.7%
MLD	.134	.142	.148	+10.4%
Western offshoots				
Theil	.191	.225	.230	+20.4%
MLD	.218	.256	.257	+17.9%
Southern Europe				
Theil	.162	.163	.171	+5.6%
MLD	.207	.212	.233	+12.6%
Eastern Europe				
Theil	.095	.103	.185	+94.7%
MLD	.100	.107	.219	+119.0%
Latin America				
Theil	.417	.466	.458	+9.8%
MLD	.458	.517	.507	+10.7%
Asia				
Theil	.167	.182	.189	+13.2%
MLD	.150	.173	.184	+22.7%
—China				
Theil	.126	.184	.195	
MLD	.136	.196	.214	
—India				
Theil	.141	.131	.145	
MLD	.141	.129	.143	
Africa				
Theil	—	.389	.360	−7.5%
MLD	—	.311	.287	−7.7%

Source: Inequality indexes are calculated from within-nation quintile income data from the Deininger-Squire (1996) compilation. Because the analysis is weighted, it is especially critical to obtain good inequality data for China and India. For both countries the inequality data are based on national samples, and the data are given the highest rating ("good") by Deininger and Squire.

Note: N = 57 nations, each with quintile income data. Average within-nation Theil is income-weighted and average within-nation MLD is population-weighted (see text).

a. Change for Africa is 1989–1995.

Change in Within-Nation Income Inequality for the Entire World

Change in within-nation income inequality for the entire world refers to change over time in the level of income inequality in the (weighted) average nation of the world. When nations are grouped by region, change in income inequality in the weighted-average nation is the weighted average of change in within-nation income inequality for regions. We have already concluded that within-nation income inequality must have increased since 1980 for the entire world, because it has increased in all regions except Africa. This conclusion does not mean that inequality has been growing in every nation, or even in most nations. But income inequality has grown in key large nations, such as China, and in key rich nations, such as the United States, so when nations are weighted by population size (as in the MLD) or by income size (as in the Theil), there is an upward trend. Hence the trend in income inequality within nations apparently is working to boost global (within-nation + between-nation) income inequality now, in contrast to its dampening effect on global income inequality in the first half of the twentieth century.

Some readers may be skeptical about the quality and comparability of inequality data for nations. Some might point, for example, to the recent analysis of Anthony Atkinson and Andrea Brandolini (2001) that calls into question the reliability of inequality data for OECD nations—presumably the best inequality data in existence. As Atkinson and Brandolini rightly point out, a "bewildering variety of estimates" makes it difficult to rank OECD nations with respect to level of income inequality, or even (in some instances) to determine whether inequality is rising or declining in a nation. But the ranking of nations on inequality is not our objective here. We are addressing instead a question at a higher level of aggregation—is income inequality growing or declining in the average nation in the world? To address this question we employ data for seven large regions of the world. The striking finding that within-nation income inequality increased for all regions except Africa is hard to dismiss as measurement error, since it is unclear why a "bewildering variety of estimates" based on different samples and different definitions of income would consistently bias estimates of change in income inequality in a positive direction. If the errors are random, they should largely cancel out within regions and across them. Even if the errors are not random, one is hard-pressed to explain why the data for all regions except one indicate an increase in within-nation income inequality. The regional data, then, buttress the point made at the beginning of the chapter, that income inequality has risen in the four most populous nations of the world, and because nearly half the world's people live in those nations, it is highly doubtful that the rise in income inequality in the four giants was offset by declining inequality in other nations.

Because the fifteen-year period from 1980 to 1995 scarcely suffices to establish a long-term trend, a high priority for future research is to verify the finding here of rising within-nation income inequality. The issue is important for predictions about whether global inequality will worsen in the future (Chapter 11). If inequality is rising within nations and continues to do so, the within-nation trend could more than offset the decline in between-nation income inequality. To set the stage for subsequent discussion of the trend in global income inequality, this section provides three sets of estimates of how much income inequality increased in the average nation from 1980 to 1995. Because of gaps in the data on national income distributions, if we restricted the analysis to nations with inequality data for coincident time intervals (for example, five-year intervals beginning with 1980), we would be limited to a small and unrepresentative sample of nations. One way to try to reduce the problem is to select the measurement points—say, 1980, 1990, and 2000 (if data were available for 2000)—and use all nations with data at those fixed points, even if the list of nations is not the same for each of the measurement points. That is Goesling's (2001) strategy, which I call the *repeated cross-sections* strategy, since in effect a new "sample" of nations is drawn at each point in time. The key assumption in the repeated cross-section strategy is that nations are substitutable, so differences in the subset of nations from one measurement point to another does not affect the estimate of change. A second strategy is to use the same *panel of nations* over time but to allow the measurement points to vary somewhat. Nation A, for example, might be measured at 1979, 1987, and 1998, whereas nation B is measured at 1981, 1989, and 1997. Both nations are included, even though the measurement points and measurement intervals do not coincide from nation to nation. The key assumption in the panel strategy is that nearby measurement points are substitutable, so it does not matter much whether we measure income inequality in 1979 or 1980 or 1981.

The second strategy is better, because it is surely the case that, with respect to income inequality, nearby measurement points are more nearly substitutable than are nations. Generally a nation's income inequality does not change dramatically from year to year, so it does not matter much whether I measure Sweden's income inequality in 1979 or 1981. But income inequality does vary greatly from nation to nation, so it does matter whether I use Sweden or Brazil. Hence fixing the measurement points and

TABLE 9.3 Change in world average within-nation income inequality since 1980: Three sets of estimates

	Theil			MLD		
	1980	1989	1995	1980	1989	199
Panel of nations	.186	.203	.215	.192	.216	.23
(n = 57 nations)						
Panel without Africa	.180	.197	.210	.178	.204	.22
(n = 47 nations)						
Repeated cross-section	.180	.210	.250	.170	.200	.24
(varying sample of nations)						

Source: Within-nation inequality is based on income quintile data from Deininger and Squire (1996), weighted by nations' income shares (Table 9.4) in the case of the Theil index and by nations' population shares (Table 9.4) in the case of the MLD (see text for calculation formulas). *Panel of nations* is based o the 57 nations listed in Table 9.1; *repeated cross-section* is based on a varying subset of nations numbering 35 nations in 1980, 53 nations in 1989, and 46 nations in 1995 (from Goesling 2001). Because the 1980 estimate for Africa is missing, the *panel of nations* estimate for 1980 with Africa assumes constant within-nation income inequality in Africa during the 1980s.

varying the nations (repeated cross-sections strategy) is more problematic than fixing the nations and varying the measurement points (panel-of-nations strategy).

Table 9.3 reports three sets of results that are based on the same data sets (primarily Deininger and Squire 1996) but employ different strategies. The first two sets of estimates are based on the preferred panel-of-nations strategy (there are two sets of estimates because one includes African nations and the other does not). The reported values for Theil and MLD were obtained by multiplying the regional Theil and MLD inequality values in Table 9.2 by appropriate weights (income shares for the Theil and population shares for the MLD) and summing. It is immediately apparent from the weights (Table 9.4) that change in income distributions in Asia will have a greater effect on change in the MLD than on change in the Theil, since the population shares for Asia are much larger than the income shares for Asia. On the other hand, change in income distributions in Western Europe and the Western offshoots will have a greater effect on change in the Theil, since the nations in those two regions claim over 40 percent of the world's income while containing less than one-eighth of the world's population in 1995.

All three sets of estimates indicate rising inequality in the average nation from 1980 to 1995. With calculations based on the panel-of-nations strategy, the increase from 1980 to 1995 was about 16 percent as measured by the Theil and about 20 percent as measured by the MLD, indicating that

TABLE 9.4 Population and income shares for the seven regions (weights for calculating average within-nation income inequality for the world)

Region	Population share			Income share		
	1980	1989	1995	1980	1989	1992
Western Europe	6.56	5.74	5.35	20.52	18.70	18.77
Western offshoots	6.11	5.72	5.50	23.97	23.37	22.71
Southern Europe	2.40	2.30	2.20	3.51	3.46	3.63
Eastern Europe	9.06	8.29	7.55	12.52	10.75	7.18
Latin America	8.11	8.44	8.52	9.26	7.85	7.95
Asia	57.24	57.84	58.43	26.95	32.83	36.75
China	22.23	21.68	21.22	7.17	11.05	12.92
India	15.38	15.82	16.56	3.19	3.94	4.24
Africa	10.53	11.67	12.45	3.27	3.03	3.01

Source: Maddison (1995), tables G.1 (population) and G.2 (income) for regional data. Population data for 1995 extrapolated from the 1989–1992 population data.

Note: Population shares and income shares are used as weights in the calculation of income inequality for the world's average nation, based on the regional within-nation Theil and MLD index values reported in Table 9.2.

the increase in within-nation inequality was somewhat greater if we weight by population (emphasizing Asia more) as opposed to income (emphasizing the West more). To show that these results do not depend on the suspect data for Africa, Table 9.3 also reports results for the sample without Africa (*n* = 47 nations, constituting about 77 percent of the world's population). Because Africa's population share is four times greater than Africa's income share (about 12 percent versus about 3 percent), the removal of Africa affects the MLD more than it affects the Theil. The critical point here, however, regards change in the Theil and the MLD. With regard to change in the inequality measures, we observe rising within-nation income inequality for the world as a whole whether or not we include African nations in our set of observations. Goesling's (2001) results paint the same picture of growing income inequality within nations, but his estimates indicate much more rapid growth. However, because Goesling does not follow the same nations over time, some of the growth he observes could be due to a higher proportion of high-inequality nations in his 1995 sample.

In short, the best available quantitative evidence indicates that income inequality has been rising in the average nation in recent years. What remains to be seen is whether this growth in inequality within nations is large enough to produce growth in the overall level of income inequality of the world. For global inequality to rise, the growth in income inequality within nations must be sufficiently rapid to offset the decline in income inequality across nations. In other words, the popular belief that global income inequality is growing can be correct only if the late-twentieth-century reversal of the within-nation trend has been sufficiently sharp to offset the late-twentieth-century reversal of the between-nation trend. That issue is addressed in Chapter 11.

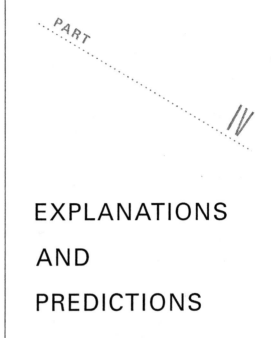

PART

IV

EXPLANATIONS

AND

PREDICTIONS

Causes of the Inequality Transition

THE INEQUALITY transition is the transition of global income inequality from within-nation to between-nation back to within-nation income inequality. This book argues that the last decades of the twentieth century mark the end of the within- to between-nation phase and the beginning of the between- to within-nation phase. Because the transition from phase 1 to phase 2 has become apparent only recently, there is no organized theoretical literature on the global inequality transition. There are, however, numerous explanations for between-nation inequality itself—why some nations are so rich and others are so poor. This is the place I begin. Sociologists sometimes refer to these explanations as theories of world (or global) stratification. The literature is so vast that I cannot hope to describe all theories, or even a few theories in much detail. Instead I group theories on the basis of their core arguments, greatly distilled.

Theories of World Stratification

A 1996 article in *The Economist* entitled "Economic Growth: The Poor and the Rich" begins by observing that "researchers have moved closer to answering the most important question in economics: why are some countries richer than others?" (p. 23). From the widely divergent explanations that continue to attract followers, however, it appears that the question of why some countries are richer than others is as contentious as ever. This section reviews some of the major answers that have been proposed and assesses the relevance of these explanations for the inequality transition.

DEPENDENCY THEORY

A possible explanation for why some nations or regions grow while others stagnate is that growth and stagnation are part of a common process that produces winners and losers. The view of development as an inherently uneven process that creates national winners and losers goes back at least to V. I. Lenin's theory of exploitation (Lenin 1939). Recent research in the new economic geography literature points to possible asymmetries in development that result in the clustering of economic activity in some parts of a region and stagnation in other parts of the region (Fujita, Krugman, and Venables 1999). But these refer for the most part to uneven development within locales; as Melchior, Telle, and Wiig (2000, p. 6) observe, there is no empirical research showing that, for example, "growth in Asia and stagnation in Africa are two sides of the same coin."

The notion that growth and stagnation for major world regions are in fact two sides of the same coin is most closely associated with dependency theory. Although there is much less interest in world system/dependency theory now than in the 1970s and 1980s, this theory serves to illustrate divergence arguments in sociology and political science, where the theory once attracted much attention (for example, Wallerstein 1974; Chase-Dunn 1975; see the appendix to this chapter for a summary of the theory). If development is in effect a zero-sum game—so growth in some major regions comes at the expense of other regions—then one expects to find global income divergence. And that is precisely what dependency theories predict—"all [dependency theories] would agree that world income inequality becomes more pronounced over time" (Korzeniewicz and Moran 1997, p. 1004). Globalization in particular provides a critical test of the theory. If rich nations benefit more from international exchange, and this exchange is the primary source of global income inequality (as dependency theory argues), then as economic exchange between rich and poor nations continues to grow we expect global income inequality to continue to grow as well. Hence the failure of weighted between-nation income inequality to grow in recent decades calls into question central tenets of the theory. Lest one argue that the theory concerns unweighted, not weighted, between-nation inequality, note that under that argument the theory would not apply to global income inequality. On the other hand, if dependency theory is referring to weighted between-nation income inequality, as Korzeniewicz and Moran (1997) insist, then recent inequality trends are inconsistent with the theory. In any case, dependency theory does not appear to be a promising point of departure for explaining the inequality transition.

CONVERGENCE THEORY IN ECONOMICS

In economics the issue of whether national economies tend to converge or diverge over time has been a central focus since the appearance of influential work on growth theory in the 1980s. Two important economic theories appear to offer different answers to the convergence question. Neoclassical growth theory (Solow 1956) expects national economies to converge because of the principle of diminishing returns to capital and labor, while the newer endogenous growth theory (Romer 1986; Lucas 1988; for summaries, see Grossman and Helpman 1994; Romer 1994; Solow 1994; Temple 1999) posits that the principle of diminishing returns can be overcome. In the view of neoclassical growth theory (Solow 1956), as rich industrial nations begin to experience diminishing returns, poorer nations (who are farther from the point of diminishing returns) will tend to catch up economically. De Long (1988, p. 1138) puts it this way:

> Economists have always expected the "convergence" of national productivity levels. The theoretical logic behind this belief is powerful. The per capita income edge of the West is based on its application of the storehouse of industrial and administrative technology of the Industrial Revolution. . . . The benefits of tapping this storehouse are great, and so nations will strain every nerve to assimilate modern technology and their incomes will converge to those of industrial nations.

The modern economic debate over convergence assumes that convergence will occur because of income growth in poorer nations, not because of declining income in richer nations. In the eighteenth-century convergence debate between David Hume and Josiah Tucker, however, Hume argued that convergence would result because at some point scientific and thus economic progress would grind to a halt and then retrogress in more advanced nations (Elmslie 1995). Hume held that the eventual decline of the sciences was inevitable in every nation, that "the arts and sciences, like some plants, require a fresh soil; and however rich the land may be, and however you may recruit it by art or care, it will never, when once exhausted, produce any thing that is perfect or finished in the kind" (Hume 1985 [1777], p. 137). Tucker (1974 [1776], p. 31), by contrast, believed that rich nations could maintain their advantage over poor nations indefinitely, through continuing scientific progress:

No Man can pretend to set Bounds to the Progress that may yet be made both in Agriculture and Manufactures; for who can take upon him to affirm, that our Children cannot as far exceed us as we have exceeded our Gothic Forefathers? And is it not much more natural and reasonable to suppose, that we are rather at the Beginning only, and just got within the Threshold, than that we have arrived at the *ne plus ultra* of useful Discoveries?

Endogenous growth theory represents the present-day form of the argument that it is "much more natural and reasonable" to suppose that we are "at the Beginning only" of useful discoveries. Reminiscent of Tucker's argument in the eighteenth century, endogenous growth theory argues that rich nations can maintain their economic momentum indefinitely since in today's world the principle of diminishing returns can be overcome by specialized inputs made possible by research. As Romer (1994, p. 3) explains, the literature on endogenous growth "distinguishes itself from neoclassical growth by emphasizing that economic growth is an endogenous outcome of an economic system, not the result of forces that impinge from outside." Specifically, technological innovation itself is seen as the result of endogenous processes that can be modeled. Because "technological advance comes from things that people do" (Romer 1994, p. 12) it is not necessary to treat technological change as exogenous, as in the neoclassical model.

Endogenous growth theory has created excitement because it raises the possibility that income growth can be sustained over the long run, even in the face of dwindling natural resources. In that sense endogenous growth theory is a twentieth-century antithesis to eighteenth-century Malthusian theory (as well as Hume's thesis). The optimism of endogenous growth theory is strikingly apparent in Robert Lucas's "Some Macroeconomics for the Twenty-first Century," where Lucas presents a model predicting that "sooner or later everyone will join the industrial revolution . . . [and] all economies will grow at the rate common to the wealthiest economies" (Lucas 2000, p. 166). Not all endogenous growth theorists paint such a rosy picture, of course, but the theory does suggest that continuous technological innovations will lead to continued income growth. Even the richest nations need not worry as yet about an income ceiling. This message is in sharp contrast to the message of the limits-to-growth literature that was popular in the 1970s (for example, Forrester 1973; Ophuls 1977).

The booming empirical literature that followed the recent resurgence of growth theories in economics owes much to Robert Barro's (1991) distinction between conditional and unconditional convergence. Here the term *conditional* refers to the presence of control variables and *unconditional* refers to the absence of control variables. Barro (1991) and Gregory Mankiw, David Romer, and David Weil (1992) have found that incomes do tend to grow faster in poorer nations than in richer ones (as neoclassical theory predicts) *if* one holds constant such factors as a nation's fertility rates, level of human capital (education), and government spending as a share of GDP—conditional convergence. Of course, in the real world such factors are not constant across nations, and if we do not control for them we find that *in unweighted analysis* richer nations tend to grow faster than poorer nations do—unconditional divergence (see Bernard and Durlauf 1995, 1996; Quah 1996; and Jones 1997 for evidence bearing on the convergence issue).

In general the empirical economics literature on convergence is not as directly relevant to global income inequality and the inequality transition as one might think. Economic studies of convergence very often are unweighted. The apparent rationale is that each national economy is a realization of some underlying process that we are trying to apprehend. Hence a nation is a nation is a nation, and we weight them equally. However, for someone interested in global income inequality, one can read the results of unweighted analyses and still have no idea whether global inequality is increasing or declining. Because many small, poor nations are not doing very well economically, convergence studies in economics find that there is unconditional divergence when countries are not weighted by population size, and the results in this book agree (see Figure 7.2). But these results do not apply to global income inequality. With regard to the inequality transition, then, much of the empirical literature on convergence misses the mark. Worse, findings about unconditional divergence can be misleading. The danger is that the uninitiated will infer rising global inequality from findings of unweighted divergence, and the literature does not warn sufficiently against that error. The convergence literature in economics is careful to distinguish conditional from unconditional convergence, but typically glosses over the much more critical (for global income inequality) distinction between weighted and unweighted convergence.

THE ROLE OF POPULATION GROWTH

Classical economists linked economic growth to population growth. Indeed, according to Robert Dorfman (1991, p. 577), classical economists such as Malthus (1798), John Stuart Mill (1848), Ricardo (1817) and Smith (1776) tended to view economic growth as a "race between increases in population and the capital stock." If economic growth is a race between increases in population and capital stock, then at this point in history most poor nations—with their more rapid rates of population growth—are inherently disadvantaged.

There are three essential demographic facts about the late twentieth century that bear on the trend in global income inequality. First, the world's population grew rapidly, yet per capita income continued to rise for the world as a whole. Second, the increase in world population was uneven, with populations growing much faster in poor nations than in rich nations. Third, other things equal, per capita incomes tended to grow more slowly in nations where rapid population growth resulted in a swelling of the population share at the younger ages (that is, an increase in the ratio of children to adults). From the first fact we infer that rapid population growth does not necessarily prevent growth in per capita income, and from the third fact we infer that rapid population growth can nonetheless slow the rate of growth in per capita income through its effect on the age structure of the population (Crenshaw, Ameen, and Christenson 1997; Williamson 1998). Because populations grew faster in poor nations (fact 2), the increasing ratio of children to adults in poor nations served to reduce the rate of growth in income per capita in poor nations relative to the rate in rich nations, boosting between-nation income inequality. In short, were it not for the rising children/adult ratios in most poor nations, between-nation income inequality would have declined faster than it did. This line of reasoning suggests that many poor nations will enjoy a demographic windfall in coming decades as their fertility rates decline and the bulge at the bottom of the population pyramid works its way to the middle of the pyramid. I return to this theme in Chapter 11, where I examine the role of the demographic windfall in determining how global income inequality will change in the twenty-first century.

TECHNOLOGY AND GLOBAL INEQUALITY

The most important cause of the inequality transition is the spread of industrialization to poor nations. The effect of spreading industrialization depends on which regions are industrializing. Because industrialization took root first in richer nations, the spread of industrialization historically has boosted inequality across nations, as noted in Chapter 2. Now, however, the diffusion of industrialization works to compress inequality across nations. These arguments are examined in greater detail later in the chapter.

This spreading-industrialization explanation of the inequality transition assigns a leading role to technology and the diffusion of technology. It is not technology per se that affects global inequality, but how that technology is diffused. When rich regions benefit more from a new technology, inequality grows across regions. When poor nations benefit more, inequality declines across regions. In short, there are cycles of rising and falling global inequality tied to major technological revolutions. The cycles may span centuries, as in the case of world industrialization. While most attention recently has focused on the rising part of the cycle, some earlier scholars focused on the falling-inequality part. Thorstein Veblen (1915), for example, argued that latecomers hold the advantage in development, since they can learn from the mistakes of the early developers, and Alexander Gershenkron (1952) likewise argued for the "advantage of relative backwardness." These notions of how the diffusion of technology affects inequality are key to the spreading-industrialization explanation of why the trend in between-nation income inequality reversed in the late twentieth century. Over the nineteenth century and the first part of the twentieth century richer nations benefited disproportionately from the diffusion of industrialization. More recently, as industrial technology has diffused to poorer regions of the world, East Asia in particular, poorer nations have benefited disproportionately from the diffusion of industrialization, resulting in a reversal of the trend in income inequality across nations.

Although the spreading-industrialization story told here is neither new nor profound, it fits the facts well, as will become clearer below. Some might be dissatisfied with the explanation, since it takes technological change as exogenous. There is no attempt here to explain industrialization itself—why it arose where it did and when it did. Because technological revolutions are difficult to predict, most theories of world stratification do not try, and it is left to historians and anthropologists to explain the technological march of human history. Thus it is left largely to anthropologists to explain the shift from hunting and gathering societies to agrarian societies and to historians to explain the shift from agrarian societies to industrial societies. Even during and after the fact, however, the issues involved are vexing, as witness the debate among historians over why the Industrial Revolution began in England (for example, Landes 1998, chaps. 14–15; Pomeranz 2000) and, more recently, the debate over whether we are in fact in the midst of a monumental technological shift (for example, Reich 1991; Castells 1998; contrast Gordon 2000). So economists and sociologists most often solve the problem of indeterminate technological revolution by taking technological epochs as contexts, and conditioning theories of world stratification accordingly. Max Weber's claim about the importance of state bureaucracies in industrial capitalist societies is one such example; the geographical argument that new technologies tend to diffuse east and west, along latitudes, is another. With some exceptions (endogenous growth theory, for example), world stratification theories treat technological development as exogenous, as we do here. Whatever the causes of the Industrial Revolution, we know what its consequences are: first, higher incomes, and second, an inequality transition from within-nation to between-nation income inequality (as richer regions industrialized) back to within-nation income inequality (as poorer nations industrialize).

APPROACHES EMPHASIZING THE ROLE OF GEOGRAPHY

Why is the distribution of economic activity so radically uneven across space? Part of the answer, of course, relates to physical features of the land, since oceans, polar regions, mountainous regions, and deserts are less hospitable for human habitation than are other areas of the world's surface. Yet until recently geography has played little or no role in most social science accounts of world stratification. Few mainstream theories of economic growth mention spatial location or climate, and fewer still attempt to model the effects of location or climate. Most approaches simply bracket geography out of the model. As Masahisa Fujita, Paul Krugman, and Anthony Venables (1999, p. 2) observe, "Even now, introductory textbooks seem to describe a curiously disembodied economy, without cities or regions." Although Fujita, Krugman, and Venables are referring specifically to economic theory, their point applies equally to theories of world stratification in general, whether in economics, sociology, political science, or history.

In recent years, however, economics has taken a "geographical turn" (Martin 1999). Two economics literatures have arisen that attempt to insert geography more squarely into accounts of world stratification and inequality. Both literatures are classified as geographic approaches, because spatial location figures prominently in both. One literature is a "new economic geography" literature that arose in the 1990s (Krugman 1991, 1998). This literature emphasizes geography-as-distance, which distinguishes the new economic geography from another literature that also stresses geographic location but emphasizes the physical features or endowments of location—climate, topography, the presence of ports, and so on—to explain why economic activity is so unevenly distributed across space. The approach that emphasizes natural endowments could be called the real estate theory of economic development, because it is based on the premise that income differences from continent to continent "stem ultimately from differences in real estate" (Diamond 1999, p. 401). Here, however, I use the term "new physical geography" to highlight the parallel between the genre of work that emphasizes natural endowments with the genre of work known as the new economic geography. The term *new physical* geography describes new scholarship on the effect of natural endowments on economic development that is distinct from the new economic geography, where the term "new economic geography" refers to the work of Paul Krugman and others who use equilibrium methods to model the effects of spatial concentration. Note that in the terminology used here the term "new economic geography" does not include all contemporary work in economics linking economics and geography, since economists have contributed to the new physical geography as well as to the new economic geography.

The new economic geography. New economic geography theory is not immediately recognizable as a theory of world stratification, because it does not begin with the convergence issue. Regional agglomeration is the starting point for the new economic geography, and the theory's implications for world stratification are apparent only when the theory is extended geographically to include large regional groups of nations. The agglomeration issue turns on the relative strengths of centripetal and centrifugal forces in economic production: when will agglomerative (centripetal) forces prevail over dispersal (centrifugal) forces? Consider manufacturing across countries, for example. When will manufacturing agglomerate in a nation or subset of nations, forming what new economic geographers call a "core-periphery" pattern? In the past economists have largely avoided such spatial questions as intractable, as Fujita, Krugman, and Venables (1999) note. However, a new genre of research in the last decade has added a spatial component to economic models of growth, resulting in a line of work that (according to its proponents) is "one of the most exciting areas of contemporary economics" (Fujita, Krugman, and Venables 1999, p. xi). Theorists working in this new field attempt to gain leverage on the agglomeration issue through the use of equilibrium models that are not widely known outside of economics (for summaries, see Fujita, Krugman, and Venables 1999; Neary 2001). This specialized knowledge notwithstanding, the central notion of the new economic geography is straightforward: Geography matters because distance matters. As Venables (1999, p. 239) explains:

> Conceptually, there are two very different reasons why geography might be important. One is that some regions may have an absolute disadvantage in their endowments—lack of natural resources, bad climate, poor land quality, low agricultural productivity, propensity to disease, and so on. The other is that a region may be located far from core economic centers. This distance penalty may affect the relative prices of different goods, the relative profitability of different activities, and perhaps the flow of new ideas and technologies into the region.

New economic geography theorists are emphatic that their approach is not based on the standard endowment disadvantage argument: "the dramatic spatial unevenness of the real economy . . . is surely the result not of inherent differences among locations but of some set of cumulative processes, necessarily involving some form of increasing returns, whereby geographic concentration can be self-reinforcing" (Fujita, Krugman, and Venables 1999, p. 2). Thus there must be strong agglomerative forces that operate independent of the physical features of the land. These agglomerative forces are found in the increasing returns to spatial concentration that characterize economic activity. In other words, the new economic geography assumes that the uneven spatial distribution of economic activity reflects the effect of a distance penalty (other literatures speak of the "tyranny of space")—distance increases production costs, so proximate economic activity produces more than distant economic activity for the same level of inputs. Hence the objective of the new economic geography is to model the "sources of increasing returns to spatial concentration" (ibid., p. 4).

Although the new economic geography was not designed to explain the inequality transition described in this book, its central notion—that geography matters because distance matters—is an insight that might help account for change in inequality. If geography matters because distance matters, then technology that changes the cost of distance can change the distribution of income across nations. A later section of this chapter explains that we expect such a change as emerging telecommunication technologies reduce the effect of labor immobility across national boundaries. Viewed another way, technological change might be reducing the returns to spatial concentration, especially in richer regions of the world where economic activity is increasingly "weightless" (Quah 1997). This line of reasoning suggests the relevance of the new economic geography to the inequality transition, as future work employing the tools of the new economic geography may shed light on the effects of changing returns to spatial concentration on the distribution of income across and within nations.

The new physical geography. In his best-selling book *Guns, Germs, and Steel,* the evolutionary biologist Jared Diamond argues that natural resources advantage some continents and disadvantage others. Diamond (1999, p. 405) writes that "the striking differences between the long-term histories of peoples of the different continents have been due not to innate differences in the people themselves but to differences in their environments."[1] That quotation nicely summarizes the new physical geography. In new physical geography (or real estate) theory, geographic location matters because natural endowments vary across location. Here the term "natural endowments" is used in a broad sense to include average temperature and temperature variability, annual rainfall, mineral resources, soil quality, the presence of navigable rivers, the presence of seaports, and so on. If natural endowments were uniformly distributed across the globe, then geography would not matter. This hypothetical situation reveals a key difference between the new physical geography and the new economic geography. In the new economic geography, physical distance itself is a key factor. In the new physical geography, by contrast, it is not distance or space per se that matters but rather the association of space with other physical features that matter, such as climate and topography.

The notion that variability in natural endowments across regions accounts for much of the variability in wealth across regions is not a new idea. More than two centuries ago Adam Smith pointed out the impediment to economic development caused by isolation stemming from disadvantageous natural endowments. He foresaw this problem as especially acute for the continent of Africa:

> There are in Africa none of those great inlets, such as the Baltic and Adriatic seas in Europe, the Mediterranean and Euxine [Black] seas in both Europe and Asia, and the gulphs of Arabia, Persia, India, Bengal, and Siam, in Asia, to carry maritime commerce into the interior parts of that great continent: and the great rivers of Africa are too great a distance from one another to give occasion to any considerable inland navigation. (1776, chap. 3, last para.)

Social scientists hardly need to be convinced that some regions enjoy geographic advantages over others, given the strength of the association between geography and development. The association between geography and development is evident in the world of the early nineteenth century as well as in today's world, as shown by the "moneybags" maps in Chapter 1. It is not surprising, then, that the role of physical geography on income growth has reemerged as an important theme in the economics literature on economic growth and development. The vexing issue for economists and other social scientists is threefold: why does geography matter, how much does geography matter, and how can physical geography—a near constant—account for *change* in inequality? What is new about the new physical geography is that it represents a renewed attempt to theorize about the effects of geography, beginning with attempts to identify the mechanisms that link geography to economic growth. For example, in "Geography, Demography, and Economic Growth in Africa," David Bloom and Jeffrey Sachs (1998, p. 211) attempt to identify geographic factors that account for the lagging economic performance of sub-Saharan Africa:

> At the root of Africa's poverty lies its extraordinarily disadvantageous geography.... Sub-Saharan Africa is by far the most tropical—in the simple sense of the highest proportions of land and population in the tropics—of the world's

major regions, and tropical regions in general lag far behind temperate regions in economic development. Moreover, in several dimensions its environment is without parallel in raising obstacles to growth. As consequences of its
climate, soils, topography, and disease ecology, Africa suffers from chroni-
cally low agricultural productivity (especially food production), high disease
burdens, and very low levels of international trade.

Bloom and Sachs present results from cross-national growth regressions
showing that geographic variables (percentage of nation's land area in the
tropics, density of the population close to the coast, and density of the
population in the interior) affect national growth rates net of the effects of
standard economic determinants. In "Geography and Economic Development," John Gallup, Sachs, and Andrew Mellinger (1999) note that rich
countries are concentrated in the temperate zones of the world, that poor
nations are concentrated in the tropics, and that landlocked countries generally have lower incomes than coastal countries. Lest there be any doubt
that climate is a significant factor in economic development, Robert Hall
and Charles Jones (1997) show that per capita income is strongly positively associated with a nation's distance from the equator, and Gallup,
Fernanda Llusa, and Sachs (1998) note that, for nations such as Brazil that
straddle the tropical and temperate zones, incomes are significantly higher
in the temperate regions.

Although findings like these are interesting, an emphasis on differences
in natural endowments per se does not give us leverage in explaining the
inequality transition, since natural endowments do not change very rapidly. More promising is the insight that technological change can change
the value of natural endowments, as we now see.

The changing geography-technology nexus. The unevenness in the physical features of the world's surface might account for much of the unevenness of human settlement and economic activity at a given point in time,
but it is harder to see how physical geography by itself can account for
substantial change in economic activity over time. How can the world's
surface features—which are relatively constant—account for change in the
pattern of global inequality over time? The answer lies in the changing geography-technology nexus. Although the physical features associated with
geography are fairly constant, the importance of those features can change
dramatically with technological change. Oil, for example, was not a significant natural resource until the widespread use of the internal combus-
tion engine fueled by gasoline. In this instance technological change radically altered the value of real estate in some regions of the world. The point
is that technological change can alter the relative values of natural re-

sources and, since natural resources are not uniformly distributed over the globe, the result is change in the pattern of global inequality:

changing technology → changing value of natural resources that vary geographically → changing global income inequality

In addition, technological change can alter the habitability of the world's regions. The widespread availability of air conditioning in the southern part of the United States, for example, makes the South a more pleasant place to live in the summer, and accounts in part for the nation's southward migration patterns in recent decades. In a similar way the control of mosquitoes in some other parts of the world has increased the habitability of those regions by reducing the incidence of malaria. If it is true that people produce more when they are healthy and when they are not too hot, then mosquito-controlling and air-conditioning technologies could work to alter global income inequality by altering the relative habitability of the world's regions:

changing technology → changing relative habitability of the world's regions → changing productivity by region → changing global income inequality

Hence technological change can affect the global distribution of income by altering or mitigating the effects of natural resources and physical features that vary geographically. This general principle adds a dynamic element to geographic theories of world stratification. According to physical geography theory, the global distribution of income is unequal largely because of regional variability in natural endowments (broadly defined). In other words, (1) natural endowments matter, (2) these endowments vary geographically, hence (3) geography matters. What we add here is an emphasis on the fact that technology conditions the effect of natural endowments. Natural endowments have different effects on economic activity under different technological regimes. In sum, variability in unchanging natural endowments across geographic location can result in a changing global distribution of income as technologies change.

APPROACHES EMPHASIZING THE ROLE OF CULTURE

Some scholars assign a central role to culture in economic development. In *The Wealth and Poverty of Nations*, for example, the historian David Landes (1998, p. 516) claims, "If we learn anything from the history of economic development, it is that culture makes all the difference." The most celebrated of the scholarly accounts of culture's effect on economic performance is Max Weber's (1904–1905) *The Protestant Ethic and the Spirit of Capitalism.* Weber argues that Protestantism was instrumental in launching capitalism in the West. The Protestant belief in working hard, saving, and avoiding conspicuous consumption squared well with the need for capital accumulation in a capitalist system. The Calvinists in particular embodied these beliefs. Calvinists believed that, although salvation is by faith and not by good works, the prosperity that resulted from hard work was evidence of one's salvation. Thus Calvinists had powerful incentives to work hard and prosper—not as a means of earning God's favor but as a means of showing that they had it. Work, in the Protestant view of this period, is not merely a means to earn a living but reflects God's *calling,* as we see in this excerpt from an American Quaker writing during the colonial period:

> We not only have Liberty to labour in Moderation, but . . . it is our duty to do so. The Farmer, the Tradesman, and the Merchant, do not understand by our Lord's Doctrine, that they must neglect their Calling, or grow idle in their Business, but must certainly work, and be industrious in their Callings. (Tolles 1948, p. 56, cited in Sica 2002, p. 501)

Although other examples of cultural explanations can be found among scholars, it is among the general public that cultural explanations have taken root most deeply. The cultural explanations favored by the public are far less subtle than Weber's Protestant ethic thesis. Ask people why it is that some nations are so rich and others are so poor, and you might very well hear in a rough form one of two types of cultural explanations. In the West you might hear a rightist account, that winners are winners in the global economy because of superior cultural customs (for example, people in richer nations work harder, are more willing to take risks, are more time conscious). In poorer regions of the world you might hear a leftist account that assigns moral superiority to the losers: nations that lag in the global economy do so because of laudable cultural values that put less emphasis (than we do in the West) on the accumulation of material goods. Lagging, then, results from the antimaterialistic (or at least less thoroughly materialistic) values of peoples who choose to compete less vigorously in the accumulation game. Or, in a somewhat different version of the leftist story, all are forced to compete, and in this clash of cultures the cultures based on collectivism and altruism are victimized by the cultures based on individualism and greed.

There are serious problems with both types of cultural explanations.

Rightist accounts confuse consequences with causes. To be sure, cultures do vary, but the differences that are often presumed to matter are consequences rather than causes of economic development. Nomadic herdsmen are less conscious of the hour and minute because they have less reason to be conscious of such matters. Move these herdsmen into a business occupation in the West and they will wear watches. Much of what is viewed in the West as irrational or outmoded cultural custom is in fact rational behavior given the economic circumstances of the masses in low-income nations.[2] I do not mean to suggest that cultural customs do not matter at all, since some cultural customs might reinforce poverty as part of a vicious circle of poverty → disadvantageous customs → poverty. But I do mean to suggest that most social scientists are skeptical of views that assign much weight to cultural customs in accounting for world stratification. (Deep-seated cultural differences—such as religious differences—are a different matter, as seen in Weber's theory.)

While popular rightist accounts of world stratification err in giving causal primacy to superficial cultural differences that are probably endogenous to development, popular leftist accounts err in giving causal primacy to a mythological cultural difference—the myth of a great cultural divide in the world that separates the materialistic culture of the West from the nonmaterialistic culture of other regions of the world. This myth persists despite clear evidence that the masses in low-income nations in fact are not content in their poverty, but have the same desire for improvement in their material conditions as do their counterparts in richer nations. Hadley Cantril's (1965) study of happiness in twelve communist and capitalist countries is the classic study in this regard. People were asked to describe in their own words the "best of all possible worlds." The results were amazingly similar for rich and poor countries, and for communist and capitalist countries. Most often respondents wanted somewhat more than they had—improvement in their material conditions. Here is a typical response from India (quoted in Easterlin 1996, p. 141): "I would like to construct a house of my own and have a cow for milk and ghee. I would also like to buy some better clothing for my wife. If I could do this then I would be happy." Compare this with a typical response from the United States: "I would like a reasonable enough income to maintain a house, have a new car, have a boat, and send my four children to private schools" (Easterlin 1996, p. 142). As Richard Easterlin (1996, p. 133) puts it, "clearly the general nature of the dominant factors affecting happiness is quite similar among countries, even countries differing widely in cultural, political, and socioeconomic conditions." There is no evidence here that the materialistic impulse is any less strong in low-income nations than it is in the West.

There are other problems with cultural theories of global inequality. One is that the income for migrants from poor nations—who presumably carry the culture of their homeland with them as they migrate—tends to jump dramatically after they migrate to rich nations, despite the usual language barriers and other handicaps migrants face (as Olson [1996] notes, the jump in income is much greater than can be accounted for by selection effects). Another problem is that a body of literature argues that Western culture is becoming postmaterialist, with a greater emphasis now on self-expression as opposed to survival values, and on secular-rational values as opposed to traditional values (Inglehart and Baker 2000). The thesis that Western culture is becoming more self-expressive and more secular has no obvious parallel in income inequality patterns in the West. Increasing self-expression and rising secularization do not explain why income inequality has risen in many Western nations, nor do postmaterialist values explain why incomes continue to rise in the West. In any case, even if cultural differences were an important source of global inequality, mass culture changes slowly, so cultural change is not a promising place to look for explanations for the change in global inequality that we are seeing during the inequality transition.[3]

APPROACHES EMPHASIZING THE ROLE OF INSTITUTIONS
AND INSTITUTIONAL CULTURE

Although cultural theories of the type just described hold little promise for explaining why some nations are so rich and other nations are so poor, *institutional* culture does matter. Many social scientists believe that differences in institutions and state policies play a major role in producing the disparity in per capita incomes across nations. "Growth depends on governance," as Peter Evans and James Rauch (1999, p. 748) put it. Moreover—and this is important here, since we are trying to explain *change* in global income inequality—institutional cultures change, sometimes fairly rapidly. One of the clearest examples of an institutional-culture theory of national development is sociology's world polity theory (Meyer 1980; Thomas et al. 1987; Meyer et al. 1997). World polity theory argues that development trends during the twentieth century are best explained by the spread of a global culture that encourages countries worldwide to adopt strikingly similar strategies (for example, expanding systems of mass education) to achieve similarly defined development goals—including, primarily, national economic growth, as measured by income per capita. Global culture as defined by world polity theorists is rooted in Western society, especially in its notions of progress, justice, individualism, and rationality. World polity theorists argue that their conception of global culture helps explain both the industrialization of low-income nations in the world's periphery during the second half of the twentieth century and the recent expansion of the service sectors in rich and poor nations alike—two trends that, they aver, are not well explained by other development theories (Meyer 1980).

A spreading global culture of the sort described by world polity theory is relevant to global income inequality only if, first, global culture in fact is causing convergence of institutions and, second, institutions matter. The convergence of national institutions is one of the causes of the inequality transition, as argued below. That subsequent discussion provides evidence on institutional convergence and why it matters.

Causes of the Inequality Transition: Overview

The transition from phase 1 to phase 2 of the inequality transition began during a period when average income rose significantly for the world as a whole and in all the world's major regions except sub-Saharan Africa, when world trade increased, when industrialization deepened and literacy rates increased in most poor nations, when the share of the world GDP contributed by the service sector continued to grow and the share contributed by agriculture continued to shrink, when the Internet was developed, when computers became more powerful and less expensive, when communism collapsed and the cold war ended, when the economic hegemony of the United States was challenged by economic advances in Europe and in Asia, when the world continued to urbanize, and when the world's population continued to grow and the percentage of that population living in poor regions increased because of faster population growth there. What, then, is causing the inequality transition? Why did income inequality grow within nations after a long period of decline, and decline across nations after a long period of growth?

I believe there are six causes. One cause is a demographic windfall reaped by a few poor nations in the late twentieth century (Crenshaw, Ameen, and Christenson, 1997). However, much of the demographic windfall for poor nations remains to be inherited in the future, so I postpone a discussion of the demographic windfall effect until the next chapter, which examines the future of global income inequality. The collapse of communism is a second cause. The collapse of communism served to exacerbate the growth in within-nation income inequality in the 1990s. Because the collapse of communism is a nonrecurring historical event, its effects are short term, and I discuss those effects only briefly before devoting the remainder of the chapter to discussions of the four long-term causes of the inequality transition: first and most important, the spread of industrialization to poor nations, which reduces inequality across nations and boosts inequality within nations; second, the growth of the service sector, which boosts income inequality within nations; third, the convergence of national economic institutions, which reduces inequality across nations by removing impediments to growth in some poor nations; and fourth, the emergence of space-independent technology, which reduces the dependence of productive activity on physical location and thereby works to reduce income inequality across nations by reducing the effect of labor immobility across national borders. The causes are related, of course. The convergence of national institutions prompts (and is prompted by) the spread of industrialization to poor nations, for example; the industrialization of poor nations is linked to the rising service sector in both poor and rich nations; and service sector jobs are produced by the sort of space-independent technology that reduces the effect of labor immobility.

NONRECURRING CAUSE: THE FALL OF COMMUNISM

The major institutional change that occurred in the late twentieth century was the collapse of communism. Because income inequality rose so sharply in most communist nations in the transition period that followed, the collapse of communism boosted average within-nation income inequality in the 1990s—that much is not controversial. It is important to stress that the collapse of communism does not explain the initial rise in within-nation income inequality, since within-nation inequality began to rise before communism fell. The fall of communism nonetheless exacerbated the rise of within-nation income inequality in the 1990s. Without the fall of communism, global income inequality would have fallen marginally more than it did in the 1990s—unless the fall of communism affected between-nation income inequality differently than it affected within-nation inequality.

The effect of the fall of communism on between-nation income inequality is unclear, however. Most likely the effect was modest, despite the apparent decline in per capita incomes in many ex-communist nations in the 1990s. Although there are varying estimates of the actual income levels in communist nations, most agree that communist nations tended to be in the middle of the income range for nations, with per capita income in some nations, such as the USSR, somewhat above the world mean, and per capita income in other nations, such as Romania, somewhat below the world mean. This suggests that the effects of declining income in postcommunist nations were largely offsetting. In addition, it is not clear that real incomes in ex-communist nations actually fell as much as commonly supposed. Anders Aslund (2001a,b) argues that the highly publicized collapse of incomes in ex-communist nations is a myth. According to Aslund (2001b,

p. 2), most of the observed decline in output in the former Soviet Union and other former communist countries is a statistical aberration caused by exaggerated output figures for the communist period: "Much of what communist economies produced was of little or no value. . . . For East Germany, real output under communism is now assessed at only half of the level previously estimated by West German experts. A similar situation prevailed throughout the region, and the production of goods of no real value has been reduced." If Aslund is correct, then the collapse of communism had little effect on between-nation income inequality. Even if Aslund is wrong, and real incomes fell significantly in former communist nations in the 1990s, the effect of that decline on between-nation income inequality would not be dramatic since, as noted above, estimated per capita incomes in ex-communist nations were above the world mean in some instances and below the world mean in others. It could be the case that the net effect of the fall of communism was to reduce between-nation income inequality somewhat, since ex-communist nations above the world mean tend to be larger than those below the world mean. Perversely, then, some part of the 1990s decline in between-nation income inequality could be due to economic retrogression in the former communist nations.

First Cause of the Inequality Transition: Spreading Industrialization

The most important cause of the inequality transition is the continuing spread of industrialization to the world's poorer regions. Although the importance of industrialization for economic development has long been recognized—in the words of Snow (1963, p. 30), "Industrialization is the only hope of the poor"—the continuing importance of industrialization for vast regions of the world is sometimes lost in the literature on globalization and the coming information age. In the rush to christen new historical eras, it is easy to lose sight of the continuing dominance of established technological regimes. Thus while we in the West are musing about a postindustrial information-based economic regime that presumably is predestined to sweep the world, we must keep in mind that a majority of the world's people still live in regions where farming is the dominant occupation and where industrialization is increasing. The spread of industrialization to low-income regions reduces between-nation income inequality and boosts inequality within nations.

OFF THE FARM

The world passed a significant milestone in the 1980s: if World Bank estimates are reasonably accurate, the 1980s mark the first time in this historical epoch that most of the world's labor force has been engaged primarily

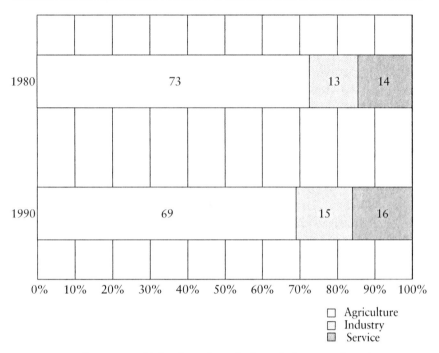

FIGURE 10.1   Percentage of labor force in agriculture, industry, and service sectors in low-income nations, 1980 versus 1990. Data from World Bank 1997, table 4.

in economic pursuits other than the production of food (the percentage of the world's labor force engaged in agriculture declined from 53 percent in 1980 to 49 percent in 1990 [World Bank 1997, table 4]). Why did it take so long for the world to reach this milestone? The answer lies in the fact that in low-income nations most people still work in agriculture. In 1980, for example, 73 percent of the labor force was engaged in agriculture in low-income nations, compared with 9 percent in high-income nations (World Bank 1997, table 4). But the percentage is declining in low-income nations, reflecting in part the deepening industrialization of those nations. In the 1980s the percentage of the labor force engaged in agriculture declined from 73 percent to 69 percent in low-income nations (Figure 10.1). Some workers shifted to industry and others shifted to the service sector.

Figure 10.1 reminds us of a point stressed in Chapter 2, that the preoccupation of the globalization literature with postindustrial technology threatens to distort the perspective of Westerners regarding the contours of the global economy. Until the last decades of the twentieth century, more than half the world's workers were engaged in agriculture as their principal source of income. So in terms of what most people do for a living, the world is barely postagricultural, much less postindustrial. Clearly the world economy *is* postagricultural, however, if we focus on production instead of on workers. Although nearly half the world's workers were engaged in agriculture in 1995, agricultural output contributed only an estimated 5 percent of the world's total output in 1995, down from an estimated 7 percent in 1980 (World Bank 1997, table 12). Even in low-income nations, where two-thirds of the labor force is engaged in agriculture, the agricultural sector contributed only one-fourth of the total output in 1995, down from one-third in 1980 (Figure 10.2 below). So even though the majority of the world's people still live in nonurban areas (World Bank 1997, table 9), and nearly half of the world's workers are engaged in agriculture, agriculture is not the engine of growth in the world economy.

THE CROSS-COUNTRY KUZNETS CURVE

If agriculture is not the engine of growth in the world economy, what is? In recent decades the world's economic growth has been driven primarily by industrialization in low-income nations and by growth in the service sector in high-income nations. As of 1980, the agricultural, industrial, and service sectors each contributed about equally to the aggregate output of low-income nations (Figure 10.2). Over the next fifteen years, the share contributed by the industrial sector grew from 32 percent of the total to 38 percent of the total and the share contributed by the service sector grew from 32 percent to 35 percent. The share contributed by agriculture shrank accordingly, from 34 percent down to 25 percent. So in low-income nations the share of the total product from agriculture declined from 1980 to 1995, the share from the service sector increased, and the share from the industrial sector increased even faster. The jump in the industrial share is key. From 1980 to 1995 the high-income and low-income nations in fact switched places with regard to industrial share of total output, with the industrial share falling from 37 percent to 32 percent in high-income nations (World Bank 1997, table 12) and growing from 32 percent to 38 percent in low-income nations. These figures indicate that by the mid-1990s low-income nations were more industrial than high-income nations in terms of the share of total output attributable to the industrial sector. Of course, per capita industrial productivity is still much greater in high-income nations. But in terms of the share of the output originating in industry, today the industrial sector is more significant for low-income nations than it is for high-income nations.

Because continued industrial growth is now concentrated in low-income nations rather than in high-income nations, we expect industrialization in

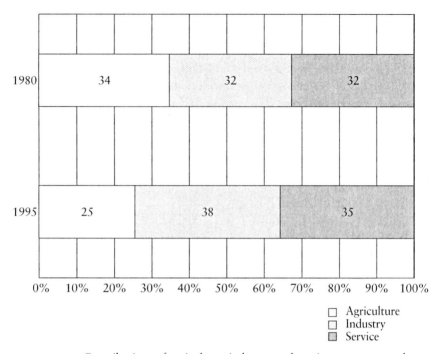

0%   10%   20%   30%   40%   50%   60%   70%   80%   90%   100%

☐ Agriculture
☐ Industry
▨ Service

FIGURE 10.2   Contributions of agriculture, industry, and service sectors to total production in low-income nations, 1980 versus 1995. Data from World Bank 1997, table 12.

today's world to *reduce* income inequality across nations.[4] This reverses the centuries-old effect of the spread of world industrialization (see Figure 2.2). The argument suggests an inverted-U trajectory for income inequality across nations that parallels the Kuznets curve for income inequality within nations. As industrialization took root first in the initially richer nations, the rich became richer and inequality shot up across nations. Now, as industrialization is spreading to poorer nations, poor regions are reaping the benefits of industrial growth, and inequality is declining across nations. In other words, the trajectory of between-nation income inequality over the course of global industrialization is tracing a Kuznets curve, with rising between-nation income inequality as industrialization took root in rich regions of the globe and declining between-nation inequality as industrialization has diffused to poorer regions of the globe in the last half of the twentieth century. If we are in phase 2 of the inequality transition then we are on the downward-sloping part of this cross-country Kuznets curve— a view consistent with the implications of Lucas's (2000, 2002) growth models. As Lucas (2000, p. 166) writes, "I think the restoration of inter-society income inequality [to its pre-Industrial Revolution level] will be one of the major economic events of the century to come."

IMPLICATIONS OF SPREADING WORLD INDUSTRIALIZATION FOR WITHIN-NATION INCOME INEQUALITY

In contrast to its compressing effect on between-nation inequality, the diffusion of industrialization to poor regions has served to increase within-nation income inequality. The industrialization of low-income regions likely boosts within-nation income inequality directly, by raising income inequality in the nations where industrialization is taking place, and perhaps indirectly, by contributing to a reduction in the industrialization of rich nations as indicated both by a declining share of the labor force engaged in industry and by a declining share of total output arising from industry in those nations (Figure 10.3, below). Both the direct and the indirect effects are based on expectations about the effects of labor force shifts from one economic sector to another. We expect the dominant sectoral shifts in both low- and high-income nations—the shift out of agriculture in the case of low-income nations and the shift into the service sector in the case of high-income nations—to boost within-nation income inequality. With regard to low-income nations, the movement of labor from the farm exacerbates income inequality in two ways. First, in line with the within-nation Kuznets curve (Chapter 5), inequality is increased as workers move from the large low-wage farm sector to the smaller higher-wage industrial sector. To be sure, as Bourguignon and Morrisson (1998) note, empirical work indicates that there is no iron law governing the relationship between inequality and development, so we cannot simply assume that income inequality will increase in all countries at early stages of industrialization. Nonetheless there is evidence that income inequality is growing in many large, poor countries, and that industrialization is one of the causes. In rural China, for example, dynamic rural industrialization close to cities is creating a dualistic rural economy and driving up inequality (Peng 1999). On the basis of results like these it is reasonable to assume that increases in income inequality will be more common than declines in income inequality as industrialization takes root in low-income regions. Even if the assumption proves to be wrong, it is unlikely that industrialization will depress inequality in those nations, so at the least income inequality is unlikely to decline as poor nations industrialize. Second, the service sector in poor nations is very diverse, ranging from marginal employment (selling pencils on the street corner) to high-paying positions, so inequality is likely to in-

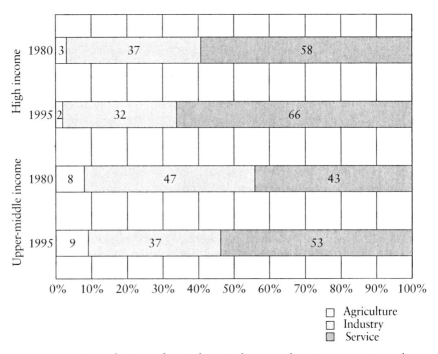

FIGURE 10.3 Contributions of agriculture, industry, and service sectors to total production in high-income and upper-middle income nations, 1980 versus 1995. Data from World Bank 1997, table 12.

crease as that sector grows. The rise of the service sector boosts income inequality in richer nations because of the heterogeneity of the service sector there as well, as we now see.

Second Cause of the Inequality Transition: Rise of the Service Sector

The late twentieth century was characterized by rapid growth of the service sector in high-income and upper-middle-income nations, as shown in Figure 10.3. From 1980 to 1995 the share of the total output contributed by the service sector grew from about 58 percent to about 66 percent in high-income nations and from about 43 percent to about 53 percent in upper-middle-income nations. For both groups of nations this growth in the service share came at the expense of industry, not agriculture (where shares were low initially). By the mid-1990s the contribution of the industrial sector had fallen to 32 percent (from 37 percent in 1980) in high-income nations and to 37 percent (from 47 percent) in upper-middle-income nations—an indication of deindustrialization, if by "deindustrialization" one means a declining share of output originating in the industrial sector.[5] In this sense of deindustrialization, then, it can be said that high-income and upper-middle-income nations deindustrialized as low-income nation industrialized in the late twentieth century.

The figures for labor force composition tell the same story of a shift toward the service sector, with the percentage of the labor force in the service sector increasing from 40 percent to 52 percent in upper-middle-income nations and from 56 percent to 64 percent in high-income nations (World Bank 1997, table 4). What are the implications for global income inequality? The principal implication is rising within-nation inequality in upper-middle-income and high-income nations. Migration into the service sector in those nations is migration into a heterogeneous category that includes any work that is neither agricultural nor industrial. Thus airline pilots, janitors, lawyers, street vendors, engineers, taxi drivers, store owners, maids, dentists, barbers, judges, bank tellers, physicians, nurses, actors, short-order cooks, high-ranking government officials, street sweepers, accountants, seamstresses, and book authors all belong to the service sector. We expect the deindustrialization of richer nations to boost income inequality, then, by moving labor from middle-income manufacturing work to this heterogeneous sector of both low- and high-paying occupations.

Third Cause of the Inequality Transition: Convergence of National Institutions

The United States and Western Europe are similar in many respects—similar cultures, similar market size (total GDP), similar technology, similar climates, similar forms of government, and roughly similar per capita incomes. Yet average income is much more unequal across nations in Western Europe than across states in the United States. That difference is so familiar that we do not think to ask why. But the question is strategic. Why do national borders create inequality contours that are not created by state or provincial borders within a country? There are two major reasons. First, institutional differences are greater across nations in Western Europe than across states in the United States. Or at least that has been the case historically—the European Union is expected to narrow these differences. Second, for a variety of reasons (including language differences), national boundaries form greater barriers to labor movement in Europe than do state boundaries in the United States. The two reasons are interrelated, since institutional differences across nations would not matter so much if labor were more mobile across nations.

These two reasons lead us to the third and fourth causes of the inequality transition. The acids of the international market tend to dissolve national differences in economic policies and institutions, thereby compressing income inequality across nations. That is the point I make in this section. The final section in this chapter examines how emerging technologies of the new global information age—to the extent that such an age has come and is coming—have mitigated and will further mitigate the effect of labor immobility across nations. Hence whether one examines globalization as economic integration or as information age, one concludes that globalization works to shrink global income inequality by reducing income inequality across nations. This conclusion is ironic, given the common perception that globalization is causing a steep rise in global inequality. Recall the Trade Protest Model of Chapter 2,

globalization → global inequality,

and the dependency version of the model,

globalization → more exploitation of poor nations by rich nations → greater global inequality.

The line of reasoning here turns these arguments on their head:

globalization → narrowing of institutional differences across nations → reduction in between-nation inequality → reduction in global inequality *(third cause of inequality transition)*.

And, to jump ahead a bit, the common theme in the globalization literature of a coming information age also turns the Trade Protest Model on its head:

globalization/emerging information age → reduction in the effect of labor immobility across national borders → reduction in between-nation inequality → reduction in global inequality *(fourth cause of inequality transition)*.

DO INSTITUTIONS MATTER?

The third cause of the inequality transition is the convergence of national institutions. The argument is that national institutions matter for economic performance (Olson 1996) and that the institutions that matter are in fact converging because of growing economic integration (Rodrik 2000). It is well established that nations with better institutions—that is, more secure property rights, an effective legal system, and less distortion-ary government policies—will tend to grow faster economically (North 1981; Knack and Keefer 1995; Rodrik 1999; Acemoglu, Johnson, and Robinson 2001). As Daron Acemoglu, Simon Johnson, and James Robin-son (2001, p. 1369) note: "At some level it is obvious that institutions mat-ter. Witness, for example, the divergent paths of North and South Korea, or East and West Germany, where one part of the economy stagnated un-der central planning and collective ownership, while the other prospered with private property and a market economy." Mancur Olson (1996) minces no words in saying that "the most important explanation of the differences in income across countries is the difference in their economic policies and institutions"(p. 7) so the "best thing a society can do to in-crease its prosperity is to wise up" (p. 21).

Two recent studies—one in sociology and one in economics—provide evidence on the importance of national institutions. In "Bureaucracy and Growth," Peter Evans and James Rauch (*American Sociological Review* 1999) use data on core state agencies in thirty-five poor nations to develop a "Weberianness" scale designed to measure how closely the agencies re-semble Max Weber's classic description of the bureaucratic organizational form. Consistent with Weber's (1904–1911) argument that economic growth under capitalism is facilitated by public administrative organiza-tions that hire on the basis of meritocracy and offer predictable, long-term career rewards, Evans and Rauch find that states high on the Weberianness scale tend to grow faster, even after controlling for the effects of initial in-come and human capital. In "The Colonial Origins of Comparative Devel-opment," Acemoglu, Johnson, and Robinson (*American Economic Re-view* 2001) find evidence of large effects of institutions on per capita income. Remarkably, "once the effect of institutions is controlled for, countries in Africa and those closer to the equator do not have lower in-comes" (p. 1369).[6]

ARE NATIONAL ECONOMIC INSTITUTIONS CONVERGING?

If institutions matter, then institutional differences across nations must ac-count for at least some of the income differences across nations, and in-comes should tend to converge across nations as institutions converge. But are institutions converging? One of the planks of world polity theory is that they are—that global culture has caused the convergence of institu-tional goals and forms over the twentieth century. The claim of world pol-ity theory is that "there exists today a level of isomorphism of social struc-tural and organizational forms across world societies that is far too great to be solely explicable in terms of functional necessity or task demands" (Buttel 2000, p. 117). Thus states in Africa and in Europe have "roughly the same roster of ministries (defense, agriculture, finance, etc.), the same tripartite organization of the military (army, navy, air force), and quite similar educational systems (state-organized schooling with strikingly similar curricula)" (ibid.). World polity theorists are on to something, but the root cause is the globalization of markets, not the diffusion of culture. With regard to global income inequality, the institutional isomorphism that matters is the isomorphism that is being forced by the "task demands" of the internationalization of economic markets. Dani Rodrik (2000, p. 180) asks the telling question here: "What would politics look like in a world in which international markets had nothing to fear from the narrower scope of political jurisdictions?" Rodrik argues that the internationalization of markets forces a choice between global federalism, on the one hand, and the maintenance of national sovereignty at the price of severely restricted political choices, on the other. Under the second option—dubbed the "Golden Straightjacket" by Thomas Friedman (1999)—national politics is exercised over an increasingly restricted range (Rodrik 2000, p. 182): "The overarching goal of nation-states in this world would be to appear attractive to international markets. . . . The price of maintaining national jurisdictional sovereignty while markets become international is that politics have to be exercised over a much narrower domain." In short, key economic institutions are converging across nations, but the convergence is dictated primarily by the growing integration of national economies, not by global culture.

Fourth Cause of the Inequality Transition: Technology That Reduces the Effect of Labor Immobility

If the steam mill gave us a capitalist class, as Marx (1976 [1847], p. 166) claimed, what will the computer give us? A common argument of the globalization literature is that there is an emerging postindustrial global economy that is largely space independent. In this view, the geography of production is changing fundamentally. Emerging postindustrial production forms are revolutionary in large part because they reduce space dependence (for example, laptop computers can easily be moved from place to place). By reducing the space dependence of productive activities, emerging technologies promise to move us to an era where (as some see it) a rising share of the world's economic output will be produced in electronic space that knows no national borders. But the effect need not be polarizing, as is commonly portrayed in the "digital divide" literature (for example, Ishaq 2001). Space-independent technology can be an equalizing force, at least with respect to the larger between-nation component of global inequality, since space-independent technology promises to compress inequality across nations by mitigating the effect of labor immobility across national borders, as we shall see.

CHANGING GEOGRAPHIES OF PRODUCTION

With the shift from hunting animals to herding them, and from gathering plants to cultivating them, human settlements became more permanent (Lenski, Nolan, and Lenski 1995, chap. 6). The technological shift from horticulture (farming without plows) to agriculture (use of plows) was especially decisive in tying humans to particular physical locations. Agriculture is a space-dependent but nonagglomerative technology. Industrialization—the shift to the use of machines powered by inanimate energy sources—did little at first to dislodge humans from their close tie to particular localities. Production in industrial societies is also space dependent, albeit for different reasons. In agricultural production, it is the land that does not move; in industrial production it is the manufacturing facility that does not move. Industrial manufacturing generally requires buildings and equipment that are not very portable. In addition, manufacturing plants are often sited near the requisite raw materials and natural resources. Because it is easier to move people than to move production facilities, people go to the work site rather than vice versa. Moreover, in industrial societies the output from one manufacturing operation often is the input for another. To save on transportation costs, manufacturing plants tend to cluster together. Whereas agriculture expands by spreading out over more land—more space—industrial production tends to agglomerate to control transportation costs. Hence industrial production can be characterized as agglomerative space-dependent production, as opposed to the nonagglomerative space dependence of agricultural production.

Is the next step the decoupling of productive activity from space? According to a vast and influential literature, the computer—along with space-compressing telecommunications technology—will give us a post-industrial world in the twenty-first century quite unlike the industrial world of the twentieth. This new world will be characterized by a global economy with information technology as its cornerstone. Importantly, the new information-based global economy will change the rules for income generation, as Robert Reich and Manuel Castells make clear:

> The standard of living of a nation's people increasingly depends on what they contribute to the world economy—on the value of their skills and insights. It depends less and less on what they own. (Reich 1991, p. 154)

> The fundamental source of wealth generation lies in an ability to create new knowledge and apply it to every realm of human activity by means of enhanced technological and organizational procedures of information process-

ing. The informational economy tends to be, in its essence, a global economy; and its structure and logic define, within the emerging world order, a new international division of labor. (Castells 1993, p. 20)

What is especially significant about Castells's version of globalization is that he is careful to link the new global economy to rising inequality. As he puts it (1998, p. 344), "inequality and polarization are prescribed in the dynamics of informational capitalism, and will prevail unless conscious action is taken to countervail these tendencies." The trade protesters in Seattle apparently took those words to heart, and decided that conscious action was necessary to reduce global inequality by targeting its presumed cause, expanding international trade. The key question for us here is whether that action was based on dubious theory. Is rising inequality in fact *prescripted* in an information-based global capitalist economy? What we need to know is how the logic of a new information-based capitalism—a form of capitalism that presumably decouples economic activity from physical space—would change the spatial contours of global income inequality.[7]

At first blush there appears to be merit in Castells's thesis that the shift to a knowledge-based global economy will tend to result in rising between-nation (and hence rising global) inequality, since with regard to technical knowledge, rich nations enjoy a substantial initial advantage over poor nations. Further reflection suggests otherwise, however. A plausible alternative hypothesis, elaborated below, is that between-nation income inequality is compressed in a global economy where income is based on knowledge that moves freely across national boundaries relative to a global economy where income is based on manufacturing, since manufactured goods flow less freely across national boundaries. Indeed, if we are in the midst of a shift to the sort of global information economy described by many writers, then we should expect to see more dramatic change in the nature of global income inequality—its distribution across and within nations—than in the level of global inequality, since space-independent technologies will reduce the importance of national borders.

THE NEW INFORMATION ECONOMY: REVOLUTION OR EVOLUTION?

Not everyone is convinced that the "growing digitization of economic activity" (Sassen 2000, p. 376) will result in the sort of qualitatively different postindustrial economy that some writers describe. Robert Gordon (2000, p. 72), for example, questions whether the invention of the computer matches the achievements of previous breakthroughs such as the "extension of day into night achieved by electric light, the revolution in factory efficiency achieved by the electric motor, the flexibility and freedom achieved by the automobile, the saving of time and shrinking of the globe achieved by the airplane . . . and the enormous improvements in life expectancy, health, and comfort achieved by urban sanitation and indoor plumbing." And with regard to telecommunications technology—the other leg of the presumed new information economy—Gordon (2000, p. 68) notes that "no current development in communications has achieved a change in communication speed comparable to the telegraph, which between 1840 and 1850 reduced elapsed time per word transmitted by a factor of 3000 (from 10 days to 5 minutes for a one-page message between New York and Chicago), and the cost by a factor of 100."

Ultimately the bottlenecks in an information-based economy will be the dual limitations of time and the capacity of the human mind for processing information. David Lyon (1988, p. 42) compares the computer revolution to the Industrial Revolution by stating that "as steam engines extended the power of human muscle, now computers are extending the capacity of human minds." Perhaps so, but there are limits. As Herbert Simon has said, "A wealth of information creates a poverty of attention" (quoted in Gordon 2000, p. 69). The exponential growth in computer speed and memory will not be matched by exponential growth in human capacity to process information.

In any case, it is doubtful that the industrial era is being rapidly superseded by a global economy that is based more on the processing of information than on the processing of raw materials (Quah 1997). Probably an information-based economy is emerging, but the break from the past is unlikely to be as radical as many globalization writers think it will be. Thus Saskia Sassen's (2000, p. 376) contention that a "growing number of economic activities are taking place in electronic space" is probably right, but there is no revolution around the corner. The question is what impact the gradual growth of information-based economic activity in electronic space will have on the differentiation of economic activity in physical space. To make defensible predictions, we must think about how production and trade in knowledge differs from more conventional commodities markets.

KNOWLEDGE MARKETS VERSUS COMMODITIES MARKETS

There are at least four significant differences between the ownership, production, and transfer of knowledge and the ownership, production, and transfer of conventional goods. One difference is the much greater mobility of knowledge, especially in today's world. With the ever-expanding use of computers and advanced telecommunications technology, knowledge can be codified and distributed worldwide virtually instantly. A second difference between knowledge and conventional goods is that knowledge is a nonrival good, that is, it can be given away without being lost. Of course, it can be argued that those with a monopoly on some form of knowledge would be foolish to share it with others, since by sharing knowledge one loses the exclusive rights to any special benefits that knowledge might confer. There is validity to this "exclusive rights" argument in some instances, as witness patent laws designed to assign the benefits of some form of special knowledge exclusively to one party. But exclusive rights to knowledge are generally more problematic than exclusive rights to conventional goods. Knowledge is hard to keep in a bottle.[8]

A third characteristic that distinguishes knowledge from conventional goods is that the notion of property rights is much more problematic in the case of knowledge. Because knowledge tends to be less tangible, property rights are more difficult to delimit and enforce. Productive knowledge may be based on understanding how natural or mathematical processes work, and nature and mathematics are generally considered to be in the public domain (at least at present). So if knowledge is power, as is often alleged, then it is generally the sort of power that is hard to keep to oneself. Finally, because knowledge is a nonrival good that moves freely across national boundaries and is hard to own, the knowledge market is harder for nations to regulate than the market for most commodities.

The implications for the global distribution of income are clear. If knowledge is increasingly a basis for producing income, and knowledge flows freely across borders, and knowledge is difficult to monopolize, then one's income is likely to be increasingly dependent on how much knowledge one obtains and uses as opposed to what one owns. Recall Reich's (1991, p. 154) claim that the "standard of living of a nation's people . . . depends less and less on what they own." If we speculate that by the end of the twenty-first century productive activity will depend as much on the processing of information as on the processing of raw materials, then if information flows relatively unimpeded across national boundaries we should expect much less inequality in income across nations and perhaps more inequality in income within nations. This is the case because we expect the variance in individuals' ability to obtain and benefit from knowledge to be substantially greater within nations than between nations. Currently, of course, inequality is greater between nations than within them, so if we are in fact moving to a true knowledge-based global economy where national differences in knowledge tend to level off over time because of the mobility of knowledge across space, we might expect to see even now some evidence of declining inequality across nations and rising inequality within nations.

We arrive at the same conclusion if we conceptualize the issue more in line with arguments of the new economic geography. In the emerging information-based global economy depicted by many globalization writers, the effect of labor immobility across national borders should decline as productive assets increasingly move to workers (thereby reducing the necessity for workers to move to the productive assets). Hence income inequality should decline across nations, even as it would decline if labor could move freely across national borders. Fujita, Krugman, and Venables (1999, p. 239) ask the right question: "As we move across geographical space, what is special about crossing a national boundary?" Their answer is that national boundaries are important economically because they present a barrier to the movement of labor, and that barrier to labor movement is the key to inequality across nations (recall the example of inequality across states in the United States versus inequality across nations in Western Europe). By restricting labor movement, national boundaries result in differences in wage rates and per capita income that "are far larger between than within countries" (ibid., p. 240). The implication is that greater labor mobility across national borders would reduce income inequality across nations as workers migrated from lower-wage to higher-wage nations. The migration of knowledge across nations would serve the same function in a global information economy by in effect moving productive assets to workers rather than vice versa. In other words, we could calibrate the distribution of labor across nations to the distribution of productive assets across nations either by moving labor or by moving productive assets. In that sense knowledge mobility across national borders in a global information economy mimics labor mobility across nations in today's world. The result would be the same in either case: reduced income inequality across nations.

Appendix A10: World System/Dependency Theory

Some long-standing theoretical traditions in sociology and political science predict economic polarization and growing income inequality. The intellectual roots of today's polarization theory can be found in Marxist theories of imperialism (Lenin 1939), in the Prebisch-Singer theory of deteriorating terms of trade for primary products (Prebisch 1950; Singer 1950), and in the Latin American dependency (for example, Frank 1966) formulations of the 1960s and 1970s. Although these theories posit somewhat different mechanisms for divergence, they all predict a worsening of global income inequality over time (Korzeniewicz and Moran 1997).

The global centrifugal forces posited by sociologists and political scientists are quite different from the forces posited by economists. In the economic version of divergence, rich nations might grow faster than poor nations because of specialized inputs into research that overcome the law of diminishing returns. In sociology and political science the orthodox divergence argument is that rich nations will tend to grow faster because they enrich themselves at the expense of poorer nations. Dependency theory and its close cousin, Immanuel Wallerstein's (1974, 1979) world system theory, are based on such exploitation arguments. The exploitation operates largely through the presence of transnational corporations in poor nations. Although some transnational corporations are headquartered in poor countries (Sklair and Robbins 2002), most are headquartered in rich countries, and profits from the host country often are remitted to corporation headquarters. Although it is not difficult to find instances where transnational corporations have harmed the local economy in poor regions, it is difficult to demonstrate in general that poor countries would be better off without transnational corporations. Dependency theory is no longer fashionable because recent patterns of growth in the world economy are hard to square with the central tenets of the theory and because the theory's signature finding—that dependence on foreign investment retards economic growth—was shown to be artifactual (Firebaugh 1992; see also De Soysa and Oneal 1999). Thus while these theories flourished in the 1970s and 1980s, today they live on largely in a few specialty journals and in summaries in college textbooks.

According to Wallerstein's world system theory, a global division of labor divides the world's nations into identifiable economic strata. Because a division of labor need not be exploitative, there is nothing inherent in the world system perspective that would rule out convergence across nations. What dependency theory adds are arguments for why the strata tend to diverge. Dependency theory rests on the premise that the development of core nations and the underdevelopment of peripheral nations are complementary processes in that core nations enrich themselves at the expense of poor nations. This state of affairs comes about because core nations differentially benefit from core-periphery economic exchange, and classic versions of dependency theory argued that poor peripheral nations are poor not because they are "less developed" but because they are "underdeveloped" by the exploitation of rich core nations (Frank 1966). While the view of global development as a zero-sum game—with gains and losses in equal amounts—is no longer taken seriously in view of the continued growth of global per capita income, the view that rich nations gain *more* from economic exchange remains a key feature of many sociological approaches to world stratification. Indeed in dependency theory the law of differential benefits from exchange (Mandel 1975)—not the law of diminishing returns—is the mainspring for trends in between-nation inequality. The law of differential benefits from exchange implies a "growing gap between core and periphery" in the world economy as a whole (Chase-Dunn 1975, p. 720). "A picture of unequal development emerges in which the core becomes progressively more developed while peripheral development is hindered as a result of its relationship to the core" (Peacock, Hoover and Killian 1988, p. 839). In effect, dependency theory argues that Karl Marx's law of uneven development applies to the world economy as a whole rather than to classes within nations (Chase-Dunn 1975). Thus dependency theory and neoclassical economic theory make opposing predictions about the root stratifying impulses of the global economy. Neoclassical theory predicts an inherent tendency toward convergence whereas dependency theory predicts an inherent tendency toward divergence.

The Future of Global Income Inequality

Assuming no cataclysmic economic collapse or global war, what is the future of global income inequality? The most likely scenario is that the twenty-first century will witness a continuation of the second phase of the inequality transition. The shift from between-nation to within-nation income inequality will continue, because the causes of that shift remain: spreading industrialization, growth of the service sector, convergence of national economic institutions, technological change that reduces the effect of labor immobility across national borders, and a demographic windfall for many poor nations. This chapter focuses on the coming demographic windfall.

Nations as Economies

THE RISE OF NATIONS AS ECONOMIC UNITS

National per capita incomes today are both dramatically larger, on average, and dramatically more unequal than they were in 1776 when Adam Smith published *The Wealth of Nations*. Smith could scarcely have foreseen the profound changes that would occur in nations' incomes over the remaining 224 years in the millennium. Nor could scholars in 1950 very easily have anticipated the income changes that would occur over the second half of the twentieth century. Japan emerged from the rubble of World War II to become an economic superpower. China's economy became one of the fastest growing in the world. Many formerly poor nations on the Pacific rim, such as South Korea, Taiwan, and Indonesia, enjoyed rapid economic growth, while poor nations in other parts of Asia and in Africa languished. Given this irregular and changing pattern of regional and national income gains and losses, it is easy to lose the big picture on changes in the global distribution of income. This study has tried to capture that big picture by studying the broad trends in income inequality across and within nations, beginning in the nineteenth century but focusing primarily on the second half of the twentieth century. Although it would be foolhardy to make predictions about income change for particular nations, from the broad trends across and within nations we can try to discern the most likely course of global income inequality in the twenty-first century.

The focus here on the rising importance of nations as sites of income production over the course of the nineteenth and early twentieth centuries distinguishes this study from a large body of work in history, political science, and sociology that focuses on the rising importance of nations as political entities. Many studies of the rise of the nation-state to prominence in recent centuries focus on countries as states (Tilly 1975; Anderson 1986; Poggi 1990), while fewer studies focus on the rise of countries as economies. Yet the rise of countries as income sites has been at least as significant as the rise of countries as political units. Because of a highly uneven pattern of growth across countries as the world industrialized, fissures in the world's income distribution developed along national boundaries and widened dramatically over the nineteenth and early twentieth centuries. World income inequality increasingly became between-nation income inequality as national boundaries formed the primary demarcation points in the old geography of global inequality. The result is the so-called passport principle—what matters most for your income is the nationality on your passport.

The last decades of the twentieth century have witnessed the emergence of a new geography of global income inequality, one in which income inequality shrinks across nations and grows within nations. These patterns most likely will continue. If current trends do continue, nations will remain significant as economic units well into the future, but their prominence will diminish so that the nation as income site will be less critical at the end of the twenty-first century than it was at the beginning.

THE DECLINE OF NATIONS AS ECONOMIC UNITS

Recall the discussion of the trend in the B/W ratio in Chapter 2, where B denotes between-nation income inequality and W denotes within-nation income inequality. A falling ratio supports the New Geography Hypothesis of the declining importance of national boundaries in the determination of individual income. A rising ratio indicates the increasing importance of national boundaries in income determination. Figure 2.1 showed the trend

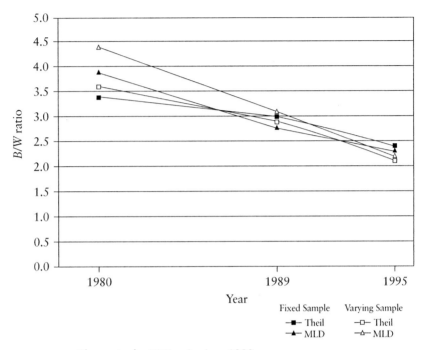

FIGURE 11.1   Change in the *B/W* ratio since 1980.

in the *B/W* ratio, based on the 33 nation groups of Bourguignon and Morrisson (1999), over the nineteenth and twentieth centuries. Over most of this period the *B/W* ratio surged upward, reflecting the rise in between-nation inequality that accompanied Western industrialization. The far right-hand side of the figure indicates a break in this upward trajectory. Growth in the *B/W* ratio was arrested in the middle of the twentieth century and now appears to be tracking downward. The decline in the ratio is steeper for the MLD than for the Theil, reflecting China's greater effect on the MLD.

If we replace the data on nation groups with data on nations themselves, we find evidence of a significant decline in the *B/W* ratio since 1980. Figure 11.1 depicts those results for 1980 to 1995, based on World Bank (1998, 1999, 2000a) income data for between-nation income inequality ($N = 125$ nations) and on Table 9.3 for change in within-nation income inequality. Using the fixed sample of 57 nations for the within-nation component, the *B/W* ratio declines from 3.4 to 2.4 for the Theil and from 3.9 to 2.3 for the MLD. The observed decline is even steeper when calculated on the basis of

Goesling's strategy of using fixed measurement points and a varying sample for the within-group component (Goesling 2001, fig. 1). Even with generous allowances for measurement error in the data, these results are hard to dismiss. Although the nationality on your passport is still critical in the determination of your income, the importance of nationality apparently has begun to erode.

The Demographic Windfall Hypothesis

The age structure of the population moves through three stages during the demographic transition: first there is a bulge of dependent children, then there is a bulge of working-age adults, finally there is a bulge of elderly (Williamson 1998). In the second half of the twentieth century some low-income nations in East Asia were in the second stage, but most in Asia and Africa were still in the first stage. In the twenty-first century the latter group of low-income nations will move to the second stage. This change in the age structure of poor nations will help to compress between-nation income inequality in the early decades of the twenty-first century.

THE DEMOGRAPHIC PENALTY IN THE LATE TWENTIETH CENTURY

Over the second half of the twentieth century populations grew rapidly in many poor nations as mortality declined and fertility remained high. What is important for change in global income inequality is not that populations grew rapidly in poor nations, but that populations grew faster in poor nations than in rich nations. The rapid population growth of poor nations produced a swelling at the bottom of the population pyramids of poor nations—reflecting an increasing ratio of children to adults—that was not characteristic of the population pyramids of richer nations.[1] The previous chapter asserted that the increasing ratio of children to adults in poor nations served to reduce the rate of growth in income per capita in poor nations relative to the rate in rich nations, so between-nation income inequality in the late twentieth century did not decline as rapidly as it would have otherwise. This chapter provides evidence for that assertion and argues that poor nations can expect a demographic windfall to boost their per capita incomes in the twenty-first century as the bulge moves to the middle of the population pyramid.[2]

We begin with the simple mathematics of growth rates. Growth rates are a strategic place to begin, since change in between-nation income inequality depends on the relative rates of growth of per capita income for richer and poorer nations. The growth rate of some quantity X from time 0 to time t can be written $g(X) = \log(X_t/X_0)$, where X_t is the value of X at time t, X_0 is the initial value of X, and log is the natural logarithm. Denoting income as Y and population as P, the growth rate of per capita income can be written as:

$$
\begin{aligned}
g(Y/P) &= \log[(Y_t/P_t) \div (Y_0/P_0)] \\
&= \log(Y_t/Y_0) - \log(P_t/P_0) \\
&= g(Y) - g(P).
\end{aligned}
\tag{11.1}
$$

Similarly, the growth rate of income per worker can be written

$$
\begin{aligned}
g(Y/W) &= \log[(Y_t/W_t) \div (Y_0/W_0)] \\
&= g(Y) - g(W),
\end{aligned}
\tag{11.2}
$$

where W denotes working-age population (generally aged fifteen to sixty-four). From the identity $g(Y) - g(P) = g(Y) - g(P) + [g(W) - g(W)]$, it follows that the growth rate of per capita income can be decomposed as follows (see Bloom and Sachs [1998, p. 252] for the same result based on first derivatives):

$$
\begin{aligned}
g(Y/P) &= [g(Y) - g(W)] + g(W) - g(P) \\
&= g(Y/W) + g(W) - g(P).
\end{aligned}
\tag{11.3}
$$

Equation 11.3 confirms the intuition that income per capita and income per worker will grow at the same rate only when the working-age population grows at the same rate as the total population. When total population grows faster than the working-age population, income per capita will grow more slowly than income per worker—the current situation in many poor nations. When the working-age population grows faster, income per capita will grow faster than income per worker—the basis of the predicted demographic windfall for poor nations over the next decades.[3]

I stated earlier that what is important for change in global inequality over recent decades is not that poor nations have experienced rapid population growth, but that population grew faster in poor nations than in rich nations. That conclusion is easy to verify from equation 11.3. Note that if $g(W) - g(P)$ were the same for all nations, then $g(Y/P) = g(Y/W) + K$ (where K is a constant), implying a perfect correlation between growth in income per capita and growth in income per worker across nations. Hence if $g(W) - g(P)$ were constant across nations, nations would be subject to the same demographic penalty or windfall, and results would be the same whether one examined the between-nation trend in income per worker or the between-nation trend in income per capita. In the last half of the twentieth century, however, the trends were not the same, as we now see.

NARROWING PRODUCTIVITY DIFFERENTIALS AND THE COMING DEMOGRAPHIC WINDFALL

For the last decades of the twentieth century we expect to find a steeper decline in between-nation inequality based on workers' productivity (GDP per worker) than on income (GDP per capita). The trends will differ because $g(W) - g(P)$ is positively correlated with income per capita, an association caused by the faster population growth in poorer nations. Because $g(W) - g(P)$ is positively correlated with income per capita, it follows from equation 11.3 that income per capita must have converged more slowly (or diverged faster) across nations than income per worker did. That is precisely what we find. When per capita GDP is used as the income measure, between-nation income inequality declined modestly from 1965 to 1989, calculated on the basis of point estimates using the Penn income data (Chapter 6). But when productivity per worker is examined—that is, when GDP per worker is used as the income measure—we find a steeper decline in between-nation inequality from 1965 to 1989. The Theil index of inequality declined by 13.0 percent for per worker income, the MLD declined by 11.2 percent, and the Gini declined by 5.8 percent. (The corresponding point estimates for income per capita are 4.7 percent decline in the Theil, 6.6 percent decline in the MLD, and 3.0 percent decline in the Gini.) These results support Sheehey's (1996) finding of faster between-nation convergence in income per worker than in income per capita. Moreover, while interval estimates in Chapter 6 indicated some uncertainty about whether inequality in per capita income declined at all across nations from 1965 to 1989, there is little doubt about the cross-country convergence of per worker income over this period (Figures 11.2–11.4). The interval estimates in the figures are based on the same simulation methods as the interval estimates reported in Chapter 6 for inequality in income per capita. The simulations indicate that declines of this magnitude are unlikely to be due to measurement error. Of the 27 interval estimates reported in the figures, not a single interval contains zero.

The narrowing of differentials in productivity across nations bodes well for the narrowing of per capita income differentials across nations. Narrowing differentials in worker productivity are translated into narrowing income differentials as workers come to constitute an increasing percentage of the total population. The key is fertility decline, and fertility is declining in Latin America (Guzmán et al. 1996), in Asia (Leete and Alam

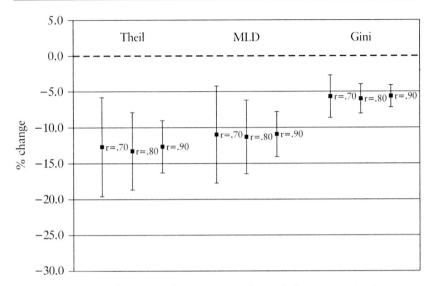

FIGURE 11.2 Interval estimates for percentage change in between-nation income inequality, 1965–1989: Simulation results for Theil, MLD, and Gini for income per worker (baseline error model).

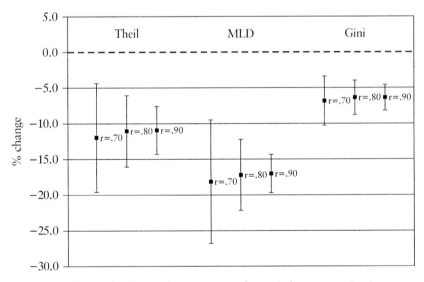

FIGURE 11.3 Interval estimates for percentage change in between-nation income inequality, 1965–1989: Simulation results for Theil, MLD, and Gini for income per worker (China-only error model).

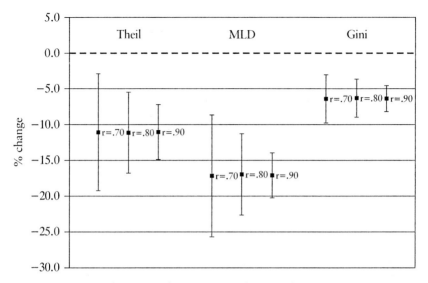

FIGURE 11.4 Interval estimates for percentage change in between-nation income inequality, 1965–1989: Simulation results for Theil, MLD, and Gini for income per worker (highest-error model).

1993) and in sub-Saharan Africa (Shapiro and Tambashe 2001). As fertility declines in poor nations we can expect the age structures of poor nations to begin to converge with the age structures of richer nations. As this gradually unfolds over time there is a sort of double windfall for per capita income in poor nations, in that the negative effect of $g(P) > g(W)$ on per capita income is replaced by the positive effect of $g(W) > g(P)$ on per capita income until the age structure stabilizes. According to David Bloom and Jeffrey Williamson (1998, p. 419), low-income nations in East Asia have already reaped some of the benefits of the demographic windfall: "The miracle [of rapid income growth in East Asia from 1965 to 1990] occurred in part because East Asia's demographic transition resulted in its working-age population growing at a much faster rate than its dependent population." Of course, the lowering of fertility rates is no magic elixir for economic growth. As Bloom and Williamson caution, the economic benefits of the demographic transition depend on institutions that permit the windfall to be realized. Nonetheless, in conjunction with the tendency toward convergence of national institutions noted in the previous chapter, there is reason to be optimistic that many poor nations will be able to reap a demographic windfall in the early decades of the twenty-first century. The stakes here are large, since Bloom and Adi Brender (1993) project that over the period 1990 to 2025, more than 96 percent of the growth in the world's labor force (defined as those aged fifteen to sixty-four) will occur in low-income countries. Because the windfall will disappear as the bulge disappears, however, its effects are nonrecurring, boosting income growth only over the next few decades.[4]

Has Global Income Inequality Peaked?

This book makes three key empirical claims:

- Income inequality across nations stabilized and then declined in the late twentieth century. It follows that the growing income gaps across nations (which no one disputes) arise from growth in income, not from growth in income inequality.

- The late twentieth century marked a turning point in the global inequality transition from within-nation to between-nation back to within-nation income inequality. Over the nineteenth and much of the twentieth century, income inequality grew across nations and was steady or declined within nations. Both trends reversed in the last decades of the twentieth century.

- Global income inequality is not growing, and may have peaked. Global inequality is no longer growing because the major component of global income inequality—between-nation income inequality—is declining.

Much of the book has been devoted to demonstrating the first two claims. We have seen evidence that income inequality has declined across nations in the late twentieth century, and that within-nation income inequality has grown. (Apparently there is no universal law that ties the growth or decline in income inequality to the growth or decline in income itself, since in the last part of the twentieth century inequality across nations declined as per capita incomes grew while in earlier periods inequality across nations increased as per capita incomes grew. It is the spread of industrialization that is determinative, as we have seen.) Since both falling inequality across nations and rising inequality within nations represent reversals of long-standing trends, it appears that the late twentieth century does mark a change in the pattern of global income inequality.

It remains only to be seen what the evidence says about global income inequality itself—is it still rising, or did it decline as between-nation inequality did in the late twentieth century? If we are indeed in the second phase of the inequality transition, as suggested in this book, then the answer depends on which is the larger effect—the decline in between-nation income inequality or the growth in within-nation income inequality. Because within-nation inequality currently is the smaller component of the total, global income inequality would grow only if within-nation income inequality grew at a faster rate than between-nation inequality declined.

THE TREND IN GLOBAL INCOME INEQUALITY AT THE END OF THE TWENTIETH CENTURY

Although confident claims of growing global income inequality are legion (Chapter 2), in fact the trend in income inequality is rarely investigated for the whole world. There are a mere handful of studies, and of these, some do not apply to the trend at the end of the twentieth century because the studies are too old (Berry, Bourguignon, and Morrisson 1983a,b) or, in the case of Korzeniewicz and Moran (1997), because the study fails to use PPP income data. To examine the trend in global income inequality at the end of the twentieth century I juxtapose the results of two recent studies that do use PPP data—Schultz (1998) and Goesling (2001)—supplemented with the results of my own further analysis of the same or similar data. Of the two published studies, Goesling's sticks more closely to the data, but at the cost of a shorter time interval and many missing cases. Schultz's study covers 1960–1989, but to obtain general coverage he must use the results of a regression analysis to impute missing within-nation inequality data. Schultz uses the Penn World Table income estimates to calculate between-nation income inequality and the Deininger and Squire (1996) data for within-nation income inequality. Goesling's study covers 1980 to 1995. Because Penn World Table estimates for the 1990s were not available when he did his study, Goesling uses PPP-adjusted income estimates from the World Bank (1998, 1999, 2000a) for between-nation income inequality. For estimates of within-nation income inequality Goesling uses the UNU/WIDER (1999) compilation, an expanded version of the Deininger-Squire data.

Both Goesling and Schultz find a downward trend in global income inequality, as does Sala-i-Martin (2002a,b) in two unpublished papers. Sala-i-Martin (2002b, table 1) finds that the global Gini increased over the 1970s from 0.63 to 0.64 and then declined over the next two decades to a value of 0.61 in 1998. The global Theil and global MLD followed the same pattern, with the Theil declining by 10 percent since 1978 and the MLD declining by 13 percent (Sala-i-Martin 2002b, table 2). In the Schultz study global inequality peaked in 1968 (Figure 11.5) with a global MLD of 0.88. By 1989 the global MLD had fallen to 0.78. The World Bank income data used by Goesling give higher estimates of between-

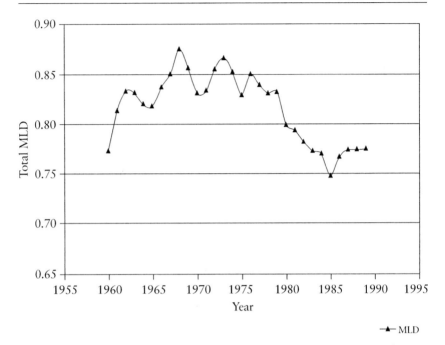

FIGURE 11.5 Trend in global income inequality, 1960–1989. Based on Schultz 1998, table A-3.

nation inequality in 1980 than do the PWT data, but the decline in global inequality is steeper, so that by 1989 the two sets of estimates almost converge. It is not clear why the deviation between the World Bank and PWT estimates are greater in the early 1980s than in the late 1980s, but it is this deviation that accounts for the steeper rate of decline in global income inequality over the 1980s in the Goesling study.[5] If we prefer the World Bank data, then we conclude that global income inequality has been declining more rapidly than the Schultz results indicate, at least for the 1980–1995 period. Either way, whether we prefer the PWT data or the World Bank data, we conclude—contrary to conventional wisdom—that global income inequality has *not* been growing.[6]

My own analysis of the data also finds that global income inequality declined in the late twentieth century. The findings reported in Table 11.1 add the 1980–1995 within-nation results from Table 9.3 to between-nation results based on World Bank income data for the 1980s and 1990s. The results directly contradict warnings of a rapid worsening of the world's income distribution. Unless existing income estimates are stupendously off the mark, global income inequality is not growing at all but is

TABLE 11.1 Estimated 1980–1995 change in global income inequality

	Theil		MLD	
	1980	Change	1980	Change
Between-nation	.65	−.13	.74	−.22
Within-nation	.19	+.03	.19	+.04
Global	.84	−.10	.93	−.18

Source: Within-nation: Estimates based on the panel-of-nations method (Table 9.3). The 57 nations in the sample have about 80 percent of the world's population. *Between-nation:* Based on the 125 nations with World Bank income data for both the 1980s and the 1990s. These nations have more than 90 percent of the world's population. Change for within-nation inequality is circa 1980 to 1995; change in between-nation inequality is for 1980 to most recent income data available (generally 1998). Note that the analysis of World Bank data in Chapter 6 was based on 156 nations. Here we have fewer nations because the Chapter 6 analysis was restricted to the 1990s.

declining. (Note that the convergence is faster when the MLD, rather than the Theil, is used, reflecting the greater effect on the MLD of the rapid income growth of large poor nations in Asia.) The margin of uncertainty for income estimates dictates the need to exercise caution before jumping to the conclusion that global income inequality is declining rapidly. It is quite apparent, however, that common concerns about exploding global income inequality are misplaced.

GLOBAL INEQUALITY PROJECTIONS

Although it is not obvious from the global trend itself, the Goesling and Schultz studies differ in terms of the proximate causes of the decline in global income inequality. In Schultz's study, global inequality declines because of downward trends in inequality both within and across nations. In Goesling's study, the downward trend in global inequality is the result of declining inequality across nations that more than offsets increases in inequality within the average nation. So Goesling and Schultz reach different conclusions about the direction of the trend for within-nation income inequality. On the basis of my analysis of the trends in within-nation income inequality (Chapter 9), I believe that the weight of the evidence points to modest growth in within-nation income inequality, a conclusion supported by Chotikapanich, Valenzuela, and Rao (1997) (using within-region inequality), by Dowrick and Akmal (2001, table 4), and by Goesling (2001), as well as by Sala-i-Martin's (2002b) recent study. So let us suppose that within-nation income inequality is growing, as I believe is most likely the case now and conjecture will be the case in the future. Let us suppose further that income inequality across nations will continue to decline, as is quite likely for the reasons given above. Then the question of whether global income inequality has peaked reduces to the question of whether growth in income inequality in the (weighted) average nation is likely to be great enough to overcome the effect of declining income inequality across nations. As we now see, rising within-nation inequality is not likely to off-set the effect of declining inequality across nations. Most likely, then, global income inequality for the industrial era peaked in the second half of the twentieth century and is now heading downward.

Three sets of projections, based on alternative scenarios regarding the global inequality transition, are given. The first scenario is that incomes across nations will converge at the same rate in the twenty-first century as they diverged from 1870 to 1970, the period of greatest international divergence. Although this scenario might seem far-fetched at first blush, it is in the spirit of the conclusion of the noted growth theorist Robert Lucas. On the basis of his models of economic development, Lucas (2002, pp. 173–75) predicts not only that between-nation income inequality has peaked, but that it will return to the level that prevailed before the Industrial Revolution:

> [The] enormous inequality of the postwar period is at its all-time peak, and will decline in the future until something like the relative incomes of 1800 are restored. . . . The legacy of economic growth that we have inherited from the industrial revolution is an irreversible gain to humanity, of a magnitude that is still unknown. It is becoming increasingly clear, I think, that the legacy of in-equality, the concomitant of this gain, is a historical transient.

The same-rate projections reported in Table 11.2 are based on the as-sumption that inequality across nations will decline over the twenty-first century at the same rate as it grew during its period of greatest growth, from 1870 to 1970. The half-rate projections are based on the assumption that between-nation income inequality will decline over the next hundred years at one-half the rate that it grew from 1870 to 1970. The quarter-rate projections are based on the conservative assumption that between-nation income inequality will decline over the next hundred years at one-fourth the rate that it grew from 1870 to 1970. According to the Bourguignon and Morrisson estimates using nation groups, the between-nation Theil in-creased by a factor of 2.6 from 1870 to 1970 and the between-nation MLD increased by a factor of 3.2. So the same-rate projections assume that over the course of the twenty-first century the between-nation Theil will shrink by 62 percent (that is, to 38 percent of its current size) and the between-nation MLD will shrink by 69 percent (to 31 percent of its cur-

TABLE 11.2 Global implications of declining between-nation income inequality: Projections based on three scenarios for the twenty-first century

Scenarios	Projected change in B over the twenty-first century		W needed for constant global inequality		
	Theil	MLD	Theil	MLD	Comments
Same rate	−0.33	−0.37	0.55	0.60	W implausible
Half rate	−0.16	−0.18	0.38	0.41	W unlikely
Quarter rate	−0.08	−0.09	0.30	0.32	W plausible

Note: B is between-nation income inequality and W is within-nation income inequality. *Same rate* assumes that between-nation income inequality declines at the same rate in the twenty-first century as it grew from 1870 to 1970, *half rate* assumes decline at half the 1870–1970 growth rate, and *quarter rate* assumes decline at one-fourth the 1870–1970 growth rate.

rent size). The half-rate projections assume that the between-nation Theil will shrink by 31 percent and the between-nation MLD by 34 percent. The quarter-rate projections assume that the Theil will shrink by 16 percent and the MLD by 17 percent.

The between-nation Theil and MLD both stood at about 0.53 in 1998 based on World Bank income data. Multiplying 0.53 by the respective shrinkage factors given above yields the projected changes in between-nation income inequality reported in Table 11.2. These declines will drive down global income inequality unless within-nation income inequality increases commensurately. Table 11.2 reports the levels of within-nation income inequality that would need to prevail to prevent global inequality from declining over the twenty-first century. Under the same-rate assumption, global inequality will decline unless W grows to at least 0.55 for Theil and 0.60 for the MLD. These are implausible levels for W, since they suggest that the level of income inequality in the average nation will exceed the world's current level of between-nation income inequality. Even in Latin American nations—where income inequality is notoriously high—income inequality in the average nation does not attain this level (see Table 9.2). Under the half-rate assumption, global inequality will decline unless W grows to at least 0.38 for the Theil and 0.41 for the MLD. This level of income inequality is also unlikely; of the world's major regions only Latin America now has a level of W higher than 0.38 (Theil) or 0.41 (MLD). Finally, if we assume that between-nation income inequality shrinks by only about 16 percent over the next hundred years—a very conservative assumption in light of the sizable declines reported by Goesling (2001) for

1980 to 1995 alone—then it is hard to say which direction global inequality will go in the twenty-first century.

The lesson of this exercise is that the direction of global income inequality in the future depends on the between-nation trend. Of course we already knew that, but these projections help to quantify the point. Because change in within-nation income inequality is a weighted composite of economic changes in many different nations—many of them offsetting—within-nation inequality is not likely to change rapidly. There is more potential for substantial change in between-nation inequality, and the likely direction is downward over this century as industrialization spreads to all parts of the world. If between-nation income inequality during the Asian industrialization period declines at the rate it grew during the Western industrialization period, then it is virtually certain that global income inequality will decline over the twenty-first century.

Finally, it is important to note that the generally rosy forecast given here for the twenty-first century—foreseen as a century that will enjoy declining inequality across nations amid continued income growth for the world's average person—needs to be tempered by several stark realities. The first reality is that the twenty-first century could be bloody (as the twentieth century was), since sustained armed conflict between nations is an ever-present possibility. The second reality is that the transfer of inequality from across nations to within nations is likely to create new problems or exacerbate old ones within nations. In addition to concerns about the capacity of the nation-state to function effectively in an era of increasing globalization (Kennedy 1993; McMichael 1996; Strange 1996; Rodrik 2000; Keohane 2001), the predicted rise in within-nation income inequality over the course of the twenty-first century will place new demands on national governments to govern effectively. Growing income inequality within nations might raise the specter of growing civil unrest and terrorism by nonstate actors at the very time that the effectiveness of national governments is weakened by transnational structures. Third, there is no apparent end in sight for human demands upon the physical environment. While doomsayers in the past—from Malthus to the Club of Rome group in the 1970s—have proved to be false prophets, it is prudent to assume that deteriorating environmental conditions could result in unforeseen constraints on human economic activity in scattered parts of the world. Last, there is no reason to be optimistic that the material desires of humans will ever be satiated (Easterlin 1996; Frank 1999). As a result, it is safe to predict that the greater affluence of the twenty-first century will fail to produce greater happiness or contentment, as the epilogue elaborates.

Epilogue:
Does Rising Income Bring Greater Happiness?

DOES RISING INCOME bring greater happiness? The question is critical because of the spectacular rise in world mean income over the past two centuries. Moreover, the world's income growth shows no signs of ceasing in the near future. Thus it is important to ask whether rising world income is likely to bring greater happiness to the world.

Many studies seem to assume that rising income results in greater happiness or satisfaction. As incomes rise and material needs are increasingly satisfied, people should move to higher levels of subjective well-being. People who really are better off should feel that they are better off.

Over the past half century several large-scale cross-national surveys have examined the relationship between income and happiness. There are two relationships of interest here. The first is the individual-level relationship: At a particular point in time in a given nation, do richer people tend to be happier than poorer people? The second is the aggregate relationship between income and happiness: Has the growth in overall income that we have seen in the past two centuries raised the general level of human happiness? I examine each in turn.

Are Richer People Happier?

Are richer people happier? The answer is yes, they are. That conclusion is based on a great deal of evidence from surveys. The surveys measure happiness by asking people how happy they are. The question used in the General Social Survey in the United States is typical: "Taken all together, how would you say things are these days—would you say that you are very

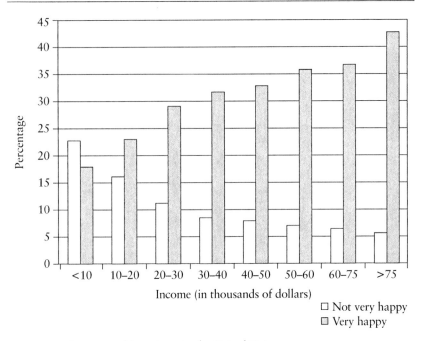

FIGURE E.1   Income and happiness in the United States.

happy, pretty happy, or not too happy?" To illustrate, Figure E.1 reports the individual-level association between income and self-reported happiness for adults in the United States in the 1990s (Davis, Smith, and Marsden, 2001). The percentage of respondents who report that they are "very happy" increases with income, and the percentage who report that they are "not too happy" declines with income. Respondents whose family income is less than $10,000 are more likely to report that they are not too happy (22.8 percent) than they are to report that they are very happy (17.9 percent). In all other income categories the number of respondents who report that they are very happy is higher than the number who report that they are not too happy. Happiness increases monotonically with income, so that respondents in the highest income category report both the highest level of happiness (42.7 percent "very happy") and the lowest level of unhappiness (5.6 percent "not too happy"). The evidence about income and happiness in the United States is consistent with findings from other nations, including non-Western cultures (Easterlin 1996, chap. 10). Ed Diener (1984, p. 553) summarizes the evidence this way: "There is an overwhelming amount of evidence that shows a positive relationship between income and SWB [subjective well-being] within countries."

The strategy of studying happiness on the basis of self-reported happiness is based on the logic that happiness refers to a type of subjective well-being, and each respondent is the best judge of his or her own subjective state. Because happiness is not directly observed, the self-report approach seems sensible. Yet the approach is not foolproof, since the use of self-reports of happiness raises the issue of comparability. How can we compare responses across individuals if each respondent sets his or her own standard of happiness? More to the point here, if the richer are more likely to say that they are happy, how confident can we be that they really are happier? Perhaps income and happiness are not really associated, but appear to be because those with more income have lower standards of happiness. Or perhaps the rich are more likely to say that they are happy because they think they should be (whether or not they actually are).

To gain leverage on the comparability issue we need to determine if other evidence is consistent with the self-reported greater happiness of those who have more income. Studies of people's preeminent concerns are a good source of such evidence, since if we know what people are most concerned about then we should have a good idea of what is needed to increase their sense of subjective well-being. For most people everywhere the preeminent concern is personal economic well-being, centered on "making a living and matters of family life" (Easterlin 1996, p. 132). Recall (Chapter 10) the results of Hadley Cantril's (1965) classic study of happiness in twelve communist and capitalist countries.[1] The study asked people to describe in their own words the "best of all possible worlds"—the conditions that would result in the greatest happiness for them. Cantril classified the responses into nine broad categories: economic, family, health, values and character, job/work, social, international, political, and status quo. He found that personal economic concerns dominated in every country.

This consistent identification of personal economic concerns as the decisive consideration in the "best of all possible worlds" suggests that people do use a fairly common set of criteria when evaluating their happiness. If so, then it is meaningful to compare self-reports of happiness across individuals. And what those self-reports indicate is that richer people tend to be happier people—precisely what one would expect given the dominance of economic themes in Cantril's study.

Are People Happier Now?

Since richer people tend to be happier, one might expect that average happiness will rise along with average income. Indeed, in view of the magnitude of the rise in per capita incomes over the past two centuries, one would expect people to be much happier now than before. Yet the evidence over time fails to support the view that people on the whole become happier as national incomes rise. Evidence comes from surveys in the United States, Western Europe, and Japan (Easterlin 1996, chap. 10). Despite rising incomes in each of these regions, there is no evidence of increasing happiness in the past half century, when surveys first began to include questions about personal happiness. Japan provides perhaps the most compelling evidence for the failure of rising incomes to produce greater happiness. From 1958 to 1987 per capita income in Japan increased fivefold. Over this thirty-year period car ownership increased from 1 percent to 60 percent, and the ownership of household consumer durables rose sharply as well (Yasuba 1991). Despite this unprecedented jump in prosperity, the average level of satisfaction among Japanese respondents was no greater in 1987 than in 1958 (Easterlin 1996, fig. 10.3).

In the aggregate, then, greater income does not bring greater happiness, even though richer people tend to be happier people. How are we to reconcile these paradoxical results? The apparent answer to the puzzle is that material aspirations are tied to the national income level. When national incomes rise, so do material aspirations. Because happiness depends on one's income relative to the income of others—a type of "frog-pond effect" (people derive satisfaction from being a big frog in a small pond: Davis 1966; Frank 1985)—then happiness varies directly with one's own income and inversely with the incomes of others. A person whose income is constant will feel poorer when others' incomes rise, even though objectively that individual remains at the same level of well-being. So well-being declines subjectively while remaining constant objectively. Easterlin (1996, p. 140) explains the frog-pond phenomenon as it pertains to income and happiness: "At any given time, the incomes of others are fixed, and those who are more affluent feel happier, on average. However, raising the incomes of all does not increase the happiness of all because the positive effect on subjective well-being of higher income for oneself is offset by the negative effect of a higher living level norm brought about by the growth in incomes generally."

This explanation of the happiness-income paradox is based on the premise that material aspirations are tied to a society's general income level. As Easterlin notes, there is ample evidence for the premise. Quotations from the Cantril cross-nation surveys are quite telling in this regard. Recall that the Cantril survey asked respondents to describe the "best of all possible worlds." Contrast these representative responses from India and the United States (quoted in Easterlin 1996, pp. 141–142):

- "I should like to have a water tap and a water supply in my house. It would also be nice to have electricity. My husband's wages must be increased if our children are to get an education and our daughter is to be married." (India)

- "I hope in the future I will not get any disease. Now I am coughing. I also hope I can purchase a bicycle . . . I also would sometime like to own a fan and maybe a radio." (India)

- "If I could earn more money I would then be able to buy our own home and have more luxury around us, like better furniture, a new car, and more vacations." (United States)

- "I would like to provide my family with an income to allow them to live well—to have the proper recreation, to go camping, to have music and dancing lessons for the children, and to have family trips. I wish we could belong to a country club and do more entertaining." (United States)

As these quotations suggest, rising living standards give birth to rising expectations, and happiness is keyed to one's expectations. Hence "raising the incomes of all . . . does not increase the happiness of all. This is because the material norms on which judgments of well-being are based increase commensurately with the growth of society's per capita income" (Easterlin 1996, p. 143).

In short, the enormous leap in incomes over the past two centuries has not been accompanied by an increase in human happiness. The leap in incomes has substantially reduced human want, as measured by the percentage of the world in poverty (Bourguignon and Morrisson 1999). Yet survey data indicate that rising national income does not translate into greater societal happiness. As incomes rise, so do one's expectations, and happiness appears to be determined by how well one is doing compared with one's expectations. There is no reason to believe that this principle will be any less evident in the future than it has been in the past.

NOTES

REFERENCES

INDEX

Notes

1. Massive Global Income Inequality

1. For most nations of the world we lack good estimates on life expectancy for the first half of the twentieth century. Life expectancy for female babies was 43.7 years in Japan in 1899, 43.7 in Italy and 49.4 in England and Wales in 1901, and 32.5 in Chile in 1909, with males having a life expectancy about 3–4 years less (Preston, Keyfitz, and Schoen 1972). Of these nations, probably life expectancy in Chile was the nearest to that for the world as a whole at the turn of the century. If so, then life expectancy virtually doubled in the twentieth century.

2. The use of 1820 as the beginning point is dictated by data availability, since Maddison's income series begins with 1820.

3. Actually there are more than 200 nations, but some are tiny and we lose very little information by omitting them or collapsing them to a single unit.

4. Inequality can be viewed as a type of variance (a scale-invariant variance, where "scale invariant" means that the measure is not affected by the metric used—whether dollar or peso etc.). Indeed, two of the standard measures of inequality—the coefficient of variation, and the variance of the logarithm—are measures of variance as well.

5. A long-standing literature in philosophy wrestles with the issue of the link between income equality and justice (for example, Rawls 1999). If some income distributions are more just than others, then we should care about both ends of the income distribution—and not just the bottom end—because justice demands it. These are vexing issues for philosophers and nonphilosophers alike. The obvious standard for a just distribution might seem to be equality, but research in sociology shows that most people deem equality to be unfair, not fair, because it underrewards those who contribute more than average and overrewards those who contribute less than average. Because "contribution" (however defined) can vary markedly from individual to individual, an equal distribution of income is seen as very unjust (see Jasso 1999 for an introduction to the growing sociological literature on evaluations of justice). We return to the justice issue briefly in a later discussion (Chapter 4) that stresses the dif-

ference between inequality and inequity—a critical distinction that is not emphasized as much as it should be, since the two terms are often confused in everyday speech.

6. The revised poverty estimates of Bourguignon and Morrisson (2002) are higher, but tell the same story.

2. The Reversal of Historical Inequality Trends

1. The business editor of the *Evening Standard* (December 1, 1999) described the demonstrators "in their Nike trainers, excitedly loading their Fuji film to take pictures with their Canons, chatting on their Nokia mobiles and dancing at the intersections to music from their Sonys" as "walking advertisements for the global economy."

2. In estimating global inequality, the key is the reliability of the data for larger nations, since global income inequality is driven largely by patterns in those nations.

3. How Is National Income Measured, and Can We Trust the Data?

1. The cross-national correlation is smaller within regions of the world (for example, within Europe), where the variance in national incomes is smaller.

2. In comparing 1960–1985 income growth rates using the Penn income estimates with income growth rates using national accounts only (involving no conversion to international prices), Nuxoll (1994) found that the discrepancy between the two growth rate series was unrelated to initial income level.

3. The LSMS surveys are described in Grosh and Glewwe (1996). My summary draws heavily on the article by Montgomery et al. (2000).

4. Daily calorie supply per capita is the calorie equivalent of the daily food supplies of an economy divided by population. The estimates are from World Bank tables, but the estimates originate with the Food and Agriculture Organization of the United Nations. *Food supplies* "comprise domestic production, imports less exports, and changes in stocks; they exclude animal feed, seeds for use in agriculture, and food lost in processing and distribution" (World Bank 1990, p. 256).

5. Ghana is a tropical nation on the west coast of Africa with heavy vegetation in the southern region that thins to savanna and dry plains in the north. The driest regions in Ghana receive more rainfall than the wettest regions in Chad. Although Ghana is one of the world's largest cocoa producers, agriculture constituted only about a half of the nation's total GDP as of the late 1980s, and most Ghanaians are not subsistence farmers.

Chad is a landlocked nation in central Africa bordered on the north by the Sahara Desert. Despite unfavorable conditions, more than 80 percent of the labor force is engaged in subsistence farming or herding. Sorghum and millet are the primary crops. Chad's subsistence farmers practice slash-and-burn agriculture in tandem with crop rotation. Herding is common in Chad's middle zone, the Sahelian region. The northern zone of Chad is populated by nomadic tribes, since rainfall in this Saharan zone is inadequate for settled farming. (These descriptions of Ghana and Chad are taken from the Library of Congress's *Country Studies*, downloaded from their website.)

6. Although sorghum is a leading cereal crop in the United States, virtually all of it is used as animal fodder. One by-product of sorghum that is used for human consumption in the United States is sorghum molasses, which is derived from the sweet juice extracted from the pithy stalk of the sorghum plant.

7. Some scholars conjecture that subsistence production is less likely (than industrial production) to be detected in official income statistics. Because subsistence production claims a declining share of nations' economic activity as they industrialize, critics might argue that the increase in inequality across nations over time was partly spurious, resulting from the greater detection of economic activity in industrializing nations. But this measurement error story cannot account for the huge differences in material living conditions (in shelter, consumer durables, transportation, and so on) that emerged across nations during the period of Western industrialization.

8. Milanovic's data set consists of 101 nations in 1988 and 119 nations in 1993, representing about 86 percent of world population in 1988 and about 91 percent of world population in 1993.

9. Sears, Roebuck and Company was a leading mail-order firm in the United States over the twentieth century. Over the century Sears prices have remained in the low to middle range (typically higher than recent "discount" stores, but less expensive than upscale retail stores), and price changes in the Sears catalog are representative of changing prices in the United States. In May 1993 Sears discontinued its large general catalog in favor of specialty catalogs (*Chicago Sun-Times*, May 28, 1993).

10. The consumer price index goes back only to 1913, so I extrapolated back to 1908. If we use 1982–1984 as the base years (CPI = 100), we find that the CPI was 130.7 in 1990 and 9.9 in 1913 ([130.7/9.9] = 13.2).

11. Some might like to see adjustments based on finer age gradations, but they are unlikely to affect results, since age structures are so closely tied to fertility rates and national fertility rates do not change overnight. More critical is the relative weight assigned to children versus adults. With regard to the comparison of national incomes, however, Summers and Heston (1999, n. 10) find that the weight they use (whether .4 or .5 or .6 for children) has no effect on their basic findings.

12. Estimates for percentage children in 1988 are as follows for selected poor countries (World Bank 1990, table 26): Benin, 47 percent; Chad, 42 percent; Madagascar, 46 percent; Mali, 47 percent; Malawi, 46 percent; Nigeria, 48 percent; Tanzania, 49 percent; Zambia, 49 percent.

13. The percentage of first-order members in the United States is 38.5 percent, derived as follows. Because the average household size is 2.6 in the United States, there are 1,000 households for every 2,600 people. It follows that, of every 2,600 people in the United States, 1,000—or 38.5 percent—are first-order members of their household (the choice of one member or another as the first-order member is arbitrary and does not matter anyway in the determination of scale economy effects). With regard to second-order members, only 753 of the

1,000 households have a second-order member, since 24.7 percent of house-holds in the United States consist of a single member. By definition there is only one second-order member per household, so it follows that 29 percent of the people in the United States (753 of every 2,600 people) are second-order members of their household. By similar logic, 16.5 percent are third-order household members—of the 1,000 households, 1000 − (247 + 323) = 430 have three or more members, and 430 is 16.5 percent of 2,600—and 9.9 per-cent are fourth-order members. The remaining 6.2 percent of the population are fifth-, sixth-, . . . nth-order household members in the United States.

The calculations for rural Swaziland follow the same logic, except that they are based on 6,000 individuals for 1,000 households (an average household size of 6.0 instead of 2.6). Because there are 6,000 individuals spread out over 1,000 households, one of every six (16.7 percent) is a first-order member. The percentage declines only slightly to 16.4 percent for second-order members, since of the 6,000 households only 84 (1.4 percent) consist of a single member. Of the 6,000 individuals, 958 (16 percent) are third-order household mem-bers, 897 (15 percent) are fourth-order, and the remaining 2,159 (36 percent) are fifth or higher order.

4. Inequality

1. In the case of inequality across households, researchers sometimes use weighted averages (additional members are given successively less weight) in view of household economies of scale. The issue bears on the estimation of between-nation income inequality, since poor nations typically have larger households (Chapter 3).
2. Note that the famous distribution principle of Marx (1996, p. 215)—"to each according to his needs"—also is consistent with the assumption that wage equality is inequitable.
3. This is not to say that individuals believe in unlimited inequality. Al-though there is no consensus on what the optimum level of income inequality would be, most agree that the current level of world income inequality is too great.
4. For example, on the basis of trends in the coefficient of variation—a measure of inequality—John Passé-Smith (1993, p. 117) concludes that "the gap be-tween rich and poor countries is growing wider." To be sure, the gap is grow-ing wider, but it muddies the waters to use an inequality measure to demon-strate the point.
5. Key contributions to the literature include Dalton (1920), Theil (1967), Atkin-son (1970), Cowell (1977), Bourguignon (1979), Shorrocks (1980), and Foster and Shneyerov (1999). See Allison (1978), Schwartz and Winship (1979), and Jenkins (1991) for summaries.
6. We can define $0 \log(0) = 0$. However, the problem of defining $\log(r_i)$ for $r_i = 0$ does not arise in the case of between-nation income inequality since national incomes are never zero.
7. For calculation of the index, it is generally more convenient to express VarLog

in its standard form as VarLog $= \Sigma_j p_j (\log X_j - E[\log X_j])^2$, where X_j is income for unit j and E is the expected value (mean).

5. What We Already Know

1. By contrast, most of the inequality in health lies within nations, not between them (Pradhan, Sahn, and Younger 2002).
2. Of course the effect of the within-nation inequality trend on the *global* inequality trend is not minor, since the within-nation trend is a component of the global trend.
3. Most of the studies of the trade-off thesis are in economics, not sociology. In sociology most studies have focused on the causes rather than on the consequences of inequality, because sociologists most often implicitly assume that income inequality is harmful. The ultimate goal of many sociological studies is amelioration, to determine what causes inequality so that we better understand how to reduce it. Cross-national research on inequality was especially fashionable in sociology during the heyday of world system and dependency theory in the 1970s and 1980s.
4. In economics a revival of interest in economic growth theory has spawned a booming literature on between-nation income differences, but much of this literature is based on unweighted analyses.

6. Income Inequality across Nations in the Late Twentieth Century

1. To be sure, incomes are stagnant or declining in some poor nations, so there are instances where income differences are widening because nations are falling behind. But that does not invalidate the point that in general it is rising income, not rising inequality, that is causing the gaps to widen.
2. Not all of the difference is due to the different sample of nations—some apparently is due also to the different income estimation methods used by the World Bank and by the PWT.
3. My purpose here is not to try to define polarization formally (see Esteban and Ray 1994 for a formal treatment) but to point out the problems with confusing polarization with widening gaps. Widening gaps do not imply polarization, nor does polarization necessarily imply widening gaps. To see the latter, note that polarization could result from tighter clustering into two groups independent of the size of the gap between the groups. For example, if nations with above-average incomes converged to the income mean for that group and nations with below-average incomes converged to the income mean for that group, we might say that polarization occurred even though the income gap remained constant. Although there is some evidence of regional income polarization in this "tighter clustering" sense (Abramovitz 1986; Baumol 1986; Baumol and Wolff 1988), this is not the sort of polarization described in the dependency and world system literatures.
4. Z-scores are appropriate here because I used random normal deviates to generate the measurement error in the simulations.
5. Kravis and Lipsey (1990, abstract) argue that the 30–35 percent margin of er-

ror for the worst PPP estimates "is still a small range of error compared to that stemming from the use of exchange rates to convert own-currency to common currency measures of output."

6. The schedule is as follows: A = ±9 percent error (18 nations); B+ = ±12 percent error (7 nations); B = ±15 percent error (8 nations); C+ = ±18 percent error (1 nation); C = ±21 percent error (34 nations); C− = ± 24 percent error (3 nations); D+ = ±27 percent error (11 nations); D = ±30 percent error (38 nations).

7. The arguments here apply to income inequality, and must be modified somewhat to apply to inequalities where there is a ceiling effect (for example, health inequality as measured by life expectancy). In the cases where ceiling effects or other strictures are present, it is often less clear what constitutes even and uneven growth.

7. Weighted versus Unweighted Inequality

1. Goesling's (2001, table 3) findings suggest that there might be less difference between the trend results for the adjusted and unadjusted data in more recent years.

2. My earlier analysis (Firebaugh 1999, app. B) attempted to separate the contributions of changing income ratios and changing population shares by employing a standard demographic decomposition method based on this equation (see Kitagawa 1955; Firebaugh 1997):

$$\Delta I = \Sigma_j \, p_{j1} \, \Delta f(r_j) + \Sigma_j \, \Delta p_j \, f(r_{j1}) + \Sigma_j \, \Delta p_j \, \Delta f(r_j),$$

where ΔI denotes change in an inequality index and r_j denotes nation j's weighted income ratio. On the basis of the results of that decomposition equation I concluded that "different rates of population growth in rich and poor nations played the predominant role in determining change in the distribution of per capita income across nations" (p. 1597). I now believe that conclusion is wrong. The decisive role was played not by changing population shares but by faster-than-world-average income growth in large poor nations in Asia.

Although the decomposition method seemed to be appropriate for the issue at hand, I failed to appreciate the importance of a hidden assumption that renders the method problematic for weighted inequality trends. The second component of the decomposition assumes fixed income ratios while population shares change. Yet because the income ratios themselves are functions of population shares in the weighted case, holding the income ratios constant while changing the population shares is impossible, unless the change in population shares is independent of the income ratios (in recent decades the two clearly have not been independent, since population growth has been much more rapid in poor nations than in rich nations). As a result this method does not work for decomposing the 1965–1989 weighted inequality trends.

3. The qualification "independent of income growth rate" is critical, since the faster population growth in poor nations has affected between-nation inequality by increasing the ratio of dependents to adults in poor nations and thus

lowering their rate of growth of per capita income. We gain leverage on that issue in Chapter 11, where we compare the inequality trends based on income per worker with the trends based on income per capita. In this section our objective has been to disentangle the effect of population growth rates from the effect of income growth rates, so we are interested here in the effect of changing population shares strictly independent of income growth.

4. The choice of inequality index can affect conclusions about the pace of change, however, since as we have noted the Gini tends to change more slowly than the Theil and the MLD do.

9. Change in Income Inequality within Nations

1. The view among most scholars is that income inequality has been growing in Japan in recent decades (for example, Smeeding 1996, p. 51; Ohtake and Saito 1999; Ohtake 2000; but see Shirahase 2002, who finds stable inequality in recent decades). If the conventional view of growing Japanese inequality is correct—and that growth is faster than the world average—then the estimates here will slightly understate the growth in income inequality in the average nation.

10. Causes of the Inequality Transition

1. In explaining why in today's world the people of Europe and North America tend to be so much richer than the people of Asia and Africa, Diamond singles out four sets of factors as the most critical. All four sets bear on physical geography. First, the number of wild plants and animal species available for domestication varies greatly across continents. This difference was critical historically because surplus food production is the key to the development of a large, specialized population that would enjoy "a military advantage through mere numbers even before they had developed any technological or political advantage" (p. 406). Second, the factors that affect the rates of diffusion and migration vary greatly across continents. The diffusion of technology and people is easiest within the same latitude, where the climate is similar. Hence diffusion was most rapid in Eurasia "because of its east-west major axis and its relatively modest ecological and geographical barriers" and slowest in Africa and the Americas "because of those continents' north-south major axes and geographic and ecological barriers" (p. 407). Third, the set of factors that affect diffusion *between* continents also varied, since the oceans differentially isolate continents from each other. Finally, the continents differ greatly in area and population size. "A larger area or population means more potential inventors, more competing societies, more innovations available to adopt—and more pressure to adopt and retain innovations, because societies failing to do so will tend to be eliminated by competing societies" (p. 407).

2. For example, large families in the world's poor agricultural regions can be viewed as a "poor person's investment" designed to ensure economic security in old age, so the cultural preference for many children is not as irrational as Westerners might think (Mamdani 1972).

3. On the basis of evidence from three waves (early 1980s, early 1990s, and late 1990s) of the World Values Survey from sixty-five nations constituting three-fourths of the world's population, Inglehart and Baker (2000, p. 49) find evidence of both cultural change and cultural persistence on their two cultural dimensions, traditional versus secular-rational and survival versus self-expression. Significantly, however, cultural change is the result of economic development, not its cause, as Inglehart and Baker (2000, p. 49) note: "Industrialization promotes a shift from traditional to secular-rational values, while the rise of postindustrial society brings a shift toward more trust, tolerance, well-being, and postmaterialist values. Economic collapse tends to propel societies in the opposite direction."

4. Although Giovanni Arrighi, Beverly Silver, and Benjamin Brewer (forthcoming) conclude that the increasing industrialization of poor nations has not reduced income inequality across nations, their analysis is flawed. First, they do not adjust income data for PPP. Second, they do not actually calculate between-nation income inequality, but rely on regression analysis to draw inferences about the inequality trend. Finally, they do not weight nations by population size in their regressions or in their figures (so their findings in fact do not bear on global income inequality—see equation 7.4).

5. High-income nations also deindustrialized in the sense of a declining percentage of workers in the industrial sector (Alderson 1999). Alternatively, deindustrialization might refer to a decline in absolute output in the industrial sector. Here a declining share does not necessarily mean declining output, since total output grew over the period. From the figures cited here it is impossible to determine if high-income nations deindustrialized in the sense of actual decline in industrial output.

6. Contrary to the physical geography school, then, Acemoglu, Johnson, and Robinson find that geographic location plays no important causal role in economic development.

7. To support his claim that the new information-based global economy has already served to raise global inequality, Castells does not calculate inequality but, like many others, draws on selected examples from development reports from the United Nations and other sources (see Castells 1998, pp. 75–82). However, as noted earlier, the examples used in development reports can be misleading, because they examine only the tails of the income distribution.

8. The difficulty of maintaining the exclusive rights to knowledge may explain in part the "sharing norm" that seems to be more common among scientists and other knowledge producers than among goods producers.

11. The Future of Global Income Inequality

1. Over the second half of the twentieth century there has been a strong inverse correlation between national income level and national population growth rate, as total population has tended to grow more rapidly in poor and middle-income nations than in rich nations (for the 120 nations used in calculating the 1965–1989 trend in between-nation inequality, the unweighted r is $-.57$ for 1965 income per capita and 1965–1989 population growth rate). The correla-

tion between initial income and growth rate of the working-age population has been much weaker ($r = -.25$ for the 120 nations, unweighted), consistent with the observed younger age structure of poor nations.

2. The demographic penalty argument is reminiscent of the view of classical economists such as Malthus (1960 [1798]) that economic growth is a race between population growth and growth in capital stock. Note, however, that the demographic penalty argument is not the same as the population trap argument mentioned in Chapter 1. To say that there is a demographic penalty is to say that rapid population growth slows income growth, but slower growth does not necessarily imply a *negative* rate of growth. (The population trap model requires periods of negative growth rates, as per capita income returns to its preexpansion level. That is, following periods of economic expansion, per capita income tracks back down to its equilibrium point as population growth outpaces economic expansion—so there is a period of declining average income.)

3. It is important to distinguish the population effects described here from those described in "Effects of Changing Population Size" (Chapter 7) and in Figure 7.3. The discussion in Chapter 7 focuses on ways faster population growth in poor countries might affect the observed between-nation trend in income inequality *independent of* the effect of population growth rate on income growth rate. The age structure effects described here are different, since they do *not* operate independent of changes in income growth rates but in fact affect between-nation inequality *through* their effects on nations' income growth rates:

> faster population growth in poor nations→higher ratio of dependents to workers in poor nations→slower rate of growth of per capita income in poor nations→greater between-nation income inequality

4. The standard world system or dependency argument for dismissing population theories—that population theories confuse proximate causes with real causes that lie in the world political-economic system—is hard to maintain with regard to the windfall hypothesis. Consider the critics' argument that the faster population growth in poor nations is the result of international forces, not domestic forces. According to this argument, if income growth is slowed in poorer nations because of their faster population growth rates, it is misleading to point to population growth as the "culprit," since the real culprit is an international system that permits rich nations to penetrate and exploit poor nations so that a privileged few capitalists in poor nations benefit while the masses languish. The predictable result of such uneven development is poor health care and high infant and child mortality rates for the masses, so couples must have many children to ensure that some will survive to adulthood. In the dependency view, then, the focus on a demographic penalty is wrongheaded, since it suggests that the solution is to focus on domestic policies, such as the promotion of birth control. If the cause of high fertility is economic dependence and exploitation it is the international political economy that needs to be fixed, not the sex practices of individuals—or so the critics argue.

While there is merit in the argument that the promotion of birth control is ineffective when couples have no incentive to limit fertility, the argument that "it's all in the world system" runs afoul of current fertility trends in poor nations. Fertility is declining in Africa, Asia, and Latin America, and that decline appears to be independent of any decline in the economic integration of those regions into the world economy. Indeed, most poor regions appear to be more integrated, not less integrated, into the world economy than they were two or three decades ago when their fertility rates were higher, and the nations most integrated into the world system often are the nations where fertility declines occurred earlier rather than later. These are not the patterns we would expect if economic integration and economic dependence were causing high fertility rates.

5. The discrepancy in estimates narrows somewhat when a common set of nations is used for both data sets.

6. An unpublished study by Dowrick and Akmal (2001) reports a decline in the between-nation Gini from about 0.57 in 1980 to about 0.52 in 1997. After noting that income series based on foreign exchange rates give a different result, Dowrick and Akmal (2001) theorize that the inconsistency is due largely to the fact that national price structures have diverged over time. They conclude that there is "no compelling evidence of a significant change in world inequality" (abstract).

Epilogue

1. The countries are Brazil, Cuba, Dominican Republic, Egypt, India, Israel, Nigeria, Panama, Philippines, United States, West Germany, and Yugoslavia.

References

Abramovitz, Moses. 1986. "Catching up, forging ahead, and falling behind." *Journal of Economic History* 46:385–406.

Acemoglu, Daron, Simon Johnson, and James A. Robinson. 2001. "The colonial origins of comparative development: An empirical investigation." *American Economic Review* 91:1369–1401.

Aghion, Philippe, Eve Caroli, and Cecilia García-Peñalosa. 1999. "Inequality and economic growth: The perspective of the new growth theories." *Journal of Economic Literature* 37:1615–60.

Ahluwalia, M. 1976a. "Income distribution and development." *American Economic Review* 66:128–135.

———— 1976b. "Inequality, poverty, and development." *Journal of Development Economics* 3:307–342.

Alderson, Arthur S. 1999. "Explaining deindustrialization: Globalization, failure, or success?" *American Sociological Review* 64:701–721.

Allison, Paul. 1978. "Measures of inequality." *American Sociological Review* 43:865–880.

Anderson, James. 1986. "Nationalism and geography." Pp. 115–142 in *The Rise of the Modern State,* ed. James Anderson. Atlantic Highlands, N.J.: Humanities Press International.

Arrighi, Giovanni, Beverly J. Silver, and Benjamin D. Brewer. Forthcoming. "Industrial convergence and the persistence of the North-South divide." *Studies in Comparative International Development.*

Aslund, Anders. 2001a. *Building Capitalism: The Transformation of the Former Soviet Bloc.* Cambridge: Cambridge University Press.

———— 2001b. "Building capitalism: Lessons of the postcommunist experience." Carnegie Policy Brief 10, Washington, D.C. December.

Atkinson, Anthony B. 1970. "On the measurement of inequality." *Journal of Economic Theory* 2:244–263.

———— 1991. "Comparing poverty rates internationally: Lessons from recent studies in developed countries." *World Bank Economic Review* 5:3–21.

Atkinson, Anthony B., and Andrea Brandolini. 2001. "Promise and pitfalls in the use of 'secondary' data-sets: Income inequality in OECD countries as a case study." *Journal of Economic Literature* 39:771–799.

Australian Treasury. 2001. "Global poverty and inequality in the twentieth century: Turning the corner?" (http://www.treasury.gov.au.)

Barro, Robert J. 1991. "Economic growth in a cross-section of countries." *Quarterly Journal of Economics* 106:407–443.

——— 2000. "Inequality and growth in a panel of countries." *Journal of Economic Growth* 5:5–32.

Baumol, William J. 1986. "Productivity growth, convergence, and welfare: What the long-run data show." *American Economic Review* 76:1072–85.

Baumol, William J., and Edward N. Wolff. 1988. "Productivity growth, convergence, and welfare: Reply." *American Economic Review* 78:1155–59.

Benabou, Roland. 1996. "Inequality and growth." *NBER Macroeconomics Annual* 11:11–74.

Ben-David, Dan, Håkan Nordström, and L. Alan Winters. 1999. *Trade, Income Inequality, and Poverty.* WTO Special Study no. 5. Geneva: World Trade Organization.

Bennett, Fran, and Chris Roche. 2000. "Developing indicators: The scope for participatory approaches." *New Economy* 7:24–28.

Bernard, Andrew B., and Steven N. Durlauf. 1995. "Convergence in international output." *Journal of Applied Econometrics* 10:97–108.

——— 1996. "Interpreting tests of the convergence hypothesis." *Journal of Econometrics* 71:161–173.

Berry, Albert, François Bourguignon, and Christian Morrisson. 1983a. "Changes in the world distribution of income between 1950 and 1977." *Economic Journal* 93:331–350.

——— 1983b. "The level of world inequality: How much can one say?" *Review of Income and Wealth* 29:217–241.

——— 1991. "Global economic inequality and its trends since 1950." Chapter 3 (pp. 60–91) in *Economic Inequality and Poverty: International Perspectives,* ed. Lars Osberg. Armonk, N.Y.: M. E. Sharpe.

Bhatta, Saurav Dev. 2002. "Has the increase in world-wide openness to trade worsened global income inequality?" *Papers in Regional Science* 81:177–196.

Blackburn, McKinley L., and David Bloom. 1987. "Earnings and income inequality in the United States." *Population and Development Review* 13:575–609.

Bloom, David, and Adi Brender. 1993. *Labor and the Emerging World Economy.* Washington, D.C.: Population Reference Bureau.

Bloom, David, and Jeffrey D. Sachs. 1998. "Geography, demography, and economic growth in Africa." *Brookings Papers on Economic Activity* 2:207–295.

Bloom, David, and Jeffrey G. Williamson. 1998. "Demographic transitions and economic miracles in emerging Asia." *World Bank Economic Review* 12:419–455.

Boltho, Andrea, and Gianni Toniolo. 1999. "The assessment: The twentieth century—achievements, failures, lessons." *Oxford Review of Economic Policy* 15:1–17.

Bourguignon, François. 1979. "Decomposable income inequality measures." *Econometrica* 47: 901–920.

Bourguignon, François, and Christian Morrisson. 1998. "Inequality and development: The role of dualism." *Journal of Development Economics* 57:233–257.

—— 1999. "The size distribution of income among world citizens: 1820–1990." Draft. June.

—— 2002. "Inequality among world citizens: 1820–1992." *American Economic Review* 92:727–744.

Buhmann, Brigitte, Lee Rainwater, Guenther Schmaus, and Timothy Smeeding. 1988. "Equivalence scales, well-being, inequality, and poverty." *Review of Income and Wealth* 34:115–142.

Buttel, Frederick H. 2000. "World society, the nation-state, and environmental protection." Special millennium issue, edited by Glenn Firebaugh, of the *American Sociological Review* 65:117–121.

Campbell, Duncan. 2001. "Can the digital divide be contained?" *International Labour Review* 140:119–141.

Cantril, Hadley. 1965. *The Pattern of Human Concerns.* New Brunswick, N.J.: Rutgers University Press.

Castells, Manuel. 1993. "The informational economy and the new international division of labor." Chapter 2 in *The New Global Economy in the Information Age,* ed. Martin Carnoy, Manuel Castells, Stephen S. Cohen, and Fernando Henrique Cardoso. University Park: Pennsylvania State University Press.

—— 1998. *End of Millennium.* Malden, Mass.: Blackwell.

Chase-Dunn, Christopher. 1975. "The effects of international economic dependence on development and inequality: A cross-national study." *American Sociological Review* 40:720–738.

Chase-Dunn, Christopher, Yukio Kawano, and Benjamin D. Brewer. 2000. "Trade globalization since 1795: Waves of integration in the world-system." Special millennium issue, edited by Glenn Firebaugh, of the *American Sociological Review* 65:77–95.

Chotikapanich, Duangkamon, Rebecca Valenzuela and D. S. Prasada Rao. 1997. "Global and regional inequality in the distribution of income: Estimation with limited and incomplete data." *Empirical Economics* 22:533–546.

Clark, Colin. 1940. *The Conditions of Economic Progress.* London: Macmillan.

Cowell, Frank A. 1977. *Measuring Inequality: Techniques for the Social Sciences.* New York: Wiley.

—— 1988. "Inequality decomposition: Three bad measures." *Bulletin of Economic Research* 40:309–312.

Crafts, Nicholas. 2000. "Globalization and growth in the twentieth century." IMF Working Paper WP/00/44. International Monetary Fund.

Crenshaw, Edward, Ansari Ameen, and Matthew Christenson. 1997. "Population dynamics and economic development: Age-specific population growth rates and economic growth in developing countries, 1965 to 1990." *American Sociological Review* 62:974–984.

Dalton, Hugh. 1920. "The measurement of the inequality of incomes." *Economic Journal* 30:348–61.

Davis, James A. 1966. "The campus as a frog pond." *American Journal of Sociology* 72:17–31.

Davis, James A., Tom W. Smith, and Peter V. Marsden. 2001. *General Social Sur-*

veys, 1972–2000 (machine-readable data file). Chicago: National Opinion Research Center.

Deininger, Klaus, and Lyn Squire. 1996. "A new data set measuring income inequality." *World Bank Economic Review* 10:565–591.

——— 1998. "New ways of looking at old issues: Inequality and growth." *Journal of Development Economics* 57:259–287.

De Long, J. Bradford. 1988. "Productivity growth, convergence, and welfare: Comment." *American Economic Review* 78:1138–54.

——— 1995. "Growth in the world economy, ca. 1870–1990." University of California, Berkeley. (http://www.j-bradford-delong.net/pdf_files/Kiel_Growth .pdf.) Retrieved June 2, 2001.

De Soysa, Indra, and John R. Oneal. 1999. "Boon or bane? Reassessing the productivity of foreign direct investment." *American Sociological Review* 64:766–782.

Diamond, Jared. 1999. *Guns, Germs, and Steel: The Fates of Human Societies.* New York: W. W. Norton.

Diener, Ed. 1984. "Subjective well-being." *Psychological Bulletin* 95: 542–575.

Dollar, David, and Aart Kraay. 2000. "Growth *is* good for the poor." Draft. March. Retrieved January 2001 from www.worldbank.org/research.

Dorfman, Robert. 1991. "Economic development from the beginning to Rostow." *Journal of Economic Literature* 29:573–591.

Dowrick, Steve, and John Quiggin. 1997. "True measures of GDP and convergence." *American Economic Review* 87:41–64.

Dowrick, Steve, and Muhammad Akmal. 2001. "Explaining contradictory trends in global income inequality: A tale of two biases." School of Economics, Australian National University. Draft. April.

Doyle, Arthur Conan. 1955. *A Treasury of Sherlock Holmes.* Selected and with an introduction by Adrian Conan Doyle. Garden City, N.Y.: Hanover House.

Easterlin, Richard A. 1996. *Growth Triumphant: The Twenty-first Century in Historical Perspective.* Ann Arbor: University of Michigan.

——— 2000. "The Worldwide Standard of Living since 1800." *Journal of Economic Perspectives* 14:7–26.

The Economist. 1996. "Economic growth: The poor and the rich." Pp. 23–25. May 25.

——— 1999. "The battle in Seattle." U.S. edition. November 27.

Eggertson, Laura. 1998. "Rich-poor gap next issue for Martin." *Toronto Star.* June 3, p. A6.

Elmslie, Bruce T. 1995. "The convergence debate between David Hume and Josiah Tucker." *Journal of Economic Perspectives* 9:207–216.

Esteban, Joan, and Debraj Ray. 1994. "On the measurement of polarization." *Econometrica* 62:819–851.

Evans, Peter, and James E. Rauch. 1999. "Bureaucracy and growth: A cross-national analysis of the effects of 'Weberian' state structures on economic growth." *American Sociological Review* 64:748–765.

Evening Standard (London). 1999. "The battle that's only begun." December 1.

Firebaugh, Glenn. 1992. "Growth effects of foreign and domestic investment." *American Journal of Sociology* 98:105–130.

——— 1997. *Analyzing Repeated Surveys*. Sage Series on Quantitative Applications in the Social Sciences, no. 07-115. Thousand Oaks, Calif.: Sage.

——— 1998. "Measuring inequality: A convenient unifying framework." Presented at the annual meeting of the Population Association of America, Chicago. April.

——— 1999. "Empirics of world income inequality." *American Journal of Sociology* 104:1597–1630.

——— 2000. "The trend in between-nation income inequality." *Annual Review of Sociology* 26:323–339.

Firebaugh, Glenn, and Frank D. Beck. 1994. "Does economic growth benefit the masses? Growth, dependence, and welfare in the Third World." *American Sociological Review* 59:631–653.

Forrester, Jay W. 1973. *World Dynamics*. 2nd ed. Cambridge, Mass.: Wright-Allen Press.

Foster, James E., and Artyom A. Shneyerov. 1999. "A general class of additively decomposable inequality measures." *Economic Theory* 14:89–111.

Frank, Andre Gunder. 1966. "The development of underdevelopment." *Monthly Review* 18:17–31.

Frank, Robert H. 1985. *Choosing the Right Pond: Human Behavior and the Quest for Status*. New York: Oxford University Press.

——— 1999. *Luxury Fever: Why Money Fails to Satisfy in an Era of Excess*. New York: Free Press.

Friedman, Thomas L. 1999. *The Lexus and the Olive Tree: Understanding Globalization*. New York: Farrar, Straus and Giroux.

Fujita, Masahisa, Paul Krugman, and Anthony J. Venables. 1999. *The Spatial Economy: Cities, Regions, and International Trade*. Cambridge: MIT Press.

Funkhouser, Edward. 1996. "The urban informal sector in Central America: Household survey evidence." *World Development* 24:1737–51.

Gallup, John L., Fernanda Llusa, and Jeffrey D. Sachs. 1998. "Economic growth across Brazilian states: How much does geography explain?" Draft. Harvard Institute for International Development.

Gallup, John L., Jeffrey D. Sachs, and Andrew D. Mellinger. 1999. "Geography and economic development." *International Regional Science Review* 22:179–232.

Gershenkron, Alexander. 1952. "Economic backwardness in historical perspective." Pp. 3–29 in *The Progress of Underdeveloped Areas*, ed. Berthold Hoselitz. Chicago: University of Chicago Press.

Giddens, Anthony. 1999. "Globalization: An irresistible force." *The Daily Yomiuri*, June 7, p. 8.

Goesling, Brian. 2000. "World income inequality: How much is between nations and how much is within?" M.A. thesis. Department of Sociology, Pennsylvania State University.

——— 2001. "Changing income inequalities within and between nations: New evidence." *American Sociological Review* 66:745–761.

Gordon, Robert J. 2000. "Does the 'new economy' measure up to the great inventions of the past?" *Journal of Economic Perspectives* 14:49–74.

Grosh, Margaret E., and Paul Glewwe. 1996. "An introduction to the World Bank's Living Standards Measurement Surveys." Living Standards Measurement Survey Working Paper 120. World Bank. Washington, D.C.

Grosh, Margaret E., and E. Wayne Nafziger. 1986. "The computation of world income distribution." *Economic Development and Cultural Change* 34:347–359.

Grossman, Gene M., and Elhanan Helpman. 1994. "Endogenous innovation in the theory of growth." *Journal of Economic Perspectives* 8:23–44.

Guillén, Mauro F. 2001. "Is globalization civilizing, destructive, or feeble? A critique of five key debates in the social science literature." *Annual Review of Sociology* 27:235–260.

Guzmán, José Miguel, Susheela Singh, Germán Rodriguéz, and Edith A. Pantelides, eds. 1996. *The Fertility Transition in Latin America.* Oxford: Clarendon Press.

Hall, Robert E., and Charles I. Jones. 1997. "Levels of economic activity across countries." *American Economic Review* 87:173–177.

Harrison, Bennett, and Barry Bluestone. 1988. *The Great U-Turn: Corporate Restructuring and the Polarizing of America.* New York: Basic Books.

Harrison, Bennett, Chris Tilly, and Barry Bluestone. 1986. "The Great U-Turn: Increasing inequality in wage and salary income in the U.S." Study prepared for the Joint Economic Committee, U.S. Congress.

Hobbes, Thomas. 1962 [1651]. *Leviathan: Or, the Matter, Forme, and Power of a Commonwealth, Ecclesiasticall and Civil.* New York: Simon and Schuster.

Horioka, Charles Yuji. 1994. "Japan's consumption and saving in international perspective." *Economic Development and Cultural Change* 42:293–316.

Hume, David. 1985 [1777]. *Essays: Moral, Political, and Literary.* Edited by Eugene Miller. Indianapolis: Liberty Classics.

Inglehart, Ronald, and Wayne E. Baker. 2000. "Modernization, cultural change, and the persistence of traditional values." Special millennium issue, edited by Glenn Firebaugh, of the *American Sociological Review* 65:19–51.

International Monetary Fund (IMF). 2000. "How we can help the poor." *Finance and Development* (December). (http://www.imf.org/external/pubs.)

Ishaq, Ashfaq. 2001. "On the global digital divide." *Finance and Development* 38:44–47.

Jasso, Guillermina. 1999. "How much injustice is there in the world? Two new justice indexes." *American Sociological Review* 64:133–168.

Jencks, Christopher. 1987. "The politics of income measurement." Pp. 83–131 in *The Politics of Numbers,* ed. William Alonso and Paul Starr. New York: Russell Sage.

Jenkins, Stephen. 1991. "The measurement of income inequality." Chapter 1 in *Economic Inequality and Poverty: International Perspectives,* ed. Lars Osberg. London: M. E. Sharpe.

Jones, Charles I. 1997. "Convergence revisited." *Journal of Economic Growth* 2:131–153.

Kaldor, Nicholas. 1956. "Alternative theories of distribution." *Review of Economic Studies* 23:83–100.

Kelley, Jonathan, and M. D. R. Evans. 1993. "The legitimation of inequality: Occupational earnings in nine nations." *American Journal of Sociology* 99:75–125.

Kennedy, Paul. 1993. *Preparing for the Twenty-first Century.* New York: Random House.

Keohane, Robert O. 2001. "Governance in a partially globalized world." Presidential address to the American Political Science Association. *American Political Science Review* 95:1–13.

Kitagawa, Evelyn. 1955. "Components of a difference between two rates." *Journal of the American Statistical Association* 30:1168–94.

Knack, Stephen, and Philip Keefer. 1995. "Institutions and economic performance: Cross-country tests using alternative institutional measures." *Economics and Politics* 7:207–227.

Kolm, Serge-Christophe. 1976. "Unequal inequalities, I." *Journal of Economic Theory* 12:416–442.

Korzeniewicz, Roberto P., and Timothy P. Moran. 1997. "World-economic trends in the distribution of income, 1965–1992." *American Journal of Sociology* 102:1000–1039.

——— 2000. "Measuring world income inequalities." *American Journal of Sociology* 106:209–214.

Kravis, Irving B., and Robert E. Lipsey. 1990. *The International Comparison Program: Current Status and Problems.* Working Paper no. 3304. Cambridge, Mass.: National Bureau of Economic Research.

Krugman, Paul. 1991. "Increasing returns and economic geography." *Journal of Political Economy* 99:483–499.

——— 1998. "What's new about the new economic geography?" *Oxford Review of Economic Policy* 14:7–17.

Kuznets, Simon. 1955. "Economic growth and income inequality." *American Economic Review* 45:1–28.

Landes, David S. 1998. *The Wealth and Poverty of Nations: Why Some Are So Rich and Some So Poor.* New York: W. W. Norton.

Leete, Richard and Iqbal Alam, eds. 1993. *The Revolution in Asian Fertility: Dimensions, Causes, and Implications.* Oxford: Clarendon Press.

Lenin, V. I. 1939. *Imperialism, the Highest Stage of Capitalism.* New York: International Publishers.

Lenski, Gerhard. 1966. *Power and Privilege: A Theory of Social Stratification.* New York: McGraw-Hill.

Lenski, Gerhard, Patrick Nolan, and Jean Lenski. 1995. *Human Societies.* 7th ed. New York: McGraw-Hill.

Levine, Ross, and David Renelt. 1992. "A sensitivity analysis of cross-country growth regressions." *American Economic Review* 82:942–963.

Levy, Frank, and Richard Murnane. 1992. "U.S. earnings levels and earnings inequality: A review of recent trends and proposed explanations." *Journal of Economic Literature* 30:1333–81.

Lindert, Peter. 1999. "Three centuries of inequality in Britain and America." In *Handbook of Income Distribution,* ed. A. B. Atkinson and F. Bourguignon. Amsterdam: Elsevier.

Lindert, Peter, and Jeffrey G. Williamson. 2000. "Does globalization make the world more unequal?" Paper presented at the "Globalization in Historical Perspective" preconference, National Bureau of Economic Research, Cambridge, Mass. November.

Lipset, Seymour Martin. 1960. *Political Man: The Social Bases of Politics.* Garden City, N.Y.: Doubleday.

Lucas, Robert E., Jr. 1988. "On the mechanics of economic development." *Journal of Monetary Economics* 22:3–42.

——— 2000. "Some macroeconomics for the twenty-first century." *Journal of Economic Perspectives* 14:159–168.

——— 2002. *Lectures on Economic Growth.* Cambridge: Harvard University Press.

Lyon, David. 1988. *The Information Society: Issues and Illusions.* Cambridge: Polity Press.

Maddison, Angus. 1995. *Monitoring the World Economy, 1820–1992.* Paris: OECD.

Malthus, Thomas R. 1960 [1798]. *On Population.* New York: Modern Library.

Mamdani, Mahmood. 1972. *The Myth of Population Control.* New York: Monthly Review Press.

Mandel, Ernest. 1975. *Late Capitalism.* New York: Monthly Review Press.

Mankiw, N. Gregory, David Romer, and David N. Weil. 1992. "A contribution to the empirics of economic growth." *Quarterly Journal of Economics* 107:407–437.

Martin, Ron. 1999. "The new 'geographical turn' in economics: Some critical reflections." *Cambridge Journal of Economics* 23:65–91.

Marx, Karl. 1996. "Critique of the Gotha programme." In *Marx: Later Political Writings*, ed. and trans. Terrell Carver. Cambridge: Cambridge University Press.

——— 1976 [1847]. *The Poverty of Philosophy: Answer to the Poverty of Philosophy by M. Proudhon.* Pp. 105–212 in *Karl Marx, Friedrich Engels: Collected Works*, vol. 6. London: Lawrence and Wishart.

Mazur, Jay. 2000. "Labor's new internationalism." *Foreign Affairs* 79:79–93.

McMichael, Philip. 1996. *Development and Social Change: A Global Perspective.* Thousand Oaks, Calif.: Pine Forge.

Melchior, Arne, and Kjetil Telle. 2001. "Global income distribution, 1965–1998: Convergence and marginalisation." *Forum for Development Studies* 1 (June): 75–98.

Melchior, Arne, Kjetil Telle, and Henrik Wiig. 2000. *Globalization and Inequality: World Income Distribution and Living Standards, 1960–1998.* Studies on Foreign Policy Issues. Oslo: Royal Norwegian Ministry of Foreign Affairs.

Meyer, John W. 1980. "The world polity and the authority of the nation-state." Pp. 109–137 in *Studies of the Modern World System*, ed. A. Bergesen. New York: Academic Press.

Meyer, John W., John Boli, George M. Thomas, and Francisco O. Ramirez. 1997. "World society and the nation-state." *American Journal of Sociology* 103:144–181.

Milanovic, Branko. 2001. "World income inequality in the second half of the twentieth century." Draft. June.

———— 2002. "True world income distribution, 1988 and 1993: First calculation based on household surveys alone." *Economic Journal* 112:51–92.

Mill, John Stuart. 1923 [1848]. *Principles of Political Economy with Some of Their Applications to Social Philosophy.* London: Longmans, Green.

Montgomery, Mark R., Michele Gragnolati, Kathleen A. Burke, and Edmundo Paredes. 2000. "Measuring living standards with proxy variables." *Demography* 37:155–174.

Morris, Martina, and Bruce Western. 1999. "Inequality in earnings at the close of the twentieth century." *Annual Review of Sociology* 25:623–657.

Morrisson, Christian. 1999. "Historical perspectives on income distribution: The case of Europe." In *Handbook of Income Distribution,* ed. A. B. Atkinson and F. Bourguignon. Amsterdam: Elsevier.

Mulhall, Michael G. 1896. *Industries and Wealth of Nations.* London and New York: Longmans, Green.

Neary, J. Peter. 2001. "Of hype and hyperbolas: Introducing the new economic geography." *Journal of Economic Literature* 39:536–561.

New Scientist. 1999. Editorial. December 4.

New York Times. 1999. "National guard is called to quell trade talk protests." December 1.

Nielsen, François, and Arthur S. Alderson. 1995. "Income inequality, development, and dualism: Results from an unbalanced cross-national panel." *American Sociological Review* 60:674–701.

———— 1997. "The Kuznets curve and the great U-turn: Income inequality in U.S. counties, 1970 to 1990." *American Sociological Review* 62:12–33.

Norris, Pippa. 2001. *Digital Divide: Civic Engagement, Information Poverty, and the Internet Worldwide.* Cambridge and New York: Cambridge University Press.

North, Douglass C. 1981. *Structure and Change in Economic History.* New York: W. W. Norton.

Nuxoll, Daniel. 1994. "Differences in relative prices and international differences in growth rates." *American Economic Review* 84:1423–36.

Ohtake, Fumio. 2000. "Income inequality during the 1990s." *Monthly Journal of the Japanese Institute of Labor* 480: 2–11.

Ohtake, Fumio, and Makoto Saito. 1999. "The background behind unequalization and its social-policy implications: Effects within age groups, effects between age groups, and the aging effect." *Quarterly of Social Security Research* 35: 65–76.

Olson, Mancur, Jr. 1996. "Big bills left on the sidewalk: Why some nations are rich, and others poor." *Journal of Economic Perspectives* 10:3–24.

Ophuls, William. 1977. *Ecology and the Politics of Scarcity.* San Francisco: W. H. Freeman.

O'Rourke, Kevin H. 2001. "Globalization and inequality: Historical trends." National Bureau of Economic Research. Draft. April.

Orshansky, Mollie. 1965. "Counting the poor: Another look at the poverty profile." *Social Security Bulletin* 28:3–31.

Passé-Smith, John T. 1993. "Could it be that the whole world is already rich? A comparison of RGDP/pc and GNP/pc measures." Chapter 9 in *Development and Underdevelopment: The Political Economy of Inequality*, ed. M. A. Seligson and J. T. Passé-Smith. Boulder: Lynne Reiner.

Peacock, Walter Gillis, Greg A. Hoover, and Charles D. Killian. 1988. "Divergence and convergence in international development: A decomposition analysis of inequality in the world system." *American Sociological Review* 53:838–852.

Peng, Yusheng. 1999. "Agricultural and nonagricultural growth and intercounty inequality in China, 1985–1991." *Modern China* 25:235–263.

Perlman, Mark. 1987. "Political purpose and the national account." Pp. 133–151 in *The Politics of Numbers*, ed. William Alonso and Paul Starr. New York: Russell Sage.

Poggi, Gianfranco. 1990. *The State: Its Nature, Development, and Prospects*. Stanford: Stanford University Press.

Pomeranz, Kenneth. 2000. *The Great Divergence: China, Europe, and the Making of the Modern World Economy*. Princeton: Princeton University Press.

Portes, Alejandro, and Richard Schauffler. 1993. "Competing perspectives on the Latin-American informal sector." *Population and Development Review* 19:33–60.

Pradhan, Menno, David E. Sahn, and Stephen D. Younger. 2002. "Decomposing world health inequality." Department of Economics, Cornell University. Draft.

Prebisch, Raul. 1950. *The Economic Development of Latin America and Its Principal Problems*. New York: United Nations.

Preston, Samuel, Nathan Keyfitz, and Robert Schoen. 1972. *Causes of Death: Life Tables for National Populations*. New York: Seminar Press.

Pritchett, Lant. 1996. "Forget convergence: Divergence past, present, and future." *Finance and Development* (June):40–43.

——— 1997. "Divergence, big time." *Journal of Economic Perspectives* 11:3–17.

Quah, Danny T. 1996. "Convergence empirics across economies with (some) capital mobility." *Journal of Economic Growth* 1:95–124.

——— 1997. "Increasingly weightless economies." *Bank of England Quarterly Bulletin* (February):49–55.

Rawls, John. 1999. *A Theory of Justice*. Rev. ed. Cambridge: Belknap Press of Harvard University Press.

Reardon, Sean F., and Glenn Firebaugh. 2002. "Measures of multi-group segregation." Pp. 33–67 in *Sociological Methodology 2002*, ed. R. Stolzenberg. Boston and Oxford: Blackwell Publishing.

Reich, Robert B. 1991. *The Work of Nations: Preparing Ourselves for Twenty-first-Century Capitalism*. New York: Knopf.

Ricardo, David. 1962 [1817]. *Works and Correspondence*, Vol. I: *On the Principles of Political Economy and Taxation*. Edited by Pierre Sraffa. Cambridge: Cambridge University Press.

Rodrik, Dani. 1999. "Where did all the growth go?" *Journal of Economic Growth* 4:385–412.

——— 2000. "How far will international economic integration go?" *Journal of Economic Perspectives* 14:177–186.

Romer, Paul. 1986. "Increasing returns and long-run growth." *Journal of Political Economy* 94:1002–1037.

———— 1994. "The origins of endogenous growth." *Journal of Economic Perspectives* 8:3–22.

Sachs, Wolfgang, ed. 1992. *The Development Dictionary: A Guide to Knowledge as Power.* London: Zed Books.

Sala-i-Martin, Xavier. 2002a. "The world distribution of income (estimated from individual country distributions)." Department of Economics, Columbia University. Draft. April.

———— 2002b. "The disturbing 'rise' of global income inequality." National Bureau of Economic Research Working Paper 8904. Draft. April.

Sassen, Saskia. 2000. "Territory and territoriality in the global economy." *International Sociology* 15:372–393.

Schultz, T. Paul. 1998. "Inequality in the distribution of personal income in the world: How it is changing and why." *Journal of Population Economics* 11:307–344.

Schwartz, Joseph, and Christopher Winship. 1979. "The welfare approach to measuring inequality." Pp. 1–36 in *Sociological Methodology 1980,* ed. Karl Schuessler. San Francisco: Jossey-Bass.

Sears, Roebuck and Company. 1969 [1908]. *1908 Catalog no. 117.* Edited by Joseph J. Schroeder, Jr. Chicago: Follett Publishing Co.

Sen, Amartya. 1973. *On Economic Inequality.* New York: Norton.

———— 1999. *Development as Freedom.* New York: Knopf.

Shapiro, David, and B. Oleko Tambashe. 2001. "Fertility transition in urban and rural sub-Saharan Africa: Preliminary evidence of a three-stage process." Draft. Department of Economics, Pennsylvania State University.

Sheehey, Edmund J. 1996. "The growing gap between rich and poor countries: A proposed explanation." *World Development* 24:1379–84.

Shirahase, Sawako. 2002. "Japanese income inequality by household type in comparative perspective." Paper presented to the Research Committee on Social Stratification of the International Sociological Association, Oxford University. April.

Shorrocks, Anthony F. 1980. "The class of additively decomposable inequality measures." *Econometrica* 48:613–625.

Sica, Alan. 2002. "Weberian theory today: The public face." Chapter 23 in *Handbook of Sociological Theory,* ed. Jonathan H. Turner. New York: Kluwer Academics/Plenum.

Singer, Hans W. 1950. "The distribution of gains between investing and borrowing countries." *American Economic Review* 40:473–485.

Sklair, Leslie, and P. T. Robbins. 2002. "Global capitalism and major corporations from the Third World." *Third World Quarterly* 23:81–100.

Smeeding, Timothy. 1996. "America's income inequality: Where do we stand?" *Challenge* (September/October): 45–53.

Smith, Adam. 1937 [1776]. *An Inquiry into the Nature and Causes of the Wealth of Nations.* With an introduction by Max Lerner. New York: Random House.

Snow, Charles Percy. 1963. *The Two Cultures: And a Second Look.* New York: Mentor.

Solow, Robert M. 1956. "A contribution to the theory of economic growth." *Quarterly Journal of Economics* 70:65–94.

———— 1994. "Perspectives on growth theory." *Journal of Economic Perspectives* 8:45–54.

Sprout, Ronald, and James H. Weaver. 1992. "International distribution of income: 1960–1987." *Kyklos* 45:237–258.

Strange, Susan. 1996. *The Retreat of the State: The Diffusion of Power in the World Economy*. New York: Cambridge University Press.

Streeten, Paul. 1995. "Human development: The debate about the index." *International Social Science Journal* 47:25–37.

Summers, Robert, and Alan Heston. 1988. "A new set of international comparisons of real product and price levels estimates for 130 countries, 1950–1985." *Review of Income and Wealth* 34:1–25.

———— 1991. "The Penn World Table (Mark 5): An expanded set of international comparisons, 1950–1988." *Quarterly Journal of Economics* 106:327–368.

———— 1999. "The world distribution of well-being dissected." Pp. 479–503 in *International and Interarea Comparisons of Income, Output, and Prices*, ed. Alan Heston and Robert E. Lipsey. Chicago: University of Chicago Press.

Summers, Robert, Alan Heston, Bettina Aten, and Daniel Nuxoll. 1994. *Penn World Table (PWT) Mark 5.6a Data* (machine-readable data files). Center for International Comparisons, Department of Economics, University of Pennsylvania.

Swaziland Statistical Office. 1995. *Swaziland Household Income and Expenditure Survey 1995 (SHIES 1995): Main Report*. Mbabane, Swaziland: Central Statistical Office.

Temple, Jonathan. 1999. "The new growth evidence." *Journal of Economic Literature* 37:112–156.

Theil, Henri. 1967. *Economics and Information Theory*. Chicago: Rand McNally.

———— 1979. "World income inequality and its components." *Economics Letters* 2:99–102.

Thomas, George M., John W. Meyer, Francisco O. Ramirez, and John·Boli. 1987. *Institutional Structure*. Newbury Park, Calif.: Sage.

Tilly, Charles, ed. 1975. *The Formation of National States in Western Europe*. Princeton, N.J.: Princeton University Press.

Todaro, Michael P. 1981. *Economic Development in the Third World*. 2nd ed. New York: Longman.

Tolles, Frederick B. 1948. *Meeting House and Counting House: The Quaker Merchants of Colonial Philadelphia*. New York: Norton.

Tucker, Josiah. 1974 [1776]. *Four Tracts on Political and Commercial Subjects*. 3rd ed. Reprint. Clifton, N.J.: Augustus M. Kelley Publishers.

United Nations. 1993. *System of National Accounts 1993*. Brussels: United Nations.

United Nations Development Program. 1999. *Human Development Report 1999*. New York: Oxford University Press.

United States Census Bureau. 1998. *Statistical Abstract of the United States: 1998*. (http://www.census.gov/prod/www/statistical-abstract-us.html.)

———— 1999. *Statistical Abstract of the United States: 1999*. Table 1435. (http://www.census.gov/prod/www/statistical-abstract-us.html.)

——— 2000. *Historical Census of Housing Tables*. http://www.census.gov/hhes/www/housing/census/historic.

UNU/WIDER. 1999. *Income Inequality Database* (machine-readable data files). Helsinki: UNU/WIDER (producer/distributor). Retrieved April 15, 2000.

UNU/WIDER. 2000. *Income Inequality Database* (machine-readable data files). Helsinki: UNU/WIDER (producer/distributor). Retrieved December 2000. (http://www.wider.unu.edu/wiid/wiid.htm.)

USDA (United States Department of Agriculture). 2002. "Farm value share and farm-to-retail price spreads for selected foods." Retrieved April 3, 2002. (http://www.ers.usda.gov/briefing/foodpricespreads/spreads/table1a.htm.)

Veblen, Thorstein. 1915. *Imperial Germany and the Industrial Revolution*. New York: Macmillan.

Venables, Anthony J. 1999. "But why does geography matter, and which geography matters?" *International Regional Science Review* 22:238–241.

Vernon, Raymond. 1987. "The politics of comparative economic statistics: Three cultures and three cases." Pp. 61–82 in *The Politics of Numbers*, ed. William Alonso and Paul Starr. New York: Russell Sage.

Wade, Robert. 2001. "Global inequality: Winners and losers." *The Economist*. April 28.

Wallerstein, Immanuel. 1974. *The Modern World-System I: Capitalist Agriculture and the Origins of the European World-Economy in the Sixteenth Century*. New York: Academic Press.

1979. *The Capitalist World-Economy*. Cambridge: Cambridge University Press.

Weber, Max. 1958 [1904–1905]. *The Protestant Ethic and the Spirit of Capitalism*. Translated by Talcott Parsons. New York: Scribner.

——— 1978 [1904–1911]. *Economy and Society*. Edited by Guenther Roth and Claus Wittich. Berkeley: University of California Press.

Whalley, John. 1979. "The worldwide income distribution: Some speculative calculations." *Review of Income and Wealth* 25:261–276.

Williamson, Jeffrey G. 1998. "Growth, distribution, and demography: Some lessons from history." *Explorations in Economic History* 35:241–71.

World Almanac. 2001. *The World Almanac and Book of Facts*. Mahwah, N.J.: World Almanac Education Group.

World Bank. 1990. *World Development Report 1990*. Oxford: Oxford University Press.

——— 1997. *World Development Report 1997: The State in a Changing World*. Oxford: Oxford University Press.

——— 1998. *World Development Indicators on CD-ROM* (machine-readable data files). Washington, D.C.: World Bank (producer/distributor).

——— 1999. *World Development Report 1999*. New York: Oxford Press.

——— 2000a. *World Development Indicators*. Washington, D.C.: World Bank.

——— 2000b. *World Development Report 2000/2001: Attacking Poverty*. New York: Oxford University Press.

Yasuba, Yasukichi. 1991. "Japan's post-war growth in historical perspective." *Japan Forum* 3:57–70.

Index